THE LURE OF EVEREST

The Lure of
EVEREST

Getting to the Bottom of Tourism on Top of the World

Clint Rogers

Mandala Publications

The Lure of EVEREST
Getting to the Bottom of Tourism on Top of the World

Published by

Mandala Publications

Kantipath, G.P.O. Box: 528, Kathmandu, Nepal
Tel: 4245570, 4249555, 4255444, Fax: 977-1-4255921
e-mail: books@mos.com.np / mandala@ccsl.com.np
www.mandalabookpoint.com

Author's email address: cb_rogers@yahoo.com

ISBN 978-99946-55-05-2

Printed & Layout by
Dongol Printers; dongolpr@mos.com.np

Contents

Contents

Author's Note

As the Maoist insurgency

As the Maoist insurgency that has hampered tourism in Nepal over the past several years appears to have drawn to an end, it seems likely that tourist numbers in the Everest region will return to and exceed the record growth experienced prior to the escalation of violence in 2001. As such, it seems that now is an opportune time to rekindle the dialogue regarding socially and environmentally responsible tourism development in Nepal's mountain highlands.

An earlier version of this manuscript was originally presented in 2000 as my Master's thesis in Geography at the University of California at Berkeley in the U.S.A. At the time, since I had only recently begun my studies of the Himalaya and had conducted limited field research of my own, I relied heavily upon the wealth of scholarly and popular literature that already existed on the Everest region, comparing and supplementing what others had written with my own firsthand experiences in the area. Plowing through the multitude of observations, analyses, and opinions of those who had gone before me was a daunting but valuable learning experience that helped lay a foundation for my own extensive fieldwork in other nearby regions of the Himalayan highlands along the Nepal-Tibet border.

Dusting off the manuscript after nearly a decade of living, traveling, and conducting research in Nepal and neighboring Himalayan countries – including stints in the Everest region in 1999, 2000, and 2003 – I found my earlier thoughts about responsible tourism development just as pertinent today as they had been several years before. Aside from re-editing and updating various sections to reflect recent events, the manuscript presented here remains much the same as what I had originally written.

For today's student of the Himalaya, the process of familiarizing oneself with the work of others is no less educational and relevant than it had been for me several years ago. As such, I thought that making this manuscript available as a low-priced book might be of some use to current and future students, researchers, and tourist visitors. When my friend Madhab Lal Maharjan at Mandala Bookpoint agreed, the ball was set in motion to print a modest number of copies. I hope that other Himalayan scholars might also see the benefit of publishing their theses, dissertations, and research papers in Kathmandu in order to make them more readily and inexpensively available in Nepal. Undoubtedly, anyone who has lived, worked, and traveled among the kindhearted people of Nepal will have received more help, more inspiration, and more personal fulfillment than he or she will ever be able to give back. Hopefully, by making the results of our work more accessible to others we can at least perpetuate the spirit of helpfulness of those who have so generously assisted us.

Clint Rogers
May 10, 2007
Kathmandu, Nepal

Overview

A great deal has been written about tourism in Nepal's Everest region, and this book is an attempt to make sense of it or, if you will, to 'get to the bottom' of it. The area to the south of Mount Everest, referred to locally as the Khumbu, is comprised of exceptionally high, snow and ice encrusted mountains and ridges that surround and separate four roughly north-south trending valleys. These valleys converge to drain the southern aspect of a dramatic and rugged 45-kilometer (30-mile) length of the Himalayan crest that forms the border between northeastern Nepal and the Tibet Autonomous Region of China. The valleys of Khumbu have been inhabited for several hundred years by members of an ethnic group called the Sherpa. The large amount of attention, literary and otherwise, that has been bestowed upon Khumbu and the Sherpas can be primarily attributed to their geographical and historical association with Mount Everest, the world's highest mountain, which lies along Khumbu's northern boundary.

Since the first attempts by British mountaineers to reach the summit of Mount Everest via the mountain's north side in the 1920s, the peak has occupied an exalted position in the crosshairs of the Western gaze. As such, the mountain's slopes have served as center stage not only for adventurous climbers endeavoring to reach 'the top of the world' but also for adventure writers trying to reach a wide audience. When the summit of Everest was finally reached for the first time in 1953 by a two-man team of a Westerner and a Sherpa, the world's attention was drawn not just to the mountain, but also to the people who inhabit the valleys at its base and who had been instrumental in the Western quest to 'conquer' the top of the world.

As a result, in addition to an enormous volume of popular literature on the climbing adventures that have taken place on the world's highest mountain, there is also an abundant literature, both popular and academic, on the Khumbu region's indigenous inhabitants, the Sherpas.

International tourism got its start in Khumbu in 1950, when the first group of Westerners visited the region. Prior to that, the Nepal side of Everest had been effectively sealed off from Western visitors by its remote geographic location and the Nepal government's strict isolationist policies. During the ensuing decade, the number of foreign visitors to Khumbu was limited by the necessity to obtain special permission from the government of Nepal. A few mountain climbing expeditions obtained such permission each year, as did a series of expeditions searching for evidence of a legendary creature known as the *yeti* (popularly referred to in the West as the 'abominable snowman'). Beyond such expeditions, Western visitors to Khumbu during the 1950s and early 1960s also included a number of researchers, journalists, and development workers. After the opening of Khumbu to commercial tourists in the mid-1960s and the construction of a nearby airstrip, tourism expanded rapidly in the early 1970s to become the leading component of the local economy. Increased development of tourism infrastructure in the 1980s and 1990s brought continued growth in Khumbu visitor numbers, with especially dramatic growth at the end of the 1990s ushering the Everest region into the realm of mass tourism.

The stream of foreign visitors that has poured into the Everest region over the past several decades has brought a plethora of implications for the Khumbu environment and the Sherpa people, and the international attention showered upon both has meant that these implications have not escaped the scrutiny of outside observers. Regardless of popular or academic genre, few of the literary works on Mount Everest and the Sherpas of Khumbu have failed to mention, and indeed several have focused directly upon, the deep and pervasive effects that tourism has had on the local environment, economy, and culture. Streams of books, articles, and films have highlighted both the positive and negative effects of tourism and today comprise a dizzying assortment of perspectives and evidence. Taken individually, these lack a collective coherence and do not serve the purpose of elucidating and explaining why tourism has developed as it has in Khumbu or the reasons that tourism has wrought the effects that it has. In other words, while many have testified about *what* tourism has done to the Everest region and the Sherpas, few have explained *why* and even fewer have explicitly drawn any practical lessons from it.

Through a generous use of the perspectives and evidence provided by others who have studied and written about the area and its inhabitants, in addition to my own firsthand experiences in the Everest region and elsewhere in the Himalaya, I try in this book to present in a clear and organized fashion the effects that tourism has had on the residents and the environment of Khumbu (the 'what'), as well as the key factors that have influenced tourism there (the 'why'). It is not my intention to impose my own subjective values by painting tourism in a positive or negative light or to try to convince you that tourism has succeeded or failed in the Everest region. Rather, it is simply my hope that you will find interesting and enlightening the myriad effects that tourism has had there and the reasons I propose for why those effects have occurred. I also hold out the humble hope that the guidance of future tourism development toward the benefit of the less advantaged residents of Khumbu, as well as other regions of the Himalaya, might profit from the lessons offered by this study.

Before getting started, let me first say a few things about how the book's content is structured. The book is comprised of nine chapters. The opening chapter introduces some basic concepts about mountains and tourism that I hope will be useful in enhancing the reader's appreciation for the significance of studying tourism in the Everest region. I begin by introducing in a very broad sense some of the valuable characteristics inherent to mountainous areas as well as some of the threats faced by such areas and the people who call them home. Since these threats have often been in the form of exploitation of mountain environments and their indigenous residents by outsiders, I also include a brief conceptual discussion of some of the forces that have driven such exploitation. While I admit that this part of the discussion is rather simplistic and one-sided, I think it is fitting to introduce the concepts in this manner because it is largely from this type of perspective that tourism has been touted as a promising alternative means to achieve economic development and environmental conservation in areas inhabited by indigenous communities. The promotion of tourism for these purposes, however, has often had disappointing results and has been the subject of considerable debate. To provide some insight into this debate, I present both the general argument for tourism and some of the negative implications that tourism can have for indigenous peoples and their natural environments.

Chapter Two offers some background information on the Khumbu area, the Sherpa people, and the evolution of tourism in the Everest region, as well as the closely related evolution of conservation and development there. To provide some historical context, two chronologies are presented. The first chronology sketches a brief outline of early Sherpa history in Khumbu, from the founding ancestors' migration from Tibet in the early 16th century to the establishment of Khumbu's first celibate monastery in the early 20th century. The second chronology provides a more detailed history of tourism, conservation, and development related events in Nepal and the Khumbu region, from the Nepal government's adoption of a strict isolationist policy in the early 19th century to the international media's present-day obsession with Mount Everest. The chapter finishes with a description of contemporary tourism in Khumbu, which lays the groundwork for describing the effects that tourism has had in the region.

In Chapters Three to Seven, I present a detailed survey of the effects that tourism has had on the Sherpa people and the Khumbu environment. I obviously couldn't include everything, but I tried to be as thorough as possible, using what I felt were the clearer examples of the various types of effects that have been discerned over the past few decades. The breadth of information presented in these chapters is a testament to the powerful potential of international tourism to bring about change in a formerly isolated area. Although there are a number of other books that discuss the implications of tourism in the Everest region, I have yet to come across a broader, more comprehensive treatment of the various effects of tourism in Khumbu than that which is presented here. To provide a coherent structure for this lengthy material, I organized the information into categories that I felt were logical and encompassing, covering in turn the effects that tourism has had on the local economy, the personal well-being and degree of self-determination of local residents, the continuity of Sherpa culture and society, and the Khumbu environment.

In Chapter Eight, I introduce and describe a set of ten key factors that I propose have been responsible for influencing the development of tourism in the Everest region. I argue that these factors explain to a great degree why tourism has developed as it has in Khumbu and why it has had the local effects that it has. While the material in the first seven chapters of the book draws heavily from the work of others, I believe this chapter forms a novel contribution to the subject of tourism in the Everest region through its attempt to offer a rationale for the particular effects that tourism has had there.

In the concluding chapter, I summarize the main points of the previous chapters, point out several important lessons that the study has to offer, and from those lessons make some specific recommendations to help guide socially and environmentally responsible tourism development in the future. Since the study is specific to the unique circumstances of the Everest region, the lessons and recommendations drawn from it are particularly relevant to the planning and management of tourism there. But I believe that the lessons are also generally applicable to tourism development in other regions of the Himalaya as well.

So, you may be wondering, what are the lessons offered by this study? When boiled down, they are really quite straightforward. Put as briefly as possible, the lessons point out the vital importance to tourism development in areas inhabited by indigenous peoples of:

- limited scale and gradual growth of tourism
- environmental protection
- visitor awareness and responsibility
- empowerment of local residents in the planning and conduct of tourism, conservation, and development
- planning and management of tourism for the benefit of the local community

Finally, there are two fundamental concepts underlying the lessons drawn from the study that merit pointing out, as both of them are subjective personal beliefs of mine rather than inherent truths. Firstly, I believe that the goal of tourism development should be consciously and explicitly directed toward providing real and fairly distributed benefits to the less advantaged members of local communities in the host region. Secondly, I think that achieving such a goal requires careful, informed, deliberate, and locally-interactive planning and management rather than merely leaving things to external agents or ad hoc market forces, which by their nature often tend to consolidate benefit among the already more advantaged. For in the end, it is my opinion that the only tourism worth developing in areas inhabited by indigenous people is tourism that purposely benefits *all* of the indigenous residents.

Chapter Outline

<u>Chapter 1 – Mountains & Tourism</u>

- The Value of Mountain Regions
- Threats to Mountain Regions
- Tourism as a Means of Economic Development & Environmental Conservation
    - Forces Driving Economic Exploitation of Indigenous Peoples & Natural Environments
    - The Argument for Tourism
    - Negative Implications of Tourism for Indigenous Peoples & Natural Environments

<u>Chapter 2 – Nepal's Everest Region & Tourism</u>

- Geographical Background of the Khumbu Region & the Sherpa People
- Historical Background of the Khumbu Region & the Sherpa People
    - Chronology of Early Sherpa History in Khumbu
    - Chronology of Tourism, Conservation, & Development Related Events in Nepal & Khumbu
- Contemporary Tourism in Khumbu
    - Forms of Tourism
    - Economic Classifications of Tourists
    - Tourism Numbers & Revenues
    - Primary Trekking Seasons & Routes

<u>Chapter 3 – Economics</u>

- Employment
- Provision of Goods & Services
- Monetization & Multiplier Effect

Chapter 6 – Self-Determination

- Liberation from Historical Subservient Relations
- Control Over Tourism Development & Operation
- Respect & Recognition
- Role Relations with Visitors
- Dependency on External Benefactors
- Education
- National Park

Chapter 7 – Cultural & Societal Continuity

- Tradition of Change
- Community Continuity & Leadership
- Cultural Encouragement & Religious Continuity
- Intrusion
- Conflict & Hospitality
- Absence, Labor Distribution, & Agropastoral Practices
- Out-Migration
- Skilled Professions & Local Crafts
- Imported Foods & Clothing
- Westernization
- Nepalization

Chapter 8 – Key Factors Influencing Tourism

- International Draw of Popular Icons & Scenery
  - Mount Everest
  - Into Thin Air, Into Thin Hair, & Into Been There
  - Shangri-La
  - Tibetan Buddhism
  - The Abominable Snowman
  - The Sherpas
  - Scenery

- Local Hosts' Characteristics Suited to Tourism
    - Familiarity with Travel
    - Cosmopolitan Perspective
    - Entrepreneurial Spirit
    - Strong Identity, Self-Confidence, & Literacy
    - Physical Prowess & Drive
    - Good-Naturedness
- Local Hosts' Involvement In & Control Over Tourism
- Limited Scale of Tourism Development
    - Lack of Infrastructure in Nepal
    - Limited Access to Khumbu
    - Rigors of Altitude, Climate, Rustic Amenities, & Travel by Footpath
    - Seasonality of Tourism
- Limited Economic Leakage of Tourism Income
    - Air Transport
    - Trekking Agencies
    - Employment, Provisions, & Lodges
    - Fees Collected by the National Government
- Types of Visitors, Their Relations with Local Hosts, & Their Concerns
- Protected Area Designation & Management
- Local Hosts' Participation in Conservation & Development Activities
- National Government's Encouragement of Tourism Development
- Lack of Local Tourism Planning & Management

Chapter 9 – Conclusion: Lessons from the Everest Region

- Summary of Tourism Effects in the Everest Region
- Summary of Key Factors Influencing Tourism in the Everest Region
- Lessons from the Everest Region
    - Limited Scale & Gradual Growth of Tourism along with
      Environmental Protection
    - Visitor Awareness & Responsibility
    - Empowerment of Local Residents
    - Planning & Management of Tourism for the Benefit of the
      Community

Acknowledgments

Over the past fifty years, quite a large number of researchers have studied and written about the Everest region and the Sherpas who live there. I owe a considerable debt to each of them, for if it were not for their collective work this study would suffer from a much narrower perspective. I have spent a relatively brief amount of time in Khumbu myself, far too short a time to make me an expert on the area or its inhabitants. Despite my relatively limited experience in the Everest region, however, I like to think that this study has taken on a bit of the expertise of each of the people to whose works it refers. To ensure that I acknowledge fully their respective contributions, I have been quite liberal with the use of footnotes in citing sources. While the Bibliography at the end of the book provides a complete listing of the referenced works, I think it is fitting to acknowledge those researchers from whose publications this study has particularly benefited. They are listed in alphabetical order below, and the years shown in parentheses denote the period spanned by the field research that informed the publications I utilized:

- Vincanne Adams,
  anthropologist at Princeton University (1982-93)

- John Aitchison,
  geographer at the University of Wales at Aberystwyth (1993-96)

- Dor Bahadur Bista,
  anthropologist at Tribhuvan University in Nepal (1957-72)

- Inger-Marie Bjønness,
  geographer at the University of Oslo in Norway (1977-83)

- Barbara Brower,
  geographer at Portland State University (1982-90)

- Alton Byers,
  geographer at The Mountain Institute in Franklin, W.Virginia (1973-95)

- James Fisher,
  anthropologist at Carleton College in Minnesota (1964-88)

- Christoph von Fürer-Haimendorf,
  anthropologist at the University of London (1953-83)

- Ramesh Raj Kunwar,
  anthropologist at Tribhuvan University in Nepal (1978-85)

- Robert Miller,
  anthropologist at the University of Wisconsin at Madison (1960s)

- Sherry Ortner,
  anthropologist at Columbia University (1966-90)

- Ivan Pawson,
  medical anthropologist at the Univ. of California at San Francisco (1982)

- Paul Rogers,
  geographer at the University of Wales at Aberystwyth (1993-96)

- Stan Stevens,
  geographer at the University of Massachusetts at Amherst (1982-95)

I would like to thank the members of my Master's thesis committee at the University of California at Berkeley – professors Michael Johns, Robert Reed, and Nelson Graburn – for their constructive review of the original manuscript. I am greatly indebted as well to the late Professor Barney Nietschmann for his early mentoring and inspiration and for allowing me the freedom to pursue what I wanted to do while fostering a sense of obligation to focus on what I believed to be important and meaningful. I would also like to thank my mother for her loving support, from which I drew great encouragement.

A grant from my graduate department in 1998 supported a year of Nepali language instruction from Minu Singh and Meenakshi Poudyal, and an Oberholtzer Fellowship from the University of California the following year helped fund my library research as well as a four-month stint in Nepal in 1999. Subsequent research grants from the University of California, the United States Department of Education's Fulbright-Hayes program, the American Alpine Club, Jon Krakauer's Everest '96 Memorial Fund and the Community Foundation supported my research in Nepal each year from 2000 through 2006.

The various people who have contributed in some way or another to my understanding of mountain tourism in the Himalaya are too many to list here, but I would be remiss not to mention Mindhu Sherpa, who at the time of my initial foray into highland Nepal helped interpret Sherpa language and customs for me. I would also like to express my appreciation to Murari Sharma and Deha Shrestha at Everest Parivar Expeditions in Kathmandu for providing much help with logistics over the years.

The greatest debt of all though is the one I owe to all of the helpful, kind, and jovial villagers who have made my stays in the mountains experiences to remember for a lifetime. When I think back over all that I have learned from them, and how little I have given in return, I am reminded of the words written by Joseph Hooker in his classic account, *Himalayan Journals*, words that remain as true today as they were in 1855:

> It is always interesting to roam with [...] a mountain people, through their thinly inhabited valleys, over their grand mountains, and to dwell with them in their gloomy and forbidding forests, and no thinking man can do so without learning much, however slender the means at his command for communion.

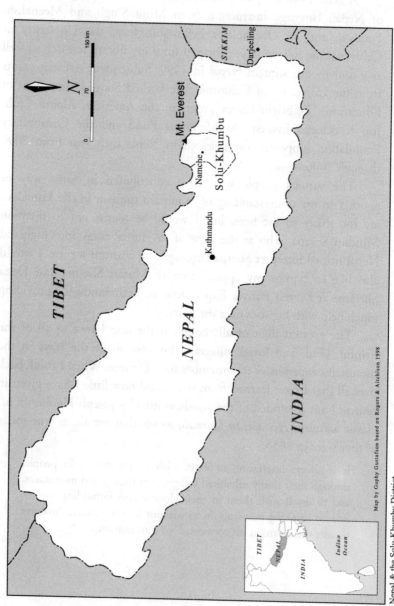

Nepal & the Solu-Khumbu District

Map by Gaphy Gustafson based on Rogers & Aitchison 1998

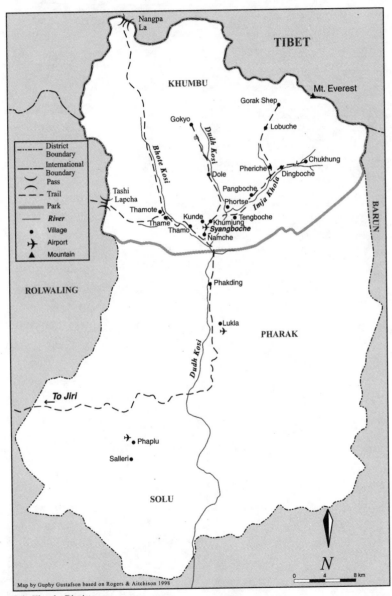

Solu-Khumbu District

CHAPTER 1

Mountains & Tourism

The ideal joy that only mountains give – the unreasoned, uncovetous, unworldly love of them we know not why, we care not why, only because they are what they are, because they move us in some way which nothing else does. And we feel that a world that can give such rapture must be a good world, a life capable of such feeling must be worth the living.

(F.W. Bourdillon, 1908, *The Alpine Journal*)

Anyone who chooses to spend his or her free time venturing into the mountains understands the special value of what these places have to offer. While to many people the intangible aspects of the mountains' inherent worth are too vast to measure and too unique to replace, mountain regions also possess a number of physically tangible characteristics whose practical value to humankind is more than sufficient to make them important enough to safeguard with all our strength and perseverance.

The Value of Mountain Regions

Mountains possess biophysical and cultural characteristics which merit special consideration and treatment in the matter of preservation and conservation. These include their three-dimensional nature involving steep slopes, altitudinal belts of varying ecosystems in a short distance, their different exposures or aspects and climates, and their frequent characteristics of spirituality, remoteness, inaccessibility, and great cultural diversity – islands in a sea of tamed and transformed environment.

(D. Poore, 1992, *Guidelines for Protected Mountain Areas*)

Mountain regions possess many unique characteristics that imbue them with special value. For starters, mountainous areas store and provide valuable physical resources such as fresh water, timber, minerals, and hydro-electric power. Among these, fresh water is arguably one of the more valuable of mountain resources, as fully half of the world's people depend on mountain watersheds for their source of water.[1] Mountain environments serve as essential reservoirs, catching and storing fresh water as snowpack and in mountain lakes and releasing it throughout the year for agricultural, hydro-power, urban, and industrial uses. The absorptive storage capacity of mountain watersheds also helps protect downstream lowland areas from catastrophic flooding.

In addition, the highly variable altitudes and aspects found in mountainous terrain create a wide range of climate zones and a correspondingly high diversity of plant and animal life. Many species of plants and animals are specifically adapted to highland environments and are only found in mountainous areas. Mountain regions also provide important migration corridors for animals and serve as safe harbors from disruptive human development that has encroached upon other more accessible landscapes. Because of these special attributes, mountains provide important locations for scientific study, education, and monitoring. As dynamic geologic and geographic features, mountainous areas offer opportunities to learn from the processes of natural change and disturbance. The extensive plant and animal diversity that results from the altitudinal and aspect variation of mountains also provides a rich laboratory for biological research. In addition, mountainous areas can serve as important locations for monitoring changes in climate and air quality, and, because of their diverse biota, mountains are excellent sites for research on the ecological impact of global climate change.[2]

Mountains also have significant cultural importance, as the physical isolation created by mountain geography has engendered an

---

1   Denniston 1995 p.5
2   compare with Hamilton 1993

abundant diversity of mountain cultures with highly specific adaptations to their local environments. Indigenous mountain peoples often possess an intimate knowledge of their natural environment and have forged unique economic and resource management systems to contend with the challenges of typically steep unstable slopes, shallow soils, and harsh climate. Because of their rugged topographies and isolated nature, mountain areas have often served as havens for the indigenous peoples who occupy them and have protected indigenous cultures from the influences of outsiders.

In many cultures, including those of lowland as well as highland peoples, mountains carry a special symbolic significance and spiritual value. Mountains are sacred religious places for more than a billion of the world's people. According to Paul Fickeler, a renowned religious geographer, mountains have played a greater role in the world's religions than all other natural sanctuaries combined and since ancient times have been considered the homes of gods who send their blessings (often in the form of natural resources) down to humankind from above.[3] Mountains have traditionally been venerated either by avoidance, according to which their disturbance is prohibited, or by pilgrimages in the form of either touring around the mountain at its foot or climbing the mountain to its peak. Even if not formalized in religious veneration, many people find personal fulfillment and enjoyment from viewing mountain scenery or pursuing the many outdoor recreational opportunities mountains offer. For many, the natural environment and open landscape found in mountains are a much-needed refuge from crowded urban settings. For others, merely the knowledge that natural environments in undeveloped mountain areas exist and are being conserved has tremendous value, even if it cannot be easily measured in traditional economic terms.

Threats to Mountain Regions

Despite their rugged terrain, mountains often harbor fragile ecosystems due to their typically thin and poorly anchored soils, harsh

---

3   Fickeler 1947

weather conditions, and short growing season. As a result, mountain environments are exceptionally sensitive to disturbance and slow to recover from damage. In recent years, mountain resources in many parts of the world have increasingly been exploited commercially. Water resources have become more and more valuable as lowland populations have surged and water-dependent development has expanded. Logging, mining, agriculture, grazing, and road construction in some mountain areas have reduced vegetative cover on mountain slopes and led to erosion, which reduces the water storage capacity of mountainous areas and increases the threat of flooding in downstream regions. Erosion also leads to greater levels of silt in streams, threatening stream integrity and damaging stream ecology. The degradation of mountain environments and the corresponding threat to both highland and lowland areas has been the subject of warnings for several decades, as exemplified by the following excerpt from a landmark article by Erik Eckholm that appeared in the world-renowned journal *Science* in the mid 1970s:

> Without a massive effort to preserve and restore the ecological integrity of the mountains, within a few decades they will not be idyllic vacation spots but, rather, barren eyesores that perennially present the lowlands with devastating torrents and suffocating loads of silt.[4]

The inherently isolated and inaccessible characteristics of mountain regions have often restricted external linkages of local economies due to poor access to markets and limited local commercial opportunities. Often, the absence of significant trade opportunities in remote mountain areas has limited economic specialization and the division of labor and hindered increases in productivity. Isolation and inaccessibility have also in many cases denied mountain communities access to the information, resources, and decision-making powers of the state governments that exercise sovereignty over their territories. As such, many mountain communities suffer from insecure land tenure rights, struggle to

---

4   Eckholm 1975 p. 764

maintain control over their resources, and have no voice in national affairs. This lack of empowerment, together with the difficulty of agricultural and pastoral production in the harsh environmental conditions innate to mountain regions, have frequently left mountain communities marginalized and impoverished. Due to their increased vulnerability to the vicissitudes of lowland market economies, some mountain peoples have been forced to deplete their own resources and environments in a vicious cycle that leaves them further marginalized, impoverished, and increasingly dependent on more wealthy and powerful outsiders. The unequal relations and terms of exchange under which many mountain peoples suffer have often reduced their degree of autonomy over local resource use and left them and their environments vulnerable to exploitation by self-interested outsiders and the power they wield.

The contemporary forces of Western-style economic development, modernization, and globalization have in many cases been introduced to remote, isolated, and formerly inaccessible mountain regions of developing countries via international tourism. International tourism has also played an important role in the spread of Western-influenced conceptions of recreational use and environmental conservation of natural areas and in many cases has directly resulted in the creation of national parks and similarly designated protected areas in remote mountain regions of developing countries. Continued growth in discretionary leisure time and income among the economically elite has led to a general increase in international tourism over the past few decades. A preference among many tourists for scenic, recreational, adventurous, and exotic destinations, along with an interest in seeking relaxation and self-discovery in natural environs as well as refuge from the stresses of crowded cities, have brought larger numbers of tourists and greater tourism development to mountainous areas. Today, one of the primary commercial uses of mountain regions is as recreational areas. In many cases, tourism development has been imposed at the expense of mountain environments, the cultures of mountain peoples, and a personal sense of solitude and nature. According to an international forum of non-governmental organizations (NGOs) focusing on mountain issues worldwide, tourism is one of the primary challenges facing the environment, traditional livelihoods, and culture of mountainous areas. As such, the international mountain forum adopted a resolution calling for additional research on the environmental, economic, and cultural impacts of mountain tourism.[5]

Tourism as a Means of Economic Development & Environmental Conservation

> It is hardly possible to overrate the value, in the present low state of human improvement, of placing human beings in contact with persons dissimilar to themselves, and with modes of thought and action unlike those with which they are familiar [...]. Such communication has always been, and is peculiarly in the present age, one of the primary sources of progress.
>
> (John Stuart Mill, 1848, *Principles of Political Economy*)

The inherent value of learning from others with different backgrounds and perspectives is by no means a new concept. Indeed, it has long been recognized as fundamental to human progress. But in the latter half of the 20th century, proponents of Western-style development and conservation began to consider international tourism, in various permutations and by a plethora of names,[6] as a savior for developing countries and impoverished rural communities. Tourism has been touted as an effective means of foreign exchange earnings and egalitarian local economic development that also provides a motive for conserving natural resources, aesthetic environments, and biologically diverse ecosystems. Proponents of tourism for these purposes have argued that tourism offers an

---

5   Mountain Forum 1995
6   Graburn (1989), Smith (1989), Whelan (1991), Smith & Eadington (1992), Honey (1998), McLaren (1998), and Mowforth & Munt (1998), among many others, have employed a variety of descriptive terms for alternative forms of tourism, including cultural tourism, historical tourism, religious tourism, nature tourism, adventure tourism, sustainable tourism, and eco tourism.

alternative to mainstream forms of economic development and environmental conservation, which they claim have in many cases led to the exploitation and further marginalization of indigenous peoples and their environments. What follows is a general conceptual perspective of economic exploitation that has been employed by some tourism advocates to promote the idea of tourism as a preferable alternative.

Forces Driving Economic Exploitation of Indigenous Peoples & Natural Environments

As Richard Butler and Thomas Hinch pointed out in the book *Tourism and Indigenous Peoples*, "the historical relationship between indigenous and non-indigenous people throughout the world [...] has been characterized by the exploitation of indigenous people for the benefit of the dominating non-indigenous groups."[7] Unfortunately, this characterization is not limited merely to historical relationships – it still rings true for indigenous peoples around the world in many cases today. Why is this? What forces continue to cause exploitative relations between those who have economic and political power and those who do not? One needs to look no further than the American Heritage Dictionary[8] to gain some clear, though perhaps uncomfortable, insight on the West's prevailing 'heritage' of imperialistic exploitation.

> exploit: *verb* – to utilize fully or advantageously in a selfish or
>   unethical way
>   *noun* – a heroic act or deed

What follows is a brief description of the types of forces that have often facilitated the exploits of the economic elite and allowed indigenous peoples and their natural resources to be exploited. While I admit that the view presented here is rather simplistic and one-sided, I think it is fitting to introduce these concepts in this manner because it is largely from this kind of perspective that tourism has

---

7   Butler & Hinch 1996 p.4
8   Third edition, 1994

been touted as an alternative means of economic development and resource conservation for indigenous communities and their natural environments.

Broadly speaking, economically and politically powerful governments of developed countries wish to promote their economic interests and political ideologies by gaining sources of raw materials, expanding global market opportunities, and creating economic dependencies to further the growth required by capitalism. Developing countries and their indigenous populations and natural environments are seen as ripe opportunities for the accomplishment of these goals, and international development agencies and lending institutions are employed by the governments of elite countries to pursue the latter's interests.

State governments in developing countries want to grow their national economies in order to accumulate capital and legitimate their control. To do this requires internal economic development and a means of attracting foreign exchange and investment to fuel economic growth. This is especially important for economically and politically weak governments burdened with debt from international development loans and economic hardship from structural adjustment programs of international lending organizations, and whose control over their constituents is threatened by disapproval or revolt by an impoverished citizenry.

Economically powerful and politically influential corporations and individuals, in both developed and developing countries, wish to gain financially by investing in new economic opportunities and expanding the market for and dependency on their own products and services. Elite private sector business interests see the economic and political weakness of developing countries as an opportunity to exploit natural and human resources without repercussions for the unjust environmental and social actions that serve their interests.

Indigenous peoples, especially those with a history of colonial exploitation of their resources and influence on their culture, are exposed to, attracted by, and made to feel inferior by the wealth, amenities, and living standards of outside economic elite. In this context, indigenous peoples become convinced that economic development will improve their lot, and they eventually are forced to yield to the power and determination of the powerful elite bent on development. Thus begins the economically motivated actions of the powerful: extraction of natural resources, promotion of capitalist ideology and consumer values, and exploitation of people who lack the economic and political means to defend themselves.

In the face of such exploitative pressures on economically and politically weak communities, multitudes of non-governmental organizations (NGOs) with a continuum of ideologies and motivations have sprung up to support and defend the rights, resources, environments, and cultures of indigenous groups. On one end of the continuum, development-minded NGOs wish to help indigenous groups with the process of economic development. On the other end, preservation-minded NGOs wish to protect indigenous groups and/or the natural environment from exploitative economic development. Unfortunately, even with the noblest intentions, the actions of NGOs and other non-indigenous organizations have in many cases resulted in, or have not been able to prevent, hardship and loss for indigenous communities.

The Argument for Tourism

The impacts on indigenous peoples and their natural environments that have occurred as a result of the conflicting interests of the various participants in the economic development process outlined above have led to considerable social and environmental problems for indigenous groups. In order to avoid such problems, many have argued that other avenues of economic development need to be sought after and employed. The general argument for tourism as an alternative means of economic development and environmental conservation can be briefly summarized as follows.

By the latter 1990s, tourism had become the world's fastest growing industry, involving an estimated 625 million people and earning receipts of nearly US$500 billion per year. Receipts from international tourist travel grew by an average annual rate of 8 percent during the 1990s, with mountain tourism accounting for an estimated 15 to 20 percent of worldwide tourism revenues by the end of the decade.[9] Contributing to the tremendous growth of international tourism is the increasing number of people in developed countries choosing to spend their leisure time and discretionary income on travel holidays to remote, unusual, or 'exotic' destinations.[10] Such international tourists often favor places marketed as having 'unspoiled' native cultures and natural environments and providing opportunities for adventure.[11] Under these circumstances, areas inhabited by indigenous peoples have been represented as enjoying a comparative advantage in the tourism business because they often possess unique cultural and natural resources that are attractive to tourist visitors.[12] Likewise, mountainous areas are also said to possess comparative advantages in tourism by virtue of their unique physical and cultural attributes.[13]

Proponents of tourism have presented it as a means of generating income and employment for indigenous communities, a source of foreign exchange earnings to increase the import capacities and economic development of developing countries, and a promising investment opportunity for a diverse array of business entities in the private sector. What's more, the money earned from tourism is expected to recirculate through the local and regional economies of the host area with a far-reaching 'multiplier' effect, thereby benefiting even those with no direct involvement in tourism.[14] Additional anticipated ancillary effects of tourism development include improvement of public infrastructure and expansion of communication and transportation links.

Optimistic advocates of tourism have portrayed it as a sustainable economic activity with a low impact on the natural environment,

---

9   World Tourism Organization 1999
10   compare with McLaren 1998 p.11
11   compare with Graburn 1989
12   compare with Butler & Hinch 1996 p.5
13   compare with Sharma 2000a p.3
14   compare with Smith 1989 p.6

especially in comparison to such extractive industrial activities as logging, mining, oil production, and the clearing of forests for animal grazing and commercial agriculture. Such proponents argue that the economic rewards of tourism will provide sufficient motive for local communities, private sector business interests, and state governments to strive to preserve the traditional culture, natural environment, and biological diversity that tourists desire, thus aligning the interests of various groups and increasing their awareness of the cultural and environmental implications of tourism development. Furthermore, tourism development is envisioned to bring about increased economic independence for indigenous peoples and result in a high degree of self-determination and cultural pride. In addition, the cross-cultural contact assumed to occur as a result of tourism is expected to increase understanding between different peoples and lead to more just and equitable relations between them.[15]

But despite the seemingly logical and compelling arguments for promoting tourism as an effective and egalitarian means of economic development for indigenous communities and conservation of natural environments, in many cases tourism development, especially when controlled by outside interests, has brought something quite different. In the following section, I point out some of the negative implications of tourism generally pointed out in critiques of tourism development.

Negative Implications of Tourism for Indigenous Peoples & Natural Environments

Governments of developing countries are typically very receptive to the economic appeal of tourism development and encourage it through policies conducive to private sector involvement. This often results in tourism development being imposed by economically and politically powerful external agents without awareness or concern for the wishes of local residents. In many cases, especially in remote regions occupied by indigenous peoples, tourism growth is not explicitly planned or managed with local community development,

---

15   compare with D'Amore 1988, Butler & Hinch 1996 p.5

environmental conservation, or protection against detrimental effects in mind, but rather is spontaneous, ad hoc, and driven by market mechanisms.

Since external private sector businesses rarely take into account the local environmental, social, or cultural costs of their activities, uncontrolled growth of tourism frequently results in environmental, social, and cultural degradation in tourism locales. Fearing a reduction in tourism revenues due to diminishing aesthetic qualities and wishing to appease powerful environmental constituents of international funding agencies, state government intervention in tourism development in remote regions of developing countries frequently takes the form of national park designation under Western-influenced concepts of balancing recreational use and strict natural resource conservation. However, because the areas where such tourism and conservation activities occur are in many cases inhabited by indigenous populations reliant on local natural resources for their subsistence, tourism and conservation objectives frequently conflict with the needs of local residents. The gazetting of lands and resources in the name of national park protection and tourism enterprise may displace indigenous peoples and/or supersede their traditional land and resource tenure rights. In addition, imported conservation ideologies and methods can undermine traditional systems of natural resource conservation and management. With their rights taken away and their self-determination lost, indigenous peoples become even more marginalized as their resources and culture are exploited by others.

Tourism in less-developed areas is typically dependent upon imported products and dominated by outside business interests that retain most or all of the economic benefits while forcing local communities and their environments to endure the costs. Thus, tourism development is rarely linked to local economic needs and revenues are seldom 'captured' by local communities; instead they 'leak' to foreign or urban-based external service providers such as tour companies, hotel owners, airlines, and the suppliers of imported goods.[16] Even the limited economic benefit available to local residents employed in low-paying tourism jobs can become a source of conflict in the local community as people are forced to compete with each other for limited opportunities. The unequal distribution of benefits accruing from tourism can thus create or exacerbate local discrepancies in wealth, power, and prestige, undermining community cohesion and cooperation.

The influx of tourists to the region, as well as outside agents drawn by the new economic opportunities afforded by tourism development, can increase the local demand for goods and services and cause inflation of local prices. This is particularly a problem for local residents when the economic benefits of tourism leak to outside interests and limited local economic growth cannot keep up with tourism-related inflation. As a result, disadvantaged local residents not participating in tourism or without sufficient means to counteract tourism-related inflation may be forced to migrate out of the area. The economic dependency of the remaining local population on tourism makes the community extremely vulnerable to potential declines in tourism business, especially declines caused by external events local residents cannot predict or control. What's more, the local infrastructure and amenity facilities developed as a result of tourism are typically priced for tourist use and, therefore, are usually not affordable for the local population. This is often the case even when the infrastructure development was subsidized by the local community through taxes and/or the diversion of limited funds away from other projects that would have been geared to the needs of local residents.

In addition, the non-biodegradable litter and human waste produced by large numbers of visitors can cause pollution and degrade local water sources. In addition, increased infrastructure development and energy demand related to tourism growth can strain the available supply of natural resources. Particularly in mountain environments, increased demand for and unsustainable use of

---

16   compare with Honey 1998, McLaren 1998

construction timber and fuel-wood can lead to local and regional deforestation, which in turn can result in increased slope erosion and irreplaceable loss of habitat and biological diversity. Increased air and noise pollution, congestion, visual scarring, and rapid growth of a new style of built environment can also affect local environmental quality and aesthetics and may discourage tourists from visiting, leaving the local population with a ruined environment *and* a bust economy.

Furthermore, the intrusion of tourists and the imposition of outside influence or control can disrupt or jeopardize indigenous peoples' traditional ceremonies and religious rites, subsistence practices, reciprocal social relations, and resource management systems. As an indigenous people's ceremonies and festivals become tourist attractions and their arts and crafts become tourist souvenirs, these aspects of traditional culture may lose their inherent meaning for local residents. As the local culture becomes a commodity designated for tourist consumption, cultural representations such as traditional ceremonies, dress, and art may be altered to reflect tourists' expectations and preferences. Tourists thus come to demand the local 'authentic' culture, no matter how contrived in reality, to fit with their stereotypical view of the tourist destination.[17]

The subservient nature that often typifies the relations between affluent visitors and impoverished local hosts may leave local residents feeling inferior, inadequate, self-conscious, and embarrassed by their relative status as 'backward' or 'undeveloped' people. Suffering from a loss of self-esteem, local people – especially youth – may rush to imitate or adopt the 'modern' tastes, behavior, dress, and material values demonstrated by Western visitors. This 'Westernization' is often aided by the increased availability in heavily touristed areas of Western consumer products. Such promotion and expansion of a Western consumer monoculture can pose a threat to local cultural identity and expression. Although cross-cultural contact from tourism may help facilitate certain visitors' awareness of the problems and

---

17   compare with MacCannell 1976

threats faced by indigenous peoples, any expected benefits from this assumes that the short-term experiences of a relatively small number of visitors will be disseminated widely in the tourists' home countries. But perhaps even more importantly, any expected benefit from such fleeting cross-cultural contact assumes that the exploitation of indigenous peoples by outsiders has been and continues to be based on ignorance rather than greed.[18]

Indeed, in one case study after another, tourism has not only failed to deliver on the ideals of local community development and environmental conservation, it has brought economic marginalization, social disruption, cultural exploitation, and environmental destruction for host communities.[19] Add to these ill effects a tendency to worsen well-being and diminish self-determination among local residents, and tourism development has come to be regarded by some as merely another weapon in the well-stocked arsenal of domination by the powerful. As such, it is not surprising that many tourism researchers and indigenous rights advocates have come to view tourism as: "a new form of imperialism,"[20] "a new form of exploitation of indigenous populations by external forces,"[21] "the new form of colonization over the poor of the world,"[22] and "a new form of Western penetration and domination of the last remaining 'untouched' parts of the world."[23]

---

18   compare with Butler & Hinch 1996 p.5
19   Examples can be found in Butler & Hinch 1996, McLaren 1998, and Sharma 2000a & 2000b, among many others.
20   Nash 1989
21   Butler & Hinch 1996 p.4
22   McLaren 1998 p.65
23   Honey 1998 p.90

CHAPTER 2

Nepal's Everest Region & Tourism

S ome Tibetan Buddhists consider the Khumbu region of Mount Everest fame to be a sacred Buddhist sanctuary designated by Padmasambhava, the illustrious Indian mystic credited with introducing Buddhism to Tibet in the 8th century. According to Tibetan Buddhist tradition, at least twenty such sacred hidden valleys or *beyul* were chosen throughout the Himalaya to serve as places of refuge for persecuted Buddhists.[1] In the case of Khumbu, history seems to match with traditional belief, as the migration of the Sherpas' ancestors from their home in eastern Tibet in the 15th century and their subsequent settlement in Khumbu are thought to have been the result of political and religious persecution in Tibet. In fact, as anthropologist Jim Fisher noted, the Khumbu region has served as "a sanctuary from the troubled outside world" for a long line of Tibetan emigrants who passed through or settled there.[2] Although this book reveals numerous ways in which tourism has brought some of the 'troubled outside world' to Khumbu, it also points out how tourism has enabled the 'sanctuary' of Khumbu to flourish.

In analyzing some of the changes that have occurred in the Everest region since the inception of tourism there in the 1950s, it is sometimes difficult to separate the changes that have been due to

---

1 Regarding Khumbu's designation as a beyul, see Reinhard 1978, Bernbaum 1980, Fisher 1990, & Diemberger 1993. For more on the beyul tradition in the Himalaya, see Macdonald 1973; Aris 1975, 1979, 1990; Reinhard 1978; Bernbaum 1980; Sacherer 1981; Brauen-Dolma 1985; Diemberger 1991, 1993, 1997; Levine & Tia Rinpoche 1993; Ehrhard 1994, 1997; Byers 1996; Sardar-Afkhami 1996, 2001; Choegyal 1998 pp.157-159; Childs 1999; Baker 2004.

2 Fisher 1990 p.xxiv

tourism from the changes brought by the many conservation and development initiatives undertaken in the region over the past few decades. The fact of the matter is that, because of the intense outside attention that has been and continues to be focused on the Everest region, there have been few developments there since the 1950s that have not been influenced in some way by the actions and interests of visitors. As a result, while there is no shortage of changes that can be directly attributed to tourism, there also exists an abundance of changes that have been indirectly affected by the attention and money outsiders have brought to the Everest region and the Sherpas.

If not for the interest shown in the region and its inhabitants by foreigners, it is doubtful that many Khumbu development projects would have been considered, planned, funded, or completed. Indeed, there are many remote areas in Nepal where the impoverished local residents could benefit from outside assistance but have received little or no support. Without the attention the Everest region has gained from foreign visitors, would the area have two airstrips, a hospital, dental and eye care clinics, a high school, grade schools in every village, a plethora of bridges made of modern construction materials, or household electricity? Without foreign-built schools and foreign-funded textbooks and teacher training, would the children's school curriculum be presented from an English and Nepali perspective rather than a Sherpa and Tibetan one? If not for tourism, would a national park have been established that encompasses the entire region and employs over two hundred Nepali soldiers to enforce Western-style land management policies and restrictions? And, in the absence of a booming tourism economy would Khumbu Sherpas have the means to afford wearing Western clothes, living in extravagant new homes, or sending their children abroad for Western educations? My point is that, in the Everest region, the effects of tourism are many and multi-faceted and permeate a vast majority of the major changes that have occurred there over the past half-century.

Geographical Background of the Khumbu Region & the Sherpa People

Although Mount Everest is typically the first thing that comes to mind when people think of northeastern Nepal's Khumbu region, there is no shortage of other impressive mountains adding to the area's magnificent geography. In addition to Everest, there are three other peaks in the vicinity with summits over 8,000 meters (26,250 feet) above sea level and numerous others above 7,000 meters (23,000 feet). In addition to the wall of giant peaks along the region's northern border that forms the Himalayan crestline as well as the political boundary between Nepal and Tibet, the remainder of the Khumbu region is virtually surrounded by mountain peaks in excess of 6,000 meters (20,000 feet). With the steep-walled gorge of the Dudh Kosi river[3] that drains the region to the south providing the only weakness in the Khumbu's fortress-like enclosure of mountains, the peaks along the region's southern flank impose a partial topographic barrier to Nepal's summer monsoon clouds, giving Khumbu a semi-arid climate with relatively low volume and low intensity precipitation within most areas.

Khumbu's relatively dry climate allows the practice of agriculture at higher altitudes than is possible in other wetter regions of the Himalaya. The average annual precipitation at 3,500 meters (11,500 feet) altitude in Namche, the southern-most and lowest altitude Khumbu village, is approximately 105 centimeters, about 80 percent of which falls during the monsoon season between June and September.[4] Precipitation within Khumbu generally decreases as one moves northward and the elevation increases (and temperature decreases) within the region's four major north-south trending valleys, such that the precipitation at 4,500 meters (15,000 feet)

---

3   In Nepali, Dudh Kosi means 'milky river,' a name that derives from the turbid color of the river due to its glacial origins and resulting high sediment load.

4   Joshi 1982 p.400. Note: The reported average annual precipitation is based on measurements during the period 1949-1977.

altitude is roughly half that at 3,600 meters (12,000 feet).[5] The region's landscape is dominated by three major types of vegetation patterns, roughly described as: 1) south-facing, sun-exposed, drier, open slopes with juniper and other shrubs and grasses, 2) north-facing, shaded, moister slopes under fir, pine, birch, and rhododendron forests, and 3) alpine areas above 4,000 meters (13,000 feet) characterized by moist, matted shrubs and grasses on northern aspects and drier variants of the same on southern aspects.[6]

The Khumbu region is inhabited by roughly 3,500 people, over 90 percent of whom belong to the indigenous Sherpa ethnic group.[7] Most of the population reside in the region's eight major villages of Khumjung, Kunde, Namche, Pangboche, Phortse, Thame, Thamo, and Thamote. In addition to these permanent villages, all of which are located between 3,500 and 4,000 meters (11,500 and 13,000 feet) in altitude, there are more than 90 seasonally occupied herding and secondary agricultural settlements at altitudes ranging up to 4,900 meters (16,000 feet).[8] Nearly all of the permanent villages include extensive cultivated land, with Namche being the sole exception. Namche residents have historically relied much less on agriculture than residents of other Khumbu villages because Namche's strategic gateway location has made it a center of commercial activity. Today, Namche hosts Khumbu's only periodic market and has by far the largest number of lodges, shops, and other services catering to tourists of any village in the region.[9]

The Khumbu region and the regions of Pharak and Solu directly to the south collectively comprise the administrative district of Solu-

---

5   A normal lapse of 3 degrees Fahrenheit per 1,000 feet of increased altitude has been observed in various local measurements. The average daily temperature at 3,500 meters (11,500 feet) in Namche during the coldest month of the year (January) is 31 degrees Fahrenheit, while that during the warmest month (July) is 54 degrees Fahrenheit.

6   Byers 1987b pp.210-211

7   Sagarmatha Pollution Control Committee 1998 Annex 14

8   Stevens 1991 p.40, Stevens 1993b p.411, Stevens 1997 p.70

9   The village of Namche is often referred to as 'Namche Bazaar,' a reference to the weekly market bazaar that occurs there. According to Stevens (1993a), the traditional Sherpa name for Namche village is actually 'Nauje'.

Khumbu. The Pharak and Solu regions are inhabited by ethnic Sherpas as well as people of Rai, Magar, Tamang, and Gurung ethnicities. Due to different geographic characteristics, including lower elevation and greater proximity to Nepal's other ethnic groups, Sherpas living in the Solu and Pharak regions historically had closer ties with lowland Nepal and Nepal's politically dominant Hindu majority than did the Sherpas living in Khumbu, who historically enjoyed closer social and cultural ties with Tibet.

The Sherpa are a people of Tibetan ancestry who migrated to and settled in a number of locales in northeastern Nepal and Sikkim over the past several centuries.[10] The original Sherpa clans are believed to have migrated to the Khumbu region from Tibet in the early 16th century, although many subsequent immigrants came from Tibet at later dates and melded into Sherpa society through intermarriage and the adoption of Sherpa language and customs. Sherpas share with other culturally Tibetan or *Bhote* peoples similarities in language, religion, social organization, and traditional dress and ornamentation.[11] Sherpas may be distinguished from other peoples of Tibetan ancestry by the Sherpas' unwritten Tibeto-Burman language dialect (referred to as Sherpa), their own system of exogamous patrilineal clans, and their own assortment of local gods, religious rites, and community festivals.[12] Sherpas are generally devout Buddhists, following the oldest of the four major sects of Tibetan Buddhism, the Nyingmapa or 'Red Hat' sect, which was introduced to Tibet in the 8th century by the Indian mystic Padmasambhava. Buddhism has traditionally been and today remains the fulcrum of Sherpa culture, and the Khumbu region boasts four

---

10 According to Fisher (1990 p.55), in addition to the over 3,000 Sherpas living in Khumbu, approximately 17,000 Sherpas live in the regions of Pharak and Solu directly south of Khumbu, another 13,000 Sherpas live in the Helambu, Langtang, and Rolwaling regions west of Khumbu, and about 7,000 Sherpas live in the Kangchenjunga and Darjeeling areas to the east of Khumbu.

11 The term 'Bhote' refers to people of Tibetan ethnicity or ancestry. The term derives from 'Bhot,' an old geographic name for Tibet used by peoples living in lower-altitude areas of Nepal and India who were not of Tibetan ethnicity.

12 Stevens 1993a pp.29, 33-35

monasteries, two nunneries, and many religious temples (*gompa*), shrines (*chorten*), prayer walls (*mani*), and village entrance gates (*kani*).

Less than 0.2 percent of the land in the Khumbu region is arable,[13] and since the ground is normally frozen for half of the year at such a high altitude only a single crop can be grown per year. The Khumbu's limited arable land and high-altitude climate historically precluded the region's inhabitants from meeting their subsistence needs through sedentary agriculture alone, instead forcing seasonal migration between dispersed crop fields and livestock grazing areas at various altitudes.[14] Over the centuries, Khumbu Sherpas developed specialized agricultural and pastoral practices particularly suited to their region's high-altitude climate and available natural resources. As a result, the specialized methods of agropastoralism developed by Khumbu Sherpas differ from those of neighboring, lower-altitude Sherpa groups as well as from Tibetans living on the drier Tibetan plateau.[15]

The accessibility of grains, wool, and salt via barter trade with adjacent regions allowed Khumbu Sherpas to focus their agricultural and pastoral production on the potato and the yak, both of which are well suited to conditions in the Khumbu region. In addition to the potato, which is the staple of the Khumbu diet, other crops grown in Khumbu include turnips, buckwheat, leafy greens, and, where there is sufficient water for irrigation, barley.[16] Crops are cultivated in late spring after fields are fertilized with a combination of tree fodder, animal manure, and composted human waste. The primary livestock kept in Khumbu include yak, which are particularly well adapted to

13 Fisher 1990 pp.55, 59; Stevens 1993a p.96
14 Fürer-Haimendorf 1963 (reprinted in Hornbein 1965 p.72); Stevens 1993a pp.76-87
15 Fürer-Haimendorf 1975 pp.24-33, Stevens 1993b p.411, Brower 1996 pp.249-255. Note: Fürer-Haimendorf (1984 pp.2-8) compared and contrasted Sherpa settlements in Khumbu, Pharak, and Solu, as well as other regions in Nepal and Sikkim.
16 According to Fisher (1990 p.59), potatoes accounted for 90 percent of all planted fields in Khumbu, buckwheat 5 percent, vegetables 4 percent, and barley 1 percent.

the cold temperatures, high altitudes, and short grasses of the alpine environment,[17] as well as yak-cattle crossbreeds that combine certain advantageous characteristics of both parents. Female crossbreeds, called *dzum*, typically produce more milk than female yak (*nak*), while handling high-altitude conditions better than cattle and low-altitude conditions better than yak. While hybrid male offspring, called *zopkio*, are typically more docile than yak for plowing and for use as pack stock and, like dzum, handle variable altitudes better than cattle and yak.[18] Milk collected from lactating bovines is used to make hard cheese (*churpi*), soft cheese (*somar*), and butter (*mar*), the last of which is especially valuable for its use in tea, cooking, and ritual practice. Goats used to be kept for meat and manure until they were outlawed in 1983 because they were thought by national park authorities to harm pasturelands. Small numbers of sheep are still kept primarily for their high quality manure used to fertilize crop fields. Chickens are also kept in small numbers primarily for their meat, as they do not produce many eggs in Khumbu's high-altitude conditions.[19]

With the exception of privately owned fields and meadows typically surrounded by stone walls, most of the open pasturelands and forests in Khumbu were traditionally regarded as communally-held resources. Over time, as the local population grew and exerted increased pressure on these limited natural resources, Khumbu residents developed systems to regulate exploitation, protect against threats, and facilitate access. Each village selected a number of local authorities (*nawa*) to enforce regulations for tree felling (*shingo nawa*)

---

17 According to Brower (1991b pp.95-96), yak adaptations to cold and altitude (relative to other bovines) include a thicker and double-layered coat of hair for warmth, thicker skin with fewer sweat glands to reduce heat loss through transpiration, a larger thoracic cavity (including an extra pair of ribs) and larger lungs to enhance respiration, smaller and more numerous red blood cells to aid circulation and oxygenation, a thinner and more mobile upper lip and specially designed tongue for grazing on short grasses, greater efficiency at metabolizing lower quality feed, and shorter legs and larger and harder hooves for traveling over rough terrain.

18 Fürer-Haimendorf 1964 p.12, 1975 p.46; Brower 1991b pp.97-98

19 Brower 1991b pp.99-105

and for livestock grazing (*osho nawa*). In addition, a considerable portion of Khumbu forests were given various types of religious and secular protected status.[20] Through this diverse assortment of locally developed systems, access to natural resources was managed in numerous ways.[21] For example, live tree felling in certain forests was limited to specific purposes, such as for house and bridge construction, and certain lands were periodically designated off-limits (*di*) to livestock in order to keep animals from disrupting crops and to allow for recuperation and regrowth of pastures.

The Khumbu region's Bhote Kosi valley and Nangpa La pass provide one of only a handful of routes across the Himalayan crest between northeastern Nepal and Tibet that are navigable by pack animals.[22] As a result, the Sherpas of Khumbu were historically able to supplement their agropastoral subsistence practices by serving as essential trade middlemen moving goods between the high plateau of Tibet and the hills of Nepal. The trans-Himalayan trade conducted by the Khumbu Sherpas typically consisted of bartering grains (such as rice, corn, millet, and wheat), butter, vegetable dyes, iron ore, paper, cotton cloth, and other manufactured items from lowland Nepal and India for salt, wool, tea, barley grain, and ritual paraphernalia from Tibet, either directly or via intermediate exchange for Sherpa livestock, woolen textiles, incense, and dried potatoes. The breeding and trading of yak-cattle hybrid livestock as part of such exchange was of particular importance to the Khumbu economy, as described by Nepali anthropologist Dor Bahadur Bista:

> The breeding of these hybrids in Khumbu was [...] constantly stimulated by demand for [hybrid] males in Tibet and females in other regions of Nepal. Khumbu is considered ideal for their breeding; Solu is not high enough [in altitude] for keeping yak, and [...] such cross-breeding was not allowed [according to

---

20   Stevens 1993a pp.196-210
21   Fürer-Haimendorf 1963 (reprinted in Hornbein 1965 pp.72, 76), 1964 pp.105-113, 1975 pp.97-98, 1984 pp.51-53; Brower 1990 pp.38-40, 1991b pp.124-126; Stevens 1993a pp.135, 159-163, 196-207
22   Bhote Kosi is Nepali for 'river from Tibet,' and Nangpa La is Tibetan/Sherpa for 'mountain pass for Buddhist people.'

custom] in traditional Tibet. This was a fortunate situation as it had helped to maintain the economy of the Khumbu Sherpas more than any other enterprise until Sherpas relatively recently began specializing in mountaineering.[23]

Virtually all Khumbu Sherpa families were involved, albeit at different levels, in trans-Himalayan trade, and some were gone for much of the year on trade expeditions that took them as far away as Calcutta and Lhasa.[24]

A combination of factors contributed to a virtual collapse in trans-Himalayan trade in the 1960s, which severely affected the economies of many of Nepal's highland peoples, including the Sherpas of Khumbu. Beginning in 1959, political and cultural turmoil in Tibet due to brutal suppression of Tibetan resistance by Communist Chinese forces led to an exodus of thousands of Tibetan refugees and significantly disrupted trading partnerships and markets in Tibet. During the 1960s, the Chinese strictly regulated trade across the Tibetan border, prohibiting trade in certain items and fixing the terms of exchange for others. These controls effectively undermined the economic incentive for Sherpa traders to engage in significant business in Tibet. The blow delivered to trans-Himalayan traders by the regulation of trade in Tibet was compounded by the substitution of Tibetan trade goods with cheaper Indian imports as foreign development aid to Nepal funded the building of roads linking the country's interior to India. Especially crucial was the growing availability in Nepal of government-subsidized iodized salt from India. This development greatly eroded the demand for Tibetan salt, which had formed a primary component of trans-Himalayan trade. By the time of the tumultuous Chinese 'Cultural Revolution' in the latter 1960s, only a few Khumbu Sherpas continued to participate in Tibetan trade.[25] Although trade across the Nangpa La pass between Nepal and Tibet did not cease altogether, in recent years it has been

---

23 Bista 1972 p.162
24 Fürer-Haimendorf 1974 pp.98-99, 1975 pp.62-73; Stevens 1993a pp.335-350
25 Fürer-Haimendorf 1974 pp.98-99, 103-104, 1975 pp.4-5; Stevens 1993a pp.350-353

conducted almost exclusively by Tibetans on a small scale and does not have anywhere near the importance it once did to the Khumbu economy.[26]

The curtailment of trans-Himalayan trade could have been devastating for Khumbu Sherpas, who had historically relied upon trade to supplement the meager returns from subsistence agropastoralism available in Khumbu's harsh environment. Indeed, the decline in Tibetan trade was a dire blow for other Himalayan highland communities, many of whose members were forced to migrate to lower altitude regions in their pursuit of alternative economic opportunities. Unlike most other highland groups, however, the Sherpas of Khumbu were fortunate to have an alternative economic opportunity emerge right in their own region. Just as trans-Himalayan trade waned in the 1960s, tourism started to come into its own in Khumbu, and the Sherpas were both well positioned and eager to take advantage of the new opportunities it afforded them.

Despite the critical importance of tourism to the modern Khumbu economy, it is worth noting that the majority of Khumbu Sherpas have continued their traditional agriculture practices, and these still provide a significant amount of their food supply. Pastoralism has also continued, although it has been deeply affected by the increased demand for and use of pack stock in tourism. Khumbu Sherpas still obtain grain and other imported products from lowland Nepal,[27] but they now do this in a market setting with cash

---

26 Rogers & Aitchison 1998 p.33. Note: According to Stevens (1993a pp.352-353), China began easing trading restrictions between Tibet and Nepal in the early 1980s, and Tibetan traders reappeared in Khumbu in 1983 for the first time in twenty years, although the scale of Tibetan trade in Khumbu in the early 1990s remained very small. Peirce (1996, as cited in Brower 1996 p.251) noted that Chinese border-crossing restrictions were relaxed for Tibetan traders crossing the Nangpa La pass in the early 1990s and subsequently re-tightened in the mid-1990s. By the late 1990s, restrictions had again been relaxed, and during my visits to the Everest region in 1999, 2000, and 2003 large numbers of Tibetan traders were crossing the Nangpa La with yak caravans.

27 Nowadays Khumbu Sherpas purchase imported foods and other items at a weekly outdoor market bazaar (*hayt*) in Namche, which was initiated in 1965.

earned from tourism instead of through the person-to-person barter exchange that was characteristic of trans-Himalayan trade.

The historical background provided in the next section sheds more light on the Khumbu Sherpas' past and helps illuminate the manner by which tourism came to become the central facet of their economy and way of life. It also lays a foundation from which to understand the myriad effects that tourism has had in Khumbu, as described in the subsequent chapters.

Historical Background of the Khumbu Region & the Sherpa People

> Men make their own history, but they do not make it just as they please; they do not make it under circumstances chosen by themselves, but under circumstances directly encountered, given, and transmitted from the past.
>
> (Karl Marx, 1869, *The Eighteenth Brumaire of Louis Bonaparte*)

As would be the case with any study of a people and a place that have undergone drastic change, an introduction to key aspects of the Khumbu Sherpas' past is necessary to provide a context in which to understand how they have come to their present situation. From the Sherpas' settlement of the Everest region to the establishment of Nepali sovereignty over the frontier border area, and from the Sherpas' extensive involvement in trans-Himalayan trade to the founding and expansion of Buddhist institutions in Khumbu, historical circumstances were critical in shaping both the Sherpas' emergent opportunities in tourism and the role that the group came to play in tourism as their home region developed into the world's most famous mountain travel destination.

Chronology of Early Sherpa History in Khumbu[28]

ca. 1480   Sherpa ancestors emigrated from the Salmo Gang region in the eastern Tibetan province of Kham.[29]

---

28 The chronology draws from Ortner (1989), Fisher (1990 p.181), Stevens (1993a pp.429-431), and other sources as footnoted.

ca. 1533   Sherpa ancestors arrived in Khumbu.[30]

ca. 1615   Tibetan Buddhist institutions formally established in Khumbu.[31]

1667   Early Buddhist temple founded at Pangboche. Another at Thame followed soon after.[32]

1717   Hindu forces from the south defeated the Sherpas in battle and collected tribute from them.[33]

1772   Hindu forces from Gorkha under the leadership of Prithvi Narayan Shah conquered eastern Nepal. The Nepali government of the Gorkhali rulers collected land taxes from Khumbu residents through local tax collectors (*pembu*) appointed by the state.

1805   First known record of a Nepali government official visiting Khumbu. The official apparently fined local Sherpa

---

29   According to Oppitz (1974 p.233), reasons for the emigration may have included political and religious tensions between the Kham and invading Mongols. Salmo Gang is located about 1300 miles east of Khumbu. The term Sherpa (or Shar-pa) means 'people from the east.'

30   According to Oppitz (1974 p.233), the Sherpa ancestors from Kham settled temporarily in the Tinkye region of central Tibet, but emigrated across the Nangpa La to Khumbu as Muslim army forces from Kashgar invaded central Tibet. Based on analysis of pollen and charcoal samples from the region, Byers (1987b) has suggested that humans may have visited Khumbu on a nomadic basis much earlier than this period.

31   Snellgrove 1957 p.213. Note: Buddhism as practiced in Khumbu adopted many of the practices and deities of the predecessor animistic religion. Adams (1996 pp.132-134) and Douglas (1997 p.109) provide background on the Sherpas' adoption of Buddhism and some of the local deities of Khumbu. For example, the Khumbu region is named after the god Khumbila Terzen Gelbu residing on the sacred mountain Khumbu Yul Lha ('Khumbu god's place'), which is located directly above the north side of the village of Khumjung. Across the valley, Khumbila Terzen Gelbu's wife Tamosermu resides on the mountain Thamserku, which is located above the south side of Tengboche.

32   Fürer-Haimendorf (1964 pp.127-129) presented some legends regarding the founding of Buddhist institutions in Khumbu by Lama Sangwa Dorje.

33   Ortner (1989 pp.84, 89) and Stevens (1993a pp.50, 445-446) provide various accounts of Sherpa conflict with Sen or Rai forces in this era.

residents for killing cattle, which are considered sacred by Hindus and protected by law in Nepal.[34]

1828 Nepal's government gave the Sherpas of Khumbu a monopoly on trade across the Nangpa La pass between Nepal and Tibet by prohibiting Sherpas from the Solu and Pharak regions south of Khumbu from trading further north than Namche and prohibiting Tibetans from trading further south than Namche.[35]

1856 Nepali forces under Prime Minister Jung Bahadur Rana defeated the Tibetans in a border war, helping to consolidate Nepali control over certain border areas. Prior to this, the Sherpas of Khumbu had paid taxes to the governments of both Nepal and Tibet.[36]

ca. 1860 The potato was introduced to Khumbu.[37] The potato's high yields in Khumbu significantly raised local agricultural production, enabling the support of a larger population residing in permanent agricultural villages.[38]

1916 The first celibate Buddhist monastery in Khumbu was founded at Tengboche. Tengboche monks received their training at Tibet's Rongphu (sometimes referred to as Rongbuk) monastery just north of Mount Everest.[39]

34 Stiller 1973 p.265, as cited in Stevens 1993a p.440. Note: The relevant historical Nepali government document has been translated to English and appears as part of the Regmi Research Series papers.
35 Fürer-Haimendorf 1975 pp.60-62. Note: The relevant historical Nepali government document has been translated to English and appears as part of the Regmi Research Series papers.
36 Stevens 1993a pp.34, 440
37 Hooker 1905 p.167, as cited in Fürer-Haimendorf 1964 pp.8-9; Stevens 1993a pp.217-221. Note: The potato, which was first domesticated in the Andes mountains of South America, had been introduced by the British to Kathmandu and to Darjeeling, from where it spread throughout Nepal.
38 According to Fürer-Haimendorf (1964 p.10, 1975 p.44), after the potato was introduced, the immigration of Tibetans to Khumbu increased and the Khumbu population grew from 169 households in 1836 to 596 households (2205 people) by 1957.
39 According to Fürer-Haimendorf (1960, as cited in Fisher 1990 p. 60; and 1964 pp.10-11, 130-132, 172-174), the increased agricultural production following the introduction of potatoes enabled the Khumbu economy to grow to the point

Chronology of Tourism, Conservation, & Development Related Events in Nepal & Khumbu[40]

> Perhaps nowhere in Asia is the contrast between a dignified, decaying past and a brash, effervescent present as violent as in Nepal; and one knows that here too eventually, the present will have its shoddy triumph.
>
> (Dervla Murphy, 1967, *The Waiting Land: A Spell in Nepal*)

As a result of their Tibetan ancestry, Tibetan Buddhist religion, and trading contact with Tibet, as well as the continued migration of Tibetans to Khumbu and the Khumbu region's remoteness from Nepal's capital of Kathmandu, the Sherpas of Khumbu were traditionally affected a great deal more by the Buddhist culture and society of Tibet than by the Hindu culture and caste-based society of lowland Nepal.[41] Although Khumbu Sherpas paid modest land taxes to the Nepali government, their remote location enabled them for centuries to enjoy a great deal of effective autonomy over their own affairs. All that changed in the middle of the 20th century, when Nepal's government took a more active role in the administration of rural areas of the country. Since 1950, circumstances and ideologies originating from Kathmandu and abroad have had increasingly direct effects on the lives of Khumbu Sherpas, as national and international policies associated with tourism, conservation, and development have had enormous ramifications for the Khumbu region and the Sherpa people. But it would be wrong to infer that Sherpas were unaffected by external events and policies before the 1950s. Indeed, as the following chronology illustrates, geopolitical developments in South

---

where it could provide for the building of a religious monastery and the support of a monastic community. Additional monasteries followed in other Khumbu villages, as did a nunnery at Deboche in 1925. The Tengboche monastery was destroyed by an earthquake in 1933, but was later rebuilt. Monastic training increased Khumbu's literacy rate to uncharacteristically high levels for such a remote area of Nepal, with approximately one-third of Khumbu Sherpa adult males being literate in Tibetan in the 1950s.

40 The chronology draws from Ortner (1989), Fisher (1990 p.181), Stevens (1993a pp.429-431), and other sources as footnoted.

41 Stevens 1993a pp.33-35; Brower 1996 pp.251, 254

Asia and economic opportunities in British India in the 19th and early 20th centuries also had far-reaching implications for the course of Sherpa history.

1814-1816 The expansionist Gorkhali kingdom of Nepal was defeated in a border war with British India. Rather than becoming colonized as part of the British Empire, however, Nepal was allowed to remain independent and continue controlling its own internal affairs in return for giving up territories along its southern, western, and eastern borders with India, accepting a British diplomatic resident in Kathmandu, and agreeing to provide recruits to the British army and raw materials (e.g. timber, iron) and agricultural products (e.g. sugar, jute) to the British Raj.[42] Following the war, Nepal closed its borders to Westerners for the next 133 years. All of this had little immediate direct effect on the Sherpas but did serve to further insulate the remote Khumbu region from foreign visitors while laying the groundwork for future Sherpa involvement with the British.

1835 The British established a colonial hill station in Darjeeling just across the border from eastern Nepal in an area that had formerly belonged to Nepal and that was populated by Nepali speaking people.

1846 An ambitious military officer named Jung Bahadur Kunwar Rana usurped political power in Nepal, reducing the Shah royal family to the role of figureheads and establishing a system of hereditary rule among his own family. During the following one hundred years, the Rana regime vigorously kept Nepal secluded from the outside world.

---

42 Ghimire 1992, as cited in Guthman 1997 p.48

ca. 1850   Sherpas began migrating to Darjeeling, a ten-day walk
            from Khumbu, seeking wage labor opportunities
            portering, building roads and railroads, and working on
            tea plantations developed under British colonial rule
            there. The Sherpas' resulting familiarity with the British
            Raj, as well as the establishment of a sizable Sherpa
            community in Darjeeling, facilitated subsequent
            migrations of Sherpas in the early 20th century to work
            for British mountaineering expeditions originating out
            of Darjeeling.

1852   Based upon survey bearings taken from the plains of
            India, British geographers determined the mountain
            now commonly referred to as Mount Everest to be the
            highest in the world, sparking international interest in
            climbing the peak. Approaching the mountain,
            however, was not possible since both Nepal and Tibet
            prohibited foreigners from entering their countries.[43]

---

43 Survey bearings of the mountain, which was initially referred to as Peak XV by
    the surveyors, were taken in 1849 from six different points on the plains of India
    far to the south. Three years later, in 1852, survey computations revealed that
    the peak, at a calculated altitude of 29,002 feet above mean sea level, was the
    highest in the world. The official height was later raised to 29,028 feet above
    mean sea level after additional measurements were made in 1954. In 1999,
    based upon new data from global positioning satellites and a geoid model of the
    shape of the Earth's surface, the National Geographic Society announced a
    corrected height of 29,035 feet above *inferred* sea level. According to Nepali
    geographer Harka Gurung (2003 p.8), the British had asked government
    authorities in Nepal whether the mountain had a local name, and when the
    answer came back negative the British decided to name it after Sir George
    Everest, the former head of the Great Trigonometric Survey of India.
    Apparently the British were unaware that the local Tibetan name for the
    mountain was Chomolungma or Jomolangma, which has been translated as
    'mother goddess of the world.' Alternatively, Ed Bernbaum (1997 p.7)
    translated the name Jomolungma as 'goddess of the wind' and claimed that the
    mountain's full name of Jomo Miyo Langsangma could be translated as
    'unmovable lady goddess benefactress of yaks.' Since the 1950s, the official
    Nepali government name for the mountain has been Sagarmatha, which has
    been translated as 'forehead in the sky', 'head above the ocean', or 'churning
    stick of the ocean' referring to a cosmic mountain of creation from Hindu
    mythology.

1885   Under disguise, an Indian surveyor named Hari Ram,
            who was employed by the British geographical survey of
            India, passed through Khumbu en route to Tibet.[44]

1904   As part of the political maneuvering associated with the
            so-called 'Great Game' between Britain and Russia to
            gain influence in Central Asia, British forces led by
            Francis Younghusband invaded Tibet and established
            diplomatic and trade relations with the Tibetan
            government of the 13th Dalai Lama.

1907   Under disguise, an Indian surveyor named Nath Singh,
            who was employed by the British geographical survey of
            India, visited Khumbu and made sketches of the
            southern side of Mount Everest.[45]

1907-1921   As a result of their colonization of much of the Indian
            subcontinent, the British had the advantage of access
            and were able to pioneer Himalayan mountain climbing
            during the early 20th century. One of the more prolific
            of the early British climbers was a doctor named A.M.
            Kellas, who went on seven expeditions in the Sikkim
            Himalaya between 1907 and 1921 and made first
            ascents of several peaks above 22,000 feet in altitude.
            On the first of these expeditions, in 1907, Kellas noted
            that Sherpas (who had migrated to Darjeeling from
            Khumbu) were especially suited to expedition work and
            performed far better than any of the other ethnic groups
            hired as porters.[46] Because of the economic
            opportunities offered by British mountaineering
            expeditions originating in Darjeeling, Sherpas from
            Khumbu were increasingly lured there.[47]

---

44 Choegyal 1998 p.66
45 Kunwar 1989 pp.98-99
46 Mason 1955 p.127, as cited in Stevens 1993a p.498; Kholi & Berghose 1962
    p.61, as cited in Kunwar 1989 p.98; Ahluwalia 1982 p.38, as cited in Kunwar
    1989 p.98; Rowell 1983 p.82; Cameron 1984 pp.154, 161, as cited in Stevens
    1993a p.498
47 Miller 1965 (1997 reprint p.18)

1908   Spurred by the potential for government revenue from sales of timber products to the British Raj, Nepal's Rana government issued orders throughout Nepal for localities to set aside forest reserves referred to as *rani ban* ('the Queen's forest'). These orders were received in Khumbu sometime between 1912 and 1915, and eight rani ban forests were established in the region. Although regulations varied in the different Khumbu rani ban areas, felling of trees was generally regulated by locally appointed Sherpa authorities.[48]

1921   With Tibetan government permission, a British expedition approached and attempted to climb Mount Everest from the Tibet side. Permission for the expedition had been negotiated with Tibet's 13th Dalai Lama, with whom the British had established relations following the 1904 invasion of Tibet by British forces under Francis Younghusband. By 1921, Younghusband had become president of Britain's Royal Geographical Society, which, along with the British Alpine Club, supported a series of British expeditions to Tibet to climb the world's highest peak.[49] British expeditions to Mount Everest in 1921, 1922, 1924, 1933, 1935, 1936, and 1938 all originated in Darjeeling and accessed the mountain's north side through Tibet.[50] Sherpas hired in Darjeeling as expedition porters soon gained a reputation for being tough, strong, hard-working, loyal, courageous, and proficient at high altitude.[51] These

48 Stevens 1993a pp.202-205
49 Rowell 1983 pp.81-89
50 Unsworth (1981) provided a detailed history of climbing expeditions to Mount Everest. According to Rowell (1983 p.87), the gap in expeditions between 1924 and 1933 was the result of the 13th Dalai Lama not allowing more expeditions due to the deaths that had occurred on the previous ones. Expeditions resumed following the 13th Dalai Lama's death.
51 Mason 1955 p.127 & Cameron 1984 pp.154 & 161, both as cited in Stevens 1993a p.357

characteristics became legendary among Himalayan climbers, and the employment of Sherpas by climbing expeditions became common.[52]

1925   The British India Forest Service encouraged Nepal's government to allow the commercial export of timber to support the construction of railroads in India, and intense harvesting of some of Nepal's more accessible forests in the southern Terai region near India ensued.[53]

1940s   World War II and upheavals surrounding India's independence in 1947 halted Western climbing expeditions in the Himalaya. In addition, due to fears over foreign threats, Tibet's 14th Dalai Lama did not allow any foreigners to travel in Tibet from 1947 to 1949.[54]

1947   India received its independence from Britain. The British withdrawal weakened political support for Nepal's Rana regime as newly independent India resented the assistance, mainly in the form of Gurkha military troops, that the Rana government had given Britain to help suppress the Indian independence movement.

1950   Communist Chinese forces invaded and occupied Tibet. The Chinese closing of the Tibetan border sealed off the access route Western mountain climbing expeditions had previously used to approach Mount Everest from the mountain's north side.

1950   Following the conclusion of World War II, the granting of India's independence, and the Chinese occupation of

<hr>

52 For example, according to Fisher (1990 p.59), the 1922 British expedition to Mount Everest hired about 50 Sherpas in Darjeeling. Some Khumbu Sherpas were able to make arrangements to work for British Mount Everest expeditions without having to actually go to Darjeeling, and Stevens (1993a p.357) provided the example of several dozen Khumbu Sherpas crossing the Nangpa La to join the 1933 expedition at its nearby basecamp just over the border from Khumbu.
53 Bajracharya 1983, as cited in Guthman 1997
54 Rowell 1983 p.89

Tibet, Nepal felt less threatened by Western colonial powers and more threatened by its newly emergent neighbors in Communist China and India. Lured by prospects of Western economic aid, Nepal opened its border to a limited number of foreign diplomats, tourists, and mountain climbing expeditions. Prior to this, Nepal had been the largest inhabited country in the world unexplored and virtually uninfluenced by Europeans. Foreign economists who came to Nepal during this time to assess its development potential described Nepal's economy as 'pre-feudal.'[55]

1950   Nepal's government gave permission to a small group (including American doctor Charles Houston and British climber Bill Tilman) to travel to Khumbu, and they became the first Westerners to visit the region.[56] In the same year, a French expedition led by Maurice Herzog was given permission to climb Annapurna, and they became the first to reach the summit of an 8,000-meter peak.[57] Beginning in the 1950s, after the closing of Tibet and the limited opening of Nepal, most Himalayan climbing expeditions were organized in and Sherpa staffs hired from Kathmandu rather than Darjeeling. Numerous foreign mountain climbing expeditions began visiting Khumbu and other regions of Nepal in a rush to achieve first ascents of the world's highest peaks, and the employment of Khumbu Sherpas by foreign climbing expeditions grew rapidly.

1951   A British expedition including Eric Shipton and Edmund Hillary visited the Khumbu region and reconnoitered Mount Everest's western cwm

---

55 Moran 1996 pp.30, 37
56 Tilman 1951
57 Herzog 1953. Note: There are 14 mountains in the world that exceed 8,000 meters in altitude. All of these are located in the Himalaya and Karakoram mountain regions, and 8 of the 14 are within or along the border of Nepal.

(pronounced 'coom') and southeast ridge, the climbing route that would later be used to make the first ascent of the mountain and which has since become the standard route of ascent. During this expedition, photographs were taken of large footprints claimed to be that of a large, mysterious creature called the *yeti* (or 'Abominable Snowman') sparking international attention and a spate of Western expeditions searching for the elusive creature.

1951   Nepal's figurehead king, Tribhuvan Shah, was granted asylum by India, from where he was helped in organizing a successful coup to overthrow Nepal's ruling Rana regime. Nepal's Shah royalty was reinstated as a ruling monarchy along with a democratic parliamentary coalition government. The autocratic Rana rulers, who had been in power since 1846, had kept Nepal almost totally secluded from the outside world for over 100 years, usurping the country's wealth, guarding against outside influences, and discouraging the development of modern transportation infrastructure or industry.

1951   The United States began offering economic development aid to Nepal. India also began providing aid aimed at developing Nepal's infrastructure to promote trade and developing Nepal's hydro-electric power generation potential. In an effort to counter the growing Western influence in Nepal, China began providing aid in 1956 and the Soviet Union began providing aid in 1959.[58]

1951   India's government funded the construction of an airport in Kathmandu, and, subsequently, Indian National Airways began the first airplane service in Nepal, linking Kathmandu with Patna, India.[59]

---

58 Pant 1991, as cited in Guthman 1997 p.49
59 Stevens 1988 p.70, Kansakar & Shrestha 1998 p.11

1952   The United States Agency for International Development (USAID) began financing an aggressive clearing, draining, and chemical spraying program to reduce the health threat from malarial mosquitoes in the Terai region, opening additional land for agriculture and settlement and breaking down what had been a barrier between India and Nepal. Beginning in the 1950s, with the support of foreign aid and army construction crews from India, communication links and motor vehicle roads were constructed between India and Nepal and into Nepal's interior.[60] As a result, Nepal's imports of inexpensive goods from India and exports of raw materials to its neighbor increased considerably.

1952   Nepal's King Tribhuvan Shah, whose ascendance to power in Nepal had been helped by newly independent India, snubbed the British and gave Switzerland exclusive permission for spring and autumn attempts to climb Mount Everest. The Swiss did not reach the summit, but the knowledge gained from their near success, as well as the experience gained by their Sherpa staff, paved the way for a British expedition that had permission for the following year.[61]

1953   On May 29, a British expedition led by John Hunt succeeded in placing New Zealander Edmund Hillary and Sherpa Tenzing Norgay atop the summit of Mount Everest.[62] Hillary and Tenzing Norgay became

---

60   Blaikie *et al.* 1980, as cited in Stevens 1988 p.70
61   Dittert, Chevally, & Lambert 1954
62   Tenzing Norgay was born in Tibet, migrated at a young age to the Khumbu village of Thame, and then migrated to Darjeeling where he began working for Western mountain climbing expeditions in 1935 at the age of 19. During the 1952 Swiss expedition to Mount Everest, Tenzing Norgay had reached the expedition's high point with Raymond Lambert. Because of his experience and skill, the 1953 British expedition had made Tenzing Norgay the *sirdar* in charge of their Sherpa staff.

international celebrities for being the first to reach the highest point on Earth.[63]

1955   The first foreign commercial tourists visited Nepal. The visit to Kathmandu was arranged by Britain's Thomas Cook Tours and hosted by Russian expatriate hotelier Boris Lissanivich under the permission and observance of Nepal's king, who is reported to have quickly recognized the economic potential of tourism.[64]

1957   Under the advice of forestry experts from the United Nations Food and Agriculture Organization (UN FAO), Nepal's government nationalized forests throughout Nepal, replacing traditional local land and forest management systems with national government control. In Khumbu, this resulted in a nationally directed permit system for tree felling beginning in 1965.

1958   Nepal's national airline, Royal Nepal Airlines Corporation, was created.

1959   Nepal's government created a Department of Tourism.[65]

1959   Due to fierce Chinese suppression of a Tibetan resistance movement, more than 80,000 Tibetans including the country's political and religious leader, the 14th Dalai Lama, fled across the border seeking refuge in India, Nepal, or Bhutan. Thousands more Tibetan refugees fled Tibet during the 1960s. During the initial flight of refugees, over 6,000 Tibetans crossed the Nangpa La pass to Khumbu, bringing thousands of livestock with them. The infusion of people and animals overwhelmed the local population of 2,200 Sherpas and the limited grazing resources in Khumbu. Some of the Tibetan immigrants remained in Khumbu and gradually

63   News of the success was announced in Britain a few days later on the morning of Queen Elizabeth's coronation by expedition sponsor *The Times of London*.
64   Thomas 1996 p.8
65   Banskota & Sharma 1995 p.88

integrated into Sherpa society. Along with the economic disruption in Tibet that followed the mass migration, Chinese authorities placed tight restrictions on trans-border trade, banning most imports from Nepal and prohibited the cross-border trade of hides, sugar, wool, jewelry, butter, and cattle. Some small-scale exchange of grain and salt was allowed to continue but only under Chinese price controls at official trading depots that did not permit bargaining, hence discouraging Khumbu Sherpas from engaging in trade. The curtailment of Tibetan trade had enormous negative implications for the Khumbu Sherpa economy.[66] In addition, border controls restricted the wintering of Khumbu yak herds in Tibet, putting additional pressure on the limited grazing resources of Khumbu.[67]

1960   Nepal's King Mahendra Shah dissolved Nepal's democratic parliamentary system and instituted a 'partyless' government system referred to as the *panchayat* throughout Nepal at the national, zonal, district, and village levels, effectively ending several centuries of virtual political autonomy in Khumbu.[68]

1960s   The first tourist hotels owned by international hotel chains were opened in Kathmandu.[69]

1961-1968   Edmund Hillary's Himalayan Schoolhouse Expedition built schoolhouses in all Khumbu villages and a hospital in Kunde, plus clinics, bridges, temples, and village water supply systems.[70]

---

66   Fürer-Haimendorf 1974 pp.98-99, 103-104; 1975 pp.73-74
67   Stevens 1993a p.289
68   Fisher 1990 p.66
69   Smith 1981, as cited in Stevens 1988 p.70
70   According to Fisher (1990 pp.71-73), Hillary's Himalayan Trust built, maintained, supplied, and originally staffed 16 schools in Khumbu and other nearby areas and provided assistance to an additional 6 schools. By 2003, the Himalayan Trust had built over 40 schools, granted over 100 students scholarships to pursue higher education, built and staffed two hospitals, and

1962	A tense border war between India and China bolstered the international importance of Nepal because of its strategic location between the two antagonistic giants. As a result of Nepal's strategic importance, foreign governments stepped up their development assistance to increase their political influence in the country.
1963	An American expedition successfully climbed Mount Everest and gained enormous U.S. media attention.[71]
1964	Nepal's government opened the Khumbu region to trekking tourists. Previously, Khumbu had only been open to mountain climbing expeditions and groups who had received special permission from Nepal's king. The first commercial trekking tourists arrived in Khumbu in February 1965.[72]
1964	An airstrip was built in the village of Lukla by Edmund Hillary's Himalayan Schoolhouse Expedition to facilitate the transportation of materials for building a hospital and schools in the Solu-Khumbu district.[73] The airstrip also greatly facilitated tourists' access to Khumbu.
1964	British expatriate Jimmy Roberts started Nepal's first commercial trekking agency, called Mountain Travel Nepal.[74]
1965	For the first time, Nepal's government set official planning objectives to increase the number of incoming visitors and to raise foreign exchange earnings from tourism. To meet these objectives, policies were adopted to establish hotels and expand aviation facilities in Kathmandu.[75]

---

supported the building of numerous bridges and water supply systems. For more on the work of the Himalayan Trust, see Sherpa & Höivik 2003 pp.21-30.
71 Bishop 1963
72 Stevens 1993a pp.360-361, 1993b p.412
73 Fisher 1990 p.xxii
74 Choegyal 1998 p.119
75 Banksota & Sharma 1995 p.88

1965   Nepal's government established a district office in Namche, further undermining local political autonomy in Khumbu. The new district government office regulated local trade, forest use, and land registration. The district government office also facilitated the establishment of a weekly market in Namche as well as at several other locations in the Solu-Khumbu district. Cash transactions at the new markets quickly replaced traditional barter exchange.[76]

1966   The Nepal Association of Travel Agents (NATA) and the Hotel Association of Nepal (HAN) were established.[77]

1966-1969 Nepal's government prohibited foreign mountain climbing expeditions in areas along the Tibetan border as a result of the tumult created in Tibet by the so-called Chinese 'Cultural Revolution.'[78]

1967   Khumbu's first tourist shop opened in Namche.[79]

1969   Nepal's King Mahendra Shah created a high-powered tourism development committee (chaired by two princes of the royal family) and promoted tourism to third place in Nepal's national development planning behind agriculture and manufacturing.[80]

1971   Nepal's government entered into an air services agreement with Thai Airways, which provided the first jet aircraft service to Nepal (from Bangkok) and greatly expanded access to Nepal for international tourists. The

76 Stevens 1993a pp.353-354, 449
77 Banskota & Sharma 1995 p.104
78 According to Rowell (1980, 1983 pp.99, 181), the Nepal government's ban on mountain climbing expeditions was prompted by concern over border incidents such as the one provoked by a small American group led by Woodrow Wilson Sayre (grandson of the former U.S. president) in 1962 that publicized its clandestine and illegal entry into Tibet from Nepal and attempted to climb Mount Everest from the mountain's northern side.
79 Stevens 1993a p.364, 1993b p.415. Note: The shop was owned by a Sherpa family from Namche.
80 Tuladhar 1970, as cited in Stevens 1988 p.70

following year, Nepal's national airline purchased its first jet aircraft (a Boeing 727) and began offering service between Kathmandu and Southeast Asian transport hubs.[81]

1971   Khumbu's first tourist lodge opened in Namche.[82]

1971   Japanese developers began building a luxury hotel called the Everest View Hotel as well as a private airstrip in the vicinity of Syangboche just above Namche.

1971   Nepal's government sought financial aid from Switzerland to construct a road from Kathmandu to Jiri in order to reduce ground access time to Khumbu and facilitate development in eastern Nepal.

1971   The United Nations Conference on the Human Environment led to Nepal's government setting up a task force on land use and erosion control, and continued international aid from UN FAO, United Nations Development Programme (UNDP), and USAID were contingent upon Nepal's attention to environmental conservation issues.[83]

1971   UN FAO adviser John Blower from New Zealand recommended to Nepal's government the designation of Khumbu as a national park.[84]

1972   Nepal's national park system was created.[85] National park planning and development were funded and largely determined by international agencies such as UN FAO, UNDP, World Wildlife Fund (WWF), and the International Union for the Conservation of Nature (IUCN). Nepal's early park planning and implementation followed the 'Yellowstone' nature

---

81 Kansakar & Shrestha 1998 p.12
82 Stevens 1993a p.364, 1993b p.415. Note: The lodge was owned by a Sherpa family from Namche. Its name was the Sherpa Hotel.
83 Guthman 1997 p.54
84 Blower 1971
85 His Majesty's Government of Nepal, 1973

preservation model pioneered one hundred years earlier in wilderness areas of the United States.[86]

1972   Nepal's government created a national tourism development plan with the aims of earning foreign exchange, increasing employment and purchasing power, and developing tourist centers beyond Kathmandu to encourage more tourism throughout the country.[87] Government actions to support tourism development included loosening tourist visa policies, opening previously restricted areas for trekking tourism, developing a system of national parks oriented toward tourist destinations, improving international and domestic airport facilities and air service, giving tax exemptions to both foreign and domestically owned tourist enterprises, and providing loans for restaurant and hotel development. Between 1971 and 1992, the number of hotels in Nepal increased from 11 to 203.[88] Nepal's government also created or raised various fees and taxes related to tourism, including tourist visa fees, airport and hotel taxes, national park entrance fees, mountain climbing permit fees, and a dual system for domestic airplane flight prices whereby foreigners paid two to three times the fare paid by Nepali citizens.[89]

1973   The number of trekking tourists visiting Khumbu grew by an order of magnitude from about three hundred in 1970 to over three thousand in 1973.

1973   New Zealand bilateral aid to Nepal funded the planning of a national park in Khumbu. New Zealand land and

---

86   Stevens 1997 pp. 13-30
87   Fisher 1990 p.110, Banskota & Sharma 1995 pp.88-89
88   Nepal Ministry of Tourism 1992, as cited in Banskota & Sharma 1995 p.24. Note: Of the 11 hotels in Nepal in 1971, only 3 were outside Kathmandu, while of the 203 hotels in Nepal in 1992, 87 were outside Kathmandu.
89   Stevens 1988 pp.68, 70, 76

natural resource managers significantly influenced the park's policies and regulations.

1974   A New Zealand mission to Khumbu held village meetings to inform local residents about the proposed creation of a national park there.

1974   Khumbu's first tourist lodge specifically built as an inn for international trekking visitors opened in Namche.[90]

1976   The Khumbu region was gazetted by Nepal's government and designated as Sagarmatha National Park, Sagarmatha being the official Nepali government name bestowed upon Mount Everest.

1977   The World Bank financed a study by Nepal's government to assess the potential for increasing tourism in Khumbu.[91]

1977   Nepal's government created a Ministry of Tourism, which in 1982 became the Ministry of Tourism and Civil Aviation.[92]

1978   Nepal's government designated eighteen mountain peaks as 'trekking peaks' and lessened the cost and regulation associated with obtaining a permit to climb them. To manage the issuance of permits and the collection of fees for trekking peaks, Nepal's government created the Nepal Mountaineering Association.[93]

1979   A loan from the Nepal Industrial Development Corporation, a government agency, financed the construction of an upscale lodge in Namche.[94]

1979   Nepal's government created general regulations for managing tourism in national parks.

---

90   Stevens 1993a p.364. Note: The lodge was owned by a Sherpa family from Namche. Its name was the Tawa Lodge.
91   His Majesty's Government of Nepal 1977; Pawson 1984b; Brower 1991b p.70
92   Banskota & Sharma 1995 pp.93, 99, 101-102
93   O'Connor 1989
94   The lodge was owned by a Sherpa family from Namche. Its name was the Sherpa Trekking Lodge.

1979   Sagarmatha National Park began tightly regulating forest use by local residents and visitors.

1980   The United Nations Education, Science, and Cultural Organization (UNESCO) declared Sagarmatha National Park a World Heritage Site.

1980s   The United Nations University funded a program of academic research in Khumbu on Sherpa culture, environmental degradation, and the impact of tourism and development.

1980s   The Asian Development Bank financed an expansion of Kathmandu's international airport.[95]

1982   The luxury Everest View Hotel at Syangboche closed down due to lack of business because of altitude sickness problems among its guests and the unreliability of flights to the hotel's private airstrip.

1983   A small hydro-electric scheme funded by UNESCO introduced electricity to Namche.

1984   A Swiss government aid project completed the road to Jiri, cutting in half the ground access time from Kathmandu to Khumbu and facilitating the transport of goods from Kathmandu.

1985   American mountain climber David Breashears led multi-millionaire American businessman Dick Bass on the first commercial guided climb of Mount Everest.[96]

1988   A small hydro-electric scheme funded by the American Himalayan Foundation introduced electricity to Tengboche.

1989   An electrical fire destroyed the Tengboche monastery.

1990   The luxury Everest View Hotel at Syangboche was renovated and reopened after an eight-year closure.

1990   A short but violent democratic revolution in Nepal led to the lifting of the ban on political parties and a new

95 Singh 1981, as cited in Stevens 1988 p.78
96 Bass, Wells, & Ridgeway 1986

constitution, which placed sovereignty with the people instead of the king and changed Nepal's government to a constitutional monarchy with a two-house parliament.[97] At the local level, the panchayat village government system was replaced by a system of locally elected village development committees.

1990   The Sagarmatha National Park warden established local forest management committees, which gave Khumbu village officials more authority over administering forest use in Khumbu.[98]

1990   The Asian Development Bank hired an international management consultancy (Touche Ross) to create a tourism development program for Nepal, and in 1992 the Asian Development Bank funded a US$10.4 million tourism infrastructure development project in Nepal.[99] Nepal's government also initiated a tourism promotion program aimed at a four-fold increase in the annual number of international visitors to one million by the year 2000.[100]

1990s   The popularity of international adventure tourism grew tremendously among the middle class of developed Western countries, and there was a corresponding increase in the marketing of international adventure tourism trips by Western tour companies. Travel to Nepal and trekking in Khumbu were prominently marketed and the resulting increase in tourist numbers

---

97 According to Moran (1996 pp.31-32), Nepal's democratic revolution was sparked by King Birendra's strict rule and kindled by a string of events including the Nepali government's purchase of weapons from China, a move which incensed the Indian government and led to its instituting a trade embargo that shut down supplies of fuel and other goods to Nepal's capital of Kathmandu and resulted in widespread public unrest.
98 Stevens 1993a pp.319-320
99 Banksota & Sharma 1995 pp.92-93
100 Stevens 1993a pp.356, 411; Ali 1994, as cited in Lachapelle 1998 p.56

led to a rapid increase in the number of trekking agencies in Kathmandu.

1991   The first commercial Mount Everest climbing guide service, Hall and Ball Adventure Consultants, began offering inexperienced but high paying clients the opportunity to climb the world's highest peak. During the 1990s, numerous additional commercial guide services popularized guided climbing expeditions to Mount Everest, resulting in growing crowds of climbers on the mountain during the climbing season.

1991   The first Sherpa non-governmental organization (NGO) focused on conservation and development, the Sagarmatha Pollution Control Committee (SPCC), was created with funding from the World Wildlife Fund. The SPCC, along with a large number of local Sherpa volunteers, engaged in a clean-up of Mount Everest basecamp and the main trekking route through Khumbu.[101]

1993   Following a World Bank structural adjustment program in the late 1980s, Nepal's government lifted its monopoly on domestic airline service, and numerous private carriers began providing expanded air service and seating capacity throughout the country. This eased the bottleneck of air access to Khumbu greatly facilitating the growth of tourist numbers there.

1993   Nepal's government (working with the UNDP's Parks and People Project) passed the Buffer Zone Amendment to Nepal's National Parks and Wildlife Conservation Act. The amendment authorized that up to 50 percent of national park entrance fees (which had previously gone entirely to the national government) "could" be allocated to local communities within and around

---

101 Stevens 1997 pp.91-94

national parks for conservation and development
projects.[102]

1994   A large Austrian-funded 600-kilowatt hydro-electric
        scheme near Thame introduced electricity to 5 of the 8
        main Khumbu villages, including about a third of
        Khumbu's 125 tourist lodges.[103]

1994   The Sagarmatha National Park warden helped arrange
        several kerosene depots along the main Khumbu
        trekking route and held a meeting with Khumbu lodge
        owners at which some lodge owners agreed to use
        kerosene rather than firewood for cooking.[104]

1996   Nepal's government initiated a tourism promotion
        program called 'Visit Nepal 1998.' The program was
        aimed at increasing air service to and within the
        country, encouraging the development of tourism
        infrastructure, and lessening bureaucratic impediments
        for tourist visitors.

1996   As a result of the growing popularity of commercially
        guided climbing expeditions, a record 398 climbers
        crowded the slopes of Mount Everest during the
        climbing season. A traffic jam high on the mountain on
        the day of May 9 along with competitive pressure
        between commercial guiding services led to disaster
        when a storm struck as climbers were descending from
        the summit late in the day. Eight climbers died in the
        widely publicized and controversial tragedy. A best-
        selling book by Jon Krakauer, a large-format IMAX
        movie by David Breashears and Greg MacGillivray, and
        ubiquitous   media   accounts   brought   intense
        international media attention to Mount Everest, the
        Khumbu region, and the Sherpa people.

---

102 Stevens 1997 p.95; Lhakpa Sherpa, as cited in Butt & Price 2000 p.18
103 Stevens 1997 p.309
104 Stevens 1997 p.309

1998	In an effort to boost trekking tourism, Nepal's government discontinued the requirement for tourist visitors to obtain trekking permits for traveling in the popular trekking areas of Khumbu, Annapurna, and Langtang.

1998   In an effort to boost trekking tourism, Nepal's government discontinued the requirement for tourist visitors to obtain trekking permits for traveling in the popular trekking areas of Khumbu, Annapurna, and Langtang.

1999   The frozen body of famous 1924 British climber George Leigh Mallory was found on the north side of Mount Everest, again focusing international popular attention on the mountain and adding to its mystique.

2003   The 50th anniversary of the first ascent of Mount Everest was celebrated with great fanfare and international media attention.

2006   Controversy erupted on Mount Everest as commercial guides and their clients were accused of putting their own desire to reach the summit ahead of helping a dying climber. Shortly afterward, the controversy received even more international media coverage after American climbing guide Dan Mazur gave up his and his clients' chance for the summit to help save a climber whom others had left for dead.

2006   The Kathmandu-based Trekking Agents Association of Nepal (TAAN) proposed a radical new policy referred to as the Trekking Registration Certificate (TRC) scheme requiring all foreign visitors trekking anywhere in the country to obtain a TRC permit from a TAAN office and hire the services of a guide employed by a registered trekking agency.

Contemporary Tourism in Khumbu

There will, doubtless, always be mountain-lovers and mountaineers, young as well as old, who are something more than invalids or athletes or mere tourists; who desire during their holidays to change their habits and mode of life as well as their climate.

(Douglas Freshfield, 1903, *Round Kangchenjunga*)

The Khumbu region lays claim to the world's highest mountain and perhaps the world's most famous indigenous people. Visitors come from around the world to trek[105] near and climb on the region's mountains and to experience the ambience of Sherpa culture. The entire Khumbu region lies within the boundary of Sagarmatha National Park, which has been designated by UNESCO as a World Heritage Site in recognition of the uniqueness, importance, and history of the region and the Sherpa culture.

While trekking in the Everest region was a small-scale, rustic adventure back in the 1970s, today the area has developed into a major tourism destination with many amenities catering to foreign travelers. A few dark, cramped, and smoky traditional tea houses that provided only the local staples of potatoes and rice have been replaced by a plethora of comfortable modern lodges offering a wide selection of Western and Asian cuisine. The tourist hub of Namche now has cyber cafes with satellite internet service, nightclubs and bars complete with pool tables (quite a novelty when one considers that the pool tables had to be carried in on the backs of porters from the roadhead at Jiri, a tortuous seven-day journey), an assortment of restaurants and fresh bakeries offering such Western fare as pizza, pastries, apple pies, and cappuccino (again, consider an oven carried in on the back of a porter), a movie theater, a post office, health and dental clinics, a bank, several foreign currency exchanges, a hairdresser, numerous tailor and laundry services, and hot water, electricity, and telephone service in every lodge.

Forms of Tourism

Tourism in the Everest region has evolved over the years to suit the disparate tastes, preferences, and budgets of all kinds of visitors. For purposes of description, tourism in Khumbu can be categorized into four primary types: luxury tourism, religious tourism, trekking

---

105 The term 'trek' is synonymous with 'hike' and infers a journey on foot while provisions are transported by other means. According to Thomas (1996 p.8), the word 'trek' is derived from the 'Vortrekkers,' Dutch pioneers who traveled across South Africa with oxcarts.

tourism, and climbing tourism. Luxury tourists typically spend the shortest amount of time in the region but pay the highest prices for comfort, amenities, and service during their stay. A growing number of religious tourists visit local Buddhist monasteries and retreat centers for spiritual practice, meditation, or education. Well over 90 percent of the foreign visitors to Khumbu are trekking tourists, and, correspondingly, much of the Khumbu's tourism development has catered to this form of tourism, which entails walking the region's trails and either staying in lodges or camping in tents. Although mountain climbers are far fewer in number than trekkers, they generally spend longer periods in the region than other types of visitors and employ greater levels of local support.

Luxury Tourism

Luxury visitors often fly in a small plane or helicopter directly to the private Syangboche airstrip above Namche and rarely venture far beyond the villages of Namche and Khumjung. Many of the luxury visitors to Khumbu each year are wealthy Japanese tourists who stay at the Japanese-built Everest View Hotel at Syangboche.[106] Another luxury accommodation, the Panorama Hotel, has been recently built near Syangboche as well.

Religious Tourism

A growing number of tourists are visiting the Everest region because of its strong Buddhist tradition. The Khumbu has become a destination for scholars and followers of the Tibetan Buddhist faith that came under pressure in Tibet following Chinese occupation and the brutal reforms of the Chinese 'Cultural Revolution' during the 1960s and 1970s. Due to the Khumbu Sherpas' historically strong ties to Tibet and the community's relative affluence due to involvement in trade and later in tourism, Buddhist institutions and religion have flourished in Khumbu. Today, many tourists visit the two larger Khumbu monasteries in Tengboche and Thame, as well as

---

106 Stevens 1993b p.412

a number of smaller monasteries and nunneries such as those found in Pangboche, Phortse, and Deboche. To accommodate the growing number of visitors interested in religious retreats, the monks of Tengboche began construction in 1999 of additional retreat facilities and lodgings near the monastery.

Trekking Tourism

For trekking visitors, traveling through the region usually constitutes the purpose in and of itself for the visit. Trekkers typically employ one (or sometimes a combination) of two basic styles: self-contained trekking and lodge trekking (the latter is still commonly referred to in Nepal as 'tea-house trekking'[107]).

Self-contained trekkers do not utilize the room and board services of lodges as they travel through the region (although this is not always the case, as some self-contained trekkers occasionally eat, lounge, read, and socialize inside lodges). Self-contained trekkers camp in tents, and meals are prepared by kitchen staff who travel along with them. Thus, self-contained trekkers need to make arrangements for food supplies and camping and cooking equipment to accompany them, and these arrangements are normally made in Kathmandu before the trek. Trekking agencies have proliferated in Kathmandu to cater to trekkers and climbers needing help organizing their trips and hiring staff and equipment. With the adoption of email use in the past few years by many Kathmandu-based trekking agencies, more and more foreign tourists are dealing directly with Kathmandu agents rather than booking their trips through tour companies in their home country, which are typically more expensive than Kathmandu-based trekking agencies and which usually subcontract the tour operations to Kathmandu-based trekking

---

107 In the early days of tourism in Khumbu, trekkers would often seek food and lodging in modest tea houses located along their route of travel. Trekkers typically followed routes that had been in use for many years by local residents, for whom the tea houses had traditionally provided service. As the number of foreign visitors and the demand for food and lodging increased along popular trekking routes, local entrepreneurs built larger and more comfortable lodges which have largely replaced tea houses along the more heavily traveled routes.

agencies anyway. Western tour companies sometimes provide Western guides on their trips, which differentiates them from the Kathmandu-based agencies that rely solely on Nepali guides. However, few Western tour companies provide Western guides anymore because of the increased cost this adds to the trip and the resulting difficulty in competing with lower priced agencies.

Porters or pack animals are normally employed to carry the equipment and supplies for self-contained trekkers, and a staff is usually hired to set up and break down camps and prepare meals. The expense and logistical organization required for hiring the support staff and equipment necessary for self-contained travel are more easily borne by groups who can benefit from an economy of scale, and thus self-contained trekkers often travel in groups. Prior to the construction of numerous large lodges along the popular trekking routes in Khumbu, self-contained trekking was the only reasonable way for groups to travel in the region since small tea houses could not feed or house more than a few people at a time. Despite the greater availability of lodges in recent years, a high number of commercially organized trekking groups in Khumbu still travel in the self-contained fashion because this is more profitable for the agency that organizes the tour. The self-contained style also allows a trekking group to operate independently of the established tourist lodge infrastructure and thereby offers the group a high level of control over its itinerary and schedule. It also allows a group to 'get off the beaten path' by spending the night in places away from the more crowded areas where tourist infrastructure has been developed. Relative to tea-house trekking, self-contained trekking can isolate the trekkers from other trekkers outside their group as well as from local people, while increasing their interaction with other trekkers in their group and with their staff.

The growth in number and capacity of lodges has enabled many trekking visitors to forego traveling with a self-contained group. Since lodges furnish travelers with meals and a place to sleep, the necessity of bringing along camping and cooking equipment, supplies, and the accompanying staff is eliminated for those who choose to stay in lodges. Thus the expansion of lodge infrastructure in Khumbu during the past couple of decades has made it easier for individual trekkers and small independent groups to travel economically in the region. However, because lodge trekkers are not self-reliant, they are limited to travel along the more popular trekking routes where food and lodging services have been established.

In 1978, before many Khumbu tourist lodges were built, only about 30 percent of Khumbu trekkers stayed in tea houses, while the other 70 percent camped in the self-contained style with tour groups organized by commercial trekking agencies.[108] By 1988, after a proliferation of lodge construction in Khumbu along the more popular trekking routes, the proportion of tea-house trekkers in Khumbu had risen to about 50 percent. By 1996, however, the proportion of tea-house trekkers in Khumbu had fallen back to about 40 percent, which was considerably less than the proportion of independent trekkers in Nepal's other two main trekking areas in the same year: 48 percent in the Annapurna region and 64 percent in Langtang.[109] The following graph shows the available data on the numbers of independent and agency organized trekkers in Khumbu in 1978[110] and during the period from 1988 to 1996.[111]

108 Bjønness 1979, as cited in Fisher 1990 p.142
109 Armington 1997 p.116
110 Bjønness 1979, as cited in Fisher 1990 p.142
111 Rogers & Aitchison 1998 p.41

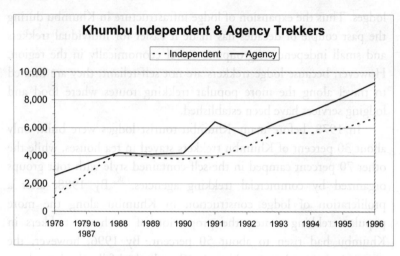

The greater growth in the number of agency-organized trekkers relative to independent tea-house trekkers in Khumbu has been influenced by the marketing power of tour companies in Western countries and trekking agencies in Kathmandu. The ubiquitousness of trekking agencies in Kathmandu and the effect that fierce competition has had on lowering prices and increasing solicitations and advertising have undoubtedly contributed to the increase in trekking agency business as a whole.

From the comparative proportions of independent and agency-organized trekkers in the Khumbu, Annapurna, and Langtang regions, it seems that trekking agencies have captured a particularly high fraction of business in Khumbu. The reasons for this difference are not completely clear, but I can offer a few possible explanations. Most trekkers access the Annapurna and Langtang regions by bus, whereas the majority of Khumbu trekkers fly to Lukla. By offering their assistance in obtaining plane tickets, often through airline business contacts, for the limited seating on flights, trekking agents attract potential trekking clients more readily for Khumbu than for Annapurna and Langtang. Many 'first-time' or 'once-in-a-lifetime' visitors to Nepal want to visit Khumbu because of their desire to see Mount Everest. Such first-time visitors are more apt to rely on a tour company or trekking agency to organize their trip than return visitors who have the benefit of previous experience in Nepal and thus a better understanding of how to do things on their own.

When approached by potential clients, tour companies and trekking agencies will typically push the self-contained camping style of trekking because it is more profitable for the organizer than the tea-house style of trekking, where more of the trekkers' money flows to local lodge owners. To market their services, trekking agencies argue that the self-contained style of trekking allows the organizer to better ensure the clients' satisfaction and also enables them to avoid the problem of crowded lodges along the most popular trekking routes. As the Everest region has become more and more crowded in recent years, this aspect of agency-organized treks has been an increasingly important selling point for tour companies and trekking agencies. Even so, some independent-minded travelers simply do not wish to join a tour group, pay for the services offered by a trekking agency, or sleep outside in a tent set up right next door to a warm and comfortable lodge. To avoid the congestion of the crowded Everest region, many such independent-minded and budget-oriented travelers choose instead to visit the Annapurna or Langtang regions since they are logistically easy to reach and have well-developed lodge infrastructure.

But regardless of where tourist visitors choose to travel in Nepal, a radical new policy proposed in the autumn of 2006 by the Trekking Agents Association of Nepal (TAAN) is likely to further bolster the power of urban-based trekking agencies to market their services and push the self-contained camping style of trekking onto independent travelers. The sweeping new policy referred to as the Trekking Registration Certificate (TRC) scheme would require all foreign visitors trekking anywhere in the country to attain a special permit and to be accompanied at all times by a licensed guide employed by a registered trekking agency. The result of self-interested lobbying by TAAN, an organization representing more than 500 registered trekking agencies, the TRC scheme represents a boon to urban-based trekking agencies, a bane to independent travelers, and a significant loss of income to local residents of trekking areas who might otherwise have been hired to accompany tourist visitors as a guide or porter. Despite strong complaints from tourists and from independent tourism workers, TAAN has defended the new policy by claiming it will improve safety for tourists and stop the operation of 'illegal' trekking businesses (i.e. individuals who do not earn enough money from tourism to meet government registration requirements and therefore do not have to report their earnings for tax purposes). Ironically, the new policy promises to have little to no effect in areas with limited lodge infrastructure where it actually makes sense for tourists to travel in a self-contained fashion. In such areas, the government already requires visitors to obtain an official trekking permit through a registered trekking agency. However, in the popular Everest, Annapurna, and Langtang areas where independent trekking is perfectly safe and where local residents are heavily reliant upon tourism for their livelihoods, the TRC scheme promises to severely undermine local tourism workers' ability to gain employment as guides or to cater services to self-contained trekking visitors who might have otherwise trekked in the tea-house style.

Mountain Climbing Tourism
Mountain climbing visitors are typically members of a group expedition with the goal of climbing a major peak for which the expedition has received a special permit from the Nepal government. As of the late 1990s there were fifteen so-called 'expedition peaks' in the Khumbu region, including Mount Everest, which require a special permit to be climbed. During the ten-year period from 1987 to 1997, the number of permits granted to expeditions for climbs of peaks in the Khumbu region averaged 50 per year and was relatively constant from year to year within a range of 40 to 58.[112]

Mountain climbing visitors trek through the region to reach the foot of their intended mountain where a basecamp is then established

---

112 Information from Reuters' Kathmandu climbing correspondent Elizabeth Hawley, as cited in Rogers & Aitchison 1998 p.44

for the duration of the climb. Supplies are normally transported to the basecamp by large numbers of porters and pack animals and then often transported up the mountain by high-altitude porters hired specifically for this task. The period of climbing normally lasts from several weeks to a couple of months while a series of higher camps are established along the climbing route and stocked with supplies and the climbers' bodies gradually become acclimated to the low oxygen conditions of increasingly higher altitudes. Although only about two percent of Khumbu visitors are members of mountain climbing expeditions,[113] these expeditions have traditionally been large groups employing large numbers of staff and requiring extensive supplies of food and fuel. While mountain climbing tourism is the most labor-intensive form of tourism in Khumbu, in recent years a growing portion of the labor has been supplied by men from outside of the Khumbu region.

Distinctions between trekking and mountain climbing visitors have been growing somewhat cloudier in recent years. For one thing, there has been an increasing trend among climbers toward smaller, more self-reliant teams employing fewer support staff. At the same time, as the popular trekking routes in Khumbu have grown more crowded, there has been an increase in the number of trekking groups leaving the main trekking trails to cross over some of the Khumbu region's high passes, which in some cases requires the use of technical climbing equipment. Furthermore, a subset of trekking groups obtain permits from the Nepal Mountaineering Association to climb some of Khumbu's smaller peaks, which have come to be referred to as 'trekking peaks.'[114] Seven of Nepal's eighteen designated trekking peaks are located in the Khumbu region. The relative ease and low cost of obtaining permits to climb Khumbu's trekking peaks, together with the accessibility of the peaks and the short time required to

---

113 Fisher 1990 p.xxv
114 Nepal's 'trekking peaks' are described by O'Connor (1989). Permits for climbing 'trekking peaks', which typically have heights less than 6,600 meters above sea level, are less expensive and include fewer regulations than permits for climbing larger 'expedition peaks' in Nepal.

climb them, have popularized trekking peak climbing among amateur mountain climbers with a yearning to climb in the Himalaya. However, although the number of trekking peak climbers increased in Khumbu by an annual rate of 6 percent during the period from 1992 to 1997, the growth among other Khumbu visitors (i.e. those *not* climbing trekking peaks) rose at an even higher annual rate of 12 percent over the same period. The following chart shows the numbers of Khumbu visitors climbing trekking peaks compared to the total number of Khumbu visitors between 1992 and 1997.[115]

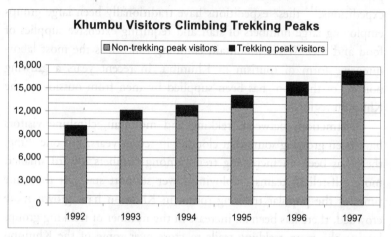

Despite the commonalities in some cases between trekkers and mountain climbers, the fraction of time visitors spend trekking versus climbing still serves to differentiate these two forms of tourism. For example, visitors climbing a trekking peak might spend just three days climbing and more than two weeks trekking, and thus may be more appropriately grouped as trekkers rather than climbers. On the other hand, an ascent of a major peak such as Mount Everest might require as much as two months on the mountain and only a week trekking to and from the basecamp. However, due to the similarities between trekking and mountain climbing visitors in terms of their method of traveling through the region and their greater reliance on

115 Nepal Mountaineering Association statistics obtained in 1998, as cited in Rogers & Aitchison 1998 p.42

local resources than is common for luxury tourists (who rely almost exclusively on imported products), I have considered trekkers and mountain climbers together broadly as trekking tourists for many purposes, making distinctions where relevant differences are significant. Since trekking visitors comprise the overwhelming majority of visitors to Khumbu, and since nearly all visitors, except for a small subset of luxury tourists, engage in trekking during at least part of their time in Khumbu, the majority of the material in this book generally deals with the trekking form of tourism.

Economic Classifications of Tourists

A World Bank commissioned study of Khumbu tourism conducted in 1977 by the Nepal government categorized tourists in the Everest region according to their methods of arranging travel and their expenditure levels. The four general classifications determined by the study are summarized below.[116] The data on expenditure levels, length of stay, and percent of visitors in each category are from the time of the study in 1977, although updated approximate expenditure levels corresponding to the various categories have been footnoted.

(1) 'Luxury' class visitors arrange their visit through a personal travel agent, fly in a small plane or helicopter to the private Syangboche airstrip, stay at the Everest View Hotel, and spend about US$125 per day while in Khumbu, nearly all of which is spent at the hotel. These visitors stay in Khumbu for only a few days and represent 25 percent of the total number of visitors or about 2 percent of the total visitor days in the region.[117]

---

116 His Majesty's Government of Nepal 1977, as cited in Pawson *et al.* 1984b pp.240-241

117 According to Armington (1997 p.196), in 1997 the Everest View Hotel rate was about US$135 per night, one day's meals of breakfast, lunch, and dinner cost about US$45, and there was an extra charge for bottled oxygen or the use of a pressurized chamber (i.e. Gamow Bag) to help guests with altitude sickness problems.

(2) 'Standard' class visitors arrange their trip through a trekking agency in their home country or in Kathmandu, fly to Lukla, stay in lodges or established group camps along their trek, pay daily rates to their trekking agency of between US$15 and US$75, and spend about US$10 per day locally. They stay in Khumbu for an average of 16 days and represent 25 percent of the total number of visitors or about 28 percent of the total visitor days in the region.[118]

(3) 'Economy' class visitors make their own arrangements, fly to Lukla, hire a local guide, and sleep and eat in lodges along the main trekking route for about US$6 per day. Their average length of stay in Khumbu is 18 days, and they represent 32 percent of the total number of visitors or about 42 percent of the total visitor days in the region.[119]

(4) 'Budget' class visitors make their own arrangements, take a public bus to the trailhead at Jiri and walk in from there, carry their own backpack, and stay and eat in tea houses for about US$1 to US$2 per day. Budget class visitors stay in Khumbu for an average of 22 days and make up 18 percent of the total number of visitors or about 28 percent of the total visitor days in the region.[120]

Based on the average duration of stay and the percent of the total number of visitors from each of the four classifications described above, the average length of stay in Khumbu at the time of the government tourism study in 1977 appears to have been about 14 days. A publication on Khumbu tourism in 1992 reported that the average visitor stay in Khumbu was 24 days.[121] The difference

---

118 Daily rates from trekking agencies in 1999 ranged from about US$50 to over US$125. Odell & Brewer (1998 p.196) estimated trekking agencies spent an average of US$7-8 locally per day per trekker for portering, supplemental food, and incidentals.
119 Daily rates for guides in 1999 ranged from about US$10 to US$20, and standard lodge rates including meals averaged about US$10 to US$15 per day.
120 Budget travelers could get by on as little as US$5 to US$10 per day in 1999.
121 Robinson 1992, as cited in Lachapelle 1998 p.53

between these two figures can be explained at least in part by the exclusion of mountain climbing visitors from the Nepal government study in 1977. Mountain climbing visitors, although relatively small in number, typically spend much longer periods of time in Khumbu than other types of visitors. Although not included in the Nepal government study, I would argue that mountain climbers comprise a fifth category of visitors who have played a significant role in Khumbu tourism and have an important effect on the Khumbu economy.

(5) Mountain climbing expeditions make permit and logistics arrangements through a trekking agency in Kathmandu, bring large quantities of equipment and supplies from their home country as well as from Kathmandu, fly to Lukla, hire large numbers of pack animals, porters, and staff, and purchase large amounts of local foods. Although they typically stay in Khumbu for much longer than other types of visitors, often a month or more, they comprised only about 2 percent of the total number of visitors in 1980.[122]

Tourism Numbers & Revenues
Khumbu Tourism Numbers
Khumbu tourist numbers have grown from zero visitors in 1949 to approximately 20 people in 1964, 600 in 1971, 5000 in 1980, 10,000 in 1991, and 25,000 in 2001. The following graph shows the growth of annual tourist numbers in Khumbu from 1971 to 1999.[123]

---

122 Fisher 1990 p.xxv. Note: In the latter 1990's, guided clients paid as much as US$65,000 to join a two-month climbing expedition to Mount Everest.
123 1964 data from Fisher (1990 pp.148-149), 1971 and 1976-1982 data from Pawson et al. (1984b p.239), 1972 and 1974 data from Hardie et al. (1987 p.25, as cited in Stevens 1993a p.362), 1973 data from Mishra (1973, as cited in Brower 1991b pp.67-68), 1983-1999 data from Sagarmatha Pollution Control Committee (1999). Note: The 1971-1979 data were collected at the Namche police checkpost and may understate actual visitor numbers since not all visitors checked in at the police checkpost. The 1980-1999 data were from the Sagarmatha National Park checkpost, which virtually all Khumbu visitors pass through. The 1976-1999 data represent fiscal years ending in June.

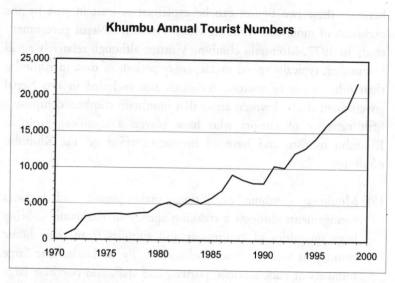

Historically, the largest numbers of foreign tourists in Khumbu have come from the United States, Japan, Germany, France, the United Kingdom, and Australia.[124] In 1999, 64 percent of Khumbu tourists were male and 36 percent were female.[125]

The number of foreign tourists entering Khumbu reflects only a portion of tourism-related visitor numbers in the region, however. Climbing expeditions and self-contained trekkers are typically accompanied by a retinue of porters, camp and cook staff, guides, and, in many cases, pack animals. Even tea-house trekkers often hire porters and guides, albeit in much lower numbers, to accompany them on their trek. The number of staff and pack animals accompanying tourist visitors is difficult to quantify precisely, since records on this have not been kept as carefully as they have been on entering tourists, who must register when paying their national park entrance fee. In the late 1970s, researcher Inger-Marie Bjønness

---

124 According to Pawson *et al.* (1984b p.240), of nearly 10,000 tourists surveyed by Sagarmatha National Park staff in 1979 and 1980, 18% came from the U.S., 17% from Japan, 11% from Germany, 10% from France, 9% from the U.K., 9% from Australia, and 26% from all other countries combined.
125 Sagarmatha Pollution Control Committee 1999

estimated a ratio of 1.7 support staff per tourist visitor in Khumbu, while, in the mid-1980s, national park warden Lhakpa Norbu Sherpa estimated a ratio of 3 to 1.[126] Other researchers have reported ratios ranging from 2 to 4 staff per self-contained trekker and from 0.5 to 1.5 staff per tea-house trekker.[127]

The national park now also tries to collect data on non-tourists passing through the park entrance station, but data collection is problematic and likely understates non-tourist numbers. The national park entrance station data for the 1997-1998 fiscal year indicate that 18,511 tourists were accompanied by 20,551 staff and 2,386 pack animals. Furthermore, an additional 13,838 commercial porters transported food and supplies into the park, much of which was consumed by non-resident visitors. According to these data, the ratio of the total number of support staff, pack animals, and commercial porters to the total number of tourists was roughly 2 to 1.[128] From my own observations in Khumbu in 1999, however, I expect the actual number of support staff is likely much higher than the park entrance data suggest. I rarely found self-contained trekking groups with fewer than 3 support staff per trekker, and I came across several groups with ratios of 6 to 1 and one as high as 8 to 1. And climbing expeditions typically have even higher staff to climber ratios. The increasing percentage of Khumbu visitors trekking with an agency in a self-contained style during the 1990s, and thus employing large numbers of support staff and pack animals, was likely responsible for the 28 percent increase in the number of trekking support staff entering Khumbu between the 1996-1997 and 1997-1998 fiscal years, while tourist numbers increased by only 6 percent.[129] What is evident from the park entrance data and my own observations is that the number of support staff and pack animals is an important

126 Bjønness 1980a & Sherpa 1985, both cited in Brower 1991b p.68
127 Banskota & Upadhyay 1991, Upadhyay 1984, Baumgartner et al. 1978, all as cited in Banskota & Sharma 1995 p.70
128 Support staff and pack animal data from Sagarmatha Pollution Control Committee 1998 Annex 10
129 Support staff and pack animal data from Sagarmatha Pollution Control Committee 1998 Annex 10

component of overall tourist visitor numbers in Khumbu and should
not be ignored when interpreting visitor numbers and their effect in
Khumbu.

Khumbu Tourism Revenues

In 1994, Khumbu attracted 59 percent of the 107 high-altitude
mountaineering expeditions visiting Nepal, and these Khumbu
climbing expeditions paid 77 percent of the fees collected from
climbing expeditions that year by the Nepal government.[130] In 1995,
13 percent of Nepal's total park entrance fees were from Sagarmatha
National Park,[131] and 18 percent of the trekking permits issued in
Nepal were for the Khumbu region. Khumbu's 15,000 trekking
permits placed it second among Nepal trekking areas, between the
50,000 permits issued for the Annapurna region and the 8,400
permits issued for Langtang.[132] It should be noted, however, that the
higher number of trekking permits issued for the Annapurna region
does not necessarily indicate a greater concentration of trekkers than
in Khumbu since the Annapurna region is much larger than Khumbu
and actually consists of numerous distinct areas such as the lower
Marsyangdi valley of Lamjung, the upper Marsyangdi valley of
Manang, the Modi Khola valley leading to the Annapurna Sanctuary,
the hill areas around Ghorepani and Sikles, the lower Kali Gandaki
valley around Tatopani, and the middle Kali Gandaki valley around
Jomson.

Nepal Tourism Numbers

Since Nepal opened its border to foreign visitors in the second half of
the 20th century, tourism in the country has been characterized by

---

130 Gurung 1998
131 Gurung 1998
132 Nepal Ministry of Tourism 1996, as cited in Sharma 1998a p.22

remarkable growth, as illustrated by the following graph of annual foreign tourist numbers from 1950 to 1998.[133]

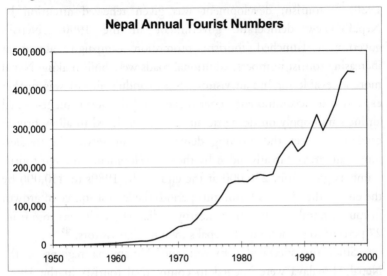

For more than a century prior to 1949, Nepal had been almost completely closed to foreign visitors. But beginning in 1949, Nepal's government began allowing entry to a limited number of foreign mountain climbing expeditions. In 1955, with the coronation of a new king, Nepal adopted a new attitude toward foreign tourism, and the first commercial tourists began to arrive. In that year, the number of foreign visitors was roughly 1,000. At first, infrastructure to accommodate tourists developed slowly in Nepal, and ten years later, in 1965, the annual number of visitors (not counting those from India) was still fewer than 10,000. In the 1970s, Nepal's government began actively promoting tourism as a focus of its development planning. Tourist visa policies were liberalized, several national parks were created, hotels were financed and built, Kathmandu's airport was enlarged to accommodate jets, and agreements were made with international airlines to provide regularly scheduled flights. As a

133 Nepal Ministry of Tourism 1998, as cited in Kansakar & Shrestha 1998 pp.12-17; Nepal Ministry of Tourism 1995, as cited in Banskota & Sharma 1995 p.20. Note: Indian tourists were not counted until 1975.

result, the number of foreign visitors grew from 35,000 in 1969 to over 165,000 in 1980. After a dip in visitor numbers in the late 1980s,[134] tourism development was given renewed attention by Nepal's new democratic government in the 1990s. Nepal's government launched tourism promotion campaigns aimed at increasing tourist numbers, additional roads were built making Nepal more accessible for Indian visitors, Kathmandu's airport was further expanded to accommodate larger planes, and the government-owned airline's monopoly on domestic air service was lifted to allow private carriers to meet the growing demand for air service in roadless mountain areas. Greatly aided by these developments, foreign tourist numbers grew from 250,000 at the end of the 1980s to 450,000 by the end of the 1990s. During this period, the largest source of growth in tourist numbers came from nearby India, whose citizens rose from 27 percent to 32 percent of Nepal's total foreign visitors.[135]

Since the spectacular Everest and Annapurna regions of the Nepal Himalaya were opened to commercial tourists in the 1960s and 1970s, increasing numbers of visitors have been drawn to Nepal by the opportunities the country offers for trekking. In 1969, only 300 tourists – less than 1 percent of visitors to Nepal – went trekking.[136] By 1977, however, the number of trekking tourists had grown to 19,000 – or 15 percent of all visitors. Even more importantly, due to the longer average duration of their stays relative to non-trekking tourists, trekkers accounted for 37 percent of the overall days spent in the country by foreign visitors in 1977.[137] During the 1980s and 1990s, the growth of trekker numbers continued to outpace the growth of non-trekkers. By 1985, the number of trekking tourists had risen to approximately 33,000 and comprised 18 percent of Nepal's foreign visitors. While, by 1996, the

---

134 Stevens (1993a p.355) attributed the slowdown in tourism growth to political friction between Nepal and India in the late 1980s and turmoil surrounding Nepal's democratic revolution in 1990.
135 1988 percentage from Nepal Ministry of Tourism (1989 p.13, as cited in Stevens 1993a p.355) and 1999 percentage from *The Hindu* (2000a)
136 Rowell 1980, as cited in Stevens 1988 p.71
137 Burger 1978, as cited in Fisher 1990 p.110

number of trekkers had grown to 89,000 and represented 21 percent of all foreign tourists.[138] A vast majority of trekkers in Nepal have come from Western countries with well-developed economies. For example, nearly two-thirds of the trekkers who visited Nepal in 1998 were from just six countries: the United Kingdom (with 17% of the total trekkers), United States (11%), Germany (10%), France (9%), Italy (8%), and Australia (7%).[139]

Nepal Tourism Revenues

Nepal's overall tourism revenues in the 1995-1996 fiscal year were US$116 million, which accounted for 3.8 percent of the country's US$3 billion gross domestic product (GDP) and 18 percent of all foreign exchange earnings.[140] By 1999, Nepal's tourism revenues had risen to US$150 million, and constituted 3.5 percent of GDP.[141] Tourism, which if considered an 'export' would have been ranked as Nepal's second largest export in 1995-1996 behind woolen carpets (many of which, it bears mentioning, are purchased by tourists), has been an important source of foreign exchange to help reduce the country's foreign trade deficit.[142] Indeed, earning foreign exchange to help the country's balance of payments has continually been the first

---

138 Nepal Ministry of Tourism 1996, as cited in Sharma 1998a p.22
139 Nepal Department of Immigration, as cited in *Himalayan News* 1999 p.8. Note: These trekking figures include climbers as well.
140 Nepal Ministry of Finance 1997, as cited in Sharma 1998a p.21
141 Lohani 1999
142 According to the Nepal Ministry of Finance (1997), Nepal's 1995-1996 tourism revenues of US$116 million would have placed tourism 'exports' (if they were considered as such) slightly behind the US$135 million in woolen carpet exports and ahead of the US$74 million in garment exports. The total value in 1995-1996 of Nepal's export products (not including tourism revenues) was US$315 million, compared to imports of approximately US$1 billion, which were primarily comprised of manufactured goods and petroleum products. According to the Nepal Ministry of Finance (1999), during the 1997-1998 fiscal year Nepal imported approximately US$1.5 billion, while exporting about US$410 million. An approximated currency exchange rate of 60 Nepali rupees per US dollar was used to convert all the reported numbers to dollars.

aim of tourism development under the Nepal government's series of 5-year planning documents.[143]

In addition to contributing much needed foreign exchange earnings to Nepal's economy, tourism has also provided revenues directly to Nepal's government in the form of government-issued tourist visas, permits for mountain climbing and trekking, and national park entrance fees. For the fiscal year 1997-1998, Nepal's government collected approximately US$10 million in revenues from tourism. Based on 11 months of data in 1998-1999, government revenues from tourism were estimated at US$15 million for the 1998-1999 fiscal year and projected to rise further to nearly US$19 million for 1999-2000.[144]

Nepal Government's Direct Tourism Revenues (US$)

	FY 1997-1998 actual	FY 1998-1999 estimated	FY 1999-2000 projected
Visas	6.3 million	10.8 million	13.6 million
Permits	3.4 million	4.1 million	5.2 million
Other	0.2 million	0.1 million	0.1 million
TOTAL	9.9 million	15.0 million	18.9 million

Primary Trekking Seasons & Routes

The main tourist season in Khumbu is during October and November (referred to as 'post-monsoon' because it follows the summer monsoon), with a secondary tourist season during March and April (referred to as 'pre-monsoon'). These seasons are popular because they avoid the summer monsoon rains and the winter cold

---

143 compare with Fisher 1990 p.110. Note: The second and third aims of tourism development according to the government's plans have been: (2nd) to increase employment by developing local arts and handicrafts and to raise people's purchasing power, and (3rd) to install tourist centers at appropriate places to promote regional balance and to encourage interregional and regional tourism.
144 Nepal Ministry of Finance 1999. Note: An approximated currency exchange rate of 60 Nepali rupees per US dollar was used to convert the reported numbers to dollars.

and snow. The graph below shows the month of entry of the nearly 22,000 tourists who entered Khumbu in the 1999 Nepal fiscal year, which is divided according to the Nepali calendar into 12 months from 14 July 1998 to 13 July 1999.[145]

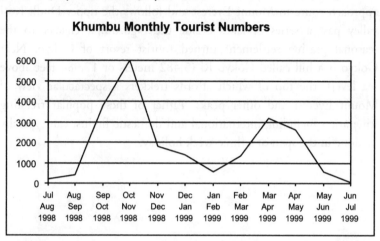

Several different routes and itineraries are possible for trekking in Khumbu, but the majority of tourists follow the standard approach to Mount Everest, a route that has taken on a sort of pilgrimage status among mountain enthusiasts. After a morning flight from Kathmandu to the village of Lukla, which is about eight miles south of the national park boundary, tourists on the main trekking route typically spend nights in the conveniently spaced locations of Phakding, Namche, Tengboche, Pangboche, Pheriche/Dingboche, Lobuche, and Gorak Shep. The latter two locations traditionally served as temporary summer settlements for yak grazing and boasted no permanent buildings until tourist lodges were built there. Visitors normally spend multiple nights in some locations to aid the body's acclimatization to the increasing altitude of the trek. From Gorak Shep, hiking up the nearby hill of Kala Patar (5,553 meters or 18,217 feet above sea level) for a dramatic close-up view of Mount Everest is very popular among trekkers. Also from Gorak Shep, trekkers can

145 Sagarmatha Pollution Control Committee 1999

visit the basecamp used by mountaineers attempting to climb Mount Everest. Trekkers then often follow their route in reverse back to Lukla, from where most fly back to Kathmandu. Another popular trekking route turns north off of the standard Imja Khola valley approach route to Mount Everest and follows the upper Dudh Kosi valley past a series of lakes beside the Ngozumpa Glacier to the seasonal grazing settlement turned tourist resort of Gokyo. Near Gokyo is a hill called Gokyo Ri (5,482 meters or 17,984 feet above sea level), the top of which affords trekkers a spectacular view of Mount Everest and other peaks. Either of these popular trekking itineraries, including international and domestic flights, can typically be done in the span of a three-week holiday.

CHAPTER 3

Economics

In Khumbu as well as in other areas of Nepal, mountain tourism has brought welcome economic opportunities to local communities and individuals. Trekking tourism alone was estimated to have generated 1.1 million person-days of employment in Nepal in 1988.[1] In addition, mountain climbing expeditions directly employed over 10,000 people in Nepal in 1995 and spent an estimated US$2.4 million on transport and provisions within the country.[2] The Everest region is one of the more popular trekking and climbing destinations in Nepal, and the great degree to which Khumbu Sherpas have been involved in mountain tourism not only in their home region but throughout Nepal has made them the wealthiest community in highland Nepal if not the entire Himalaya.[3]

Since the decline in trade with Tibet and the advent of trekking in Khumbu in the 1960s, tourism has replaced trans-Himalayan trade

---

1   Banskota & Sharma 1995 p.84

2   Nepal Ministry of Tourism 1996. Note: Interestingly, the 1995 expenditure by mountain climbing expeditions on transport and provisions within Nepal was more than four-fold higher than the corresponding 1986 expenditure level, despite a smaller number of expeditions, a lower number of climbers, and despite only employing half as many Nepali people (5,195 employed in 1995, compared to 10,415 in 1986). As a possible explanation for the lower number of Nepali people employed more recently and the seeming discrepancy with higher costs, Gurung (1998) noted that in recent years expeditions have tended to use planes and helicopters instead of porters for transporting goods, thereby reducing employment but increasing costs. The use of planes and helicopters for transporting goods and the resulting shift of revenues away from local people may be a portent for those elements of local mountain economies that have become reliant on tourism income.

3   compare with Stevens 1991 p.42

as the driver of the Khumbu Sherpas' economy. Faced with the threat of economic ruin from the downturn in trade, Khumbu Sherpas welcomed and embraced tourism and the economic opportunities it provided them.[4] Sherpas who have had capital available to invest in building a tourist lodge, acquiring pack animals, or starting a trekking agency have been rewarded economically as a result of growing visitor demands for such services. Furthermore, because of the relatively high wages that can be earned through tourism employment, even some formerly poor Sherpa families have been able to accumulate sufficient capital to purchase land or livestock for the first time and in many cases start up their own tourism businesses.[5]

As of 1995, more than 75 percent of Khumbu Sherpa households generated income from tourism.[6] In addition to wage-earning employment, tourism has also created opportunities for Khumbu Sherpas to provide goods and services to visitors. For example, retail shops sell tourist supplies, tea shops furnish refreshments, lodges prepare meals and provide rooms for the night, pack animals are rented to carry loads, and trekking agencies organize logistics, obtain permits, hire staff, arrange transportation, and manage operations for climbing and trekking groups. Based upon the enormously beneficial effect that tourism has had on the Khumbu economy, researcher Stan Stevens and national park warden Mingma Norbu Sherpa concluded in 1992 that "Khumbu is today one of the world's foremost examples of successful local economic development through tourism."[7] This chapter describes how that has happened and explores in detail the effects that tourism has had on the economy of the Khumbu region.

Employment
Although lower paying portering jobs have in recent years increasingly been filled by people from other, less-affluent

4   Fürer-Haimendorf 1975 pp.84-91
5   Fürer-Haimendorf 1975 pp.86-88
6   Stevens 1997 p.70
7   Stevens & Sherpa 1992, as quoted in Rogers & Aitchison 1998 p.35

communities, many Khumbu Sherpas continue to work as camp and cook staff, guides, and staff managers (*sirdar*) for trekking and climbing groups. Trekking and climbing employment in Khumbu has historically been dominated by males,[8] although the number of

8 The literature I came across regarding gender orientation in Khumbu Sherpa society provided a varied, and in some cases seemingly contradictory, perspective. According to Fisher (1990 p.79), the male orientation of Sherpa society could be "seen in the great joy expressed at the birth of a boy and the distinct lack of enthusiasm shown at the birth of a girl. [...] Parents think that a high school diploma is unnecessary for their daughters, who are likely to be wives and mothers, whereas higher education for their sons can yield big payoffs in tourism." Along the same lines, Carrier (1992 p.87) described a preference among Sherpa women for male children, since, according to one Sherpa mother, "[boys] can go wherever they like, and they make better money. And they're much smarter." Bias toward males in Khumbu Sherpa society was also discussed by Fürer-Haimendorf (1964 p.286, 1975 p.18, 1984 p.10), who noted how in traditional Khumbu homes women never occupied the bench by the fireplace, which is reserved for the males of the household and prominent visitors. Instead women always sat on the floor. Furthermore, Fürer-Haimendorf (1975 p.29), in describing Khumbu potato harvesting, claimed that "nearly all the work of digging and gathering is done by women. Better class men do not mind carrying the baskets to their houses, but only poor men will work in a line with women." Likewise, Stevens (1993a p.125) pointed out that in Khumbu labor was often divided along gender lines: "household agricultural tasks are strongly differentiated by sex. Men herd and perform other tasks such as plowing, hauling fertilizer to the fields, helping with grain and hay harvesting, and carrying the harvest to storage places. Women perform most of the agricultural work and assist with some aspects of pastoralism, especially milking and processing milk as well as handling most domestic chores and childcare. These roles are not totally rigid, and men may occasionally be found digging potato fields and women may herd." Barbara Brower (1991b p.53), on the other hand, gave a different slant on gender in describing the Sherpas of Khumbu as "a remarkably egalitarian society, where women and men are essentially coequal. Both women and men are property owners; daughters inherit an equal share in their parents' estate" (a point that contradicts the earlier observation by Fürer-Haimendorf (1964 pp.97-99) that most of a Khumbu family's property, excepting daughters' dowries, was traditionally split among its sons). Brower went on to claim that "Although most tasks may be allocated according to gender (women do most field-work, men construction, for instance) there are no tasks which are exclusively male or female. Men cook, clean, weed, and care for children (most often in the absence of women to do such jobs); women run businesses, trade in India and Tibet, tend livestock in remote areas, hold office in local government. In practical terms, however, there are considerable differences in the daily lives of men and women; roles are defined – if not circumscribed – by gender." These latter statements by Brower are similar to those made by Fürer-Haimendorf (1964 pp.80-81) three decades earlier: "A

females working as kitchen or camp staff or as drivers of pack animals has increased somewhat in recent years.[9] Sherpa males, typically starting around the age of fifteen,[10] work their way up through the hierarchy of positions as they gain more experience and skills in dealing with foreign visitors.

There is little opportunity cost to tourism employment in Khumbu, as other sources of wage-earning employment pay much less than tourism work. In Khumbu, the primary source of employment outside of tourism is agricultural labor, and although wages for agricultural labor have increased over the past few decades, they have remained much lower than the wages offered for even the lowest-paying job in tourism, that of portering. In 1957, when tourism was still at an early stage in Khumbu, male porters for mountaineering expeditions were paid almost four times the normal daily wage of male agricultural laborers, while tourism porters in 1971 earned over three times the daily wage for agricultural labor.[11] As of 1990, tourism porters were still earning wages approximately three times that of agricultural laborers.[12]

As the wealth, connections, and status of Khumbu Sherpas have risen, their roles in tourism employment have changed. Although the

---

Sherpa marriage is basically a partnership between two equals. [...] There is a very clear demarcation between the respective spheres of activities [of men and women], but this distinction between their tasks and interests does not involve any valuation. Sherpas do not consider a man's work of greater value or merit than that of a woman or vice versa. In certain respects, moreover, men and women do the same work; both carry loads on trading journeys and devote themselves to the care of their cattle. [...] A Sherpa woman appears as the equal partner of her husband not only in the privacy of the family circle but also in front of outsiders."

9   Stevens 1993b p.414
10   As Fisher (1990 pp.111, 120) noted, a large number of Sherpa youth quit school to pursue jobs in tourism.
11   Fürer-Haimendorf (1975 pp.42, 87) reported agricultural day wages of 2 rupees in 1957, compared to 7.5 rupees for expedition portering. By 1971, agricultural wages were 3 rupees for women (men's wages were higher, but men were generally not available since they were working in tourism), and tourism portering paid 10 rupees.
12   Stevens (1993a p.127) reported agricultural day wages of 30-40 rupees in 1990, compared to 100 rupees for tourism portering.

term 'sherpa' (uncapitalized) has come into common use by Westerners to refer to the general job category of portering regardless of the porter's ethnicity, Khumbu Sherpas seldom work as porters anymore. One reason for this is that the social and family connections of affluent Khumbu Sherpas provide them with higher paying, more prestigious, and less physically grueling employment opportunities as staff members and guides. Another reason is because most Khumbu Sherpas consider themselves above the menial status of portering work. The legacy of the Hindu caste system has produced a very structured Nepali society. According to longtime Nepal resident and Kathmandu trekking agency owner Stan Armington, this social structure "leads to people having very definite ideas, ingrained since birth, about what jobs they will and will not do. If someone considers themselves a trekking guide, they will be reluctant to carry a porter load."[13] As a result of the experience and reputation many Sherpas had gained working for foreign mountain climbing expeditions originating in Darjeeling in the 1920s and 1930s, Sherpa ideas of their status and, accordingly, what jobs they were not suited for began taking shape even before foreigners first visited Khumbu. Bill Tilman, a member of the first Western group to tour Khumbu, remarked in 1950 how Sherpas "now regard themselves as a *corps d'elite* from whom coolie [i.e. porter] work should not be expected."[14] By the late 1970s, with the growth of climbing expeditions and trekking tourism in Nepal, the Sherpas sense of status had risen even higher. For example, the leader of an American climbing expedition in Nepal in 1978 noted how Sherpas made a point to differentiate themselves from porters: "it was a matter of status: the Sherpas wouldn't carry the same loads as the porters."[15]

As a result of Khumbu Sherpas' general disinterest in portering, most of the portering jobs in Khumbu are now taken by less affluent people from regions outside of Khumbu. A large number of non-

---

13 Armington 1997 p.105
14 Tilman 1951 p.219. Note: The term 'coolie' had its origin in British colonialism in India, and referred to portering labor.
15 Blum 1980 p.87

Sherpa men from lowland areas in Nepal migrate seasonally to Kathmandu to find portering jobs with trekking agencies that hire labor for climbing and trekking expeditions. In addition, many Sherpas, Tamangs, Rais, and Magars from the Solu region travel seasonally to the Lukla airstrip to find jobs with the large number of trekkers and climbers who land there on their way to Khumbu. During the popular visitor seasons in spring and autumn, daily throngs of more than a hundred men and boys wait for visitors to arrive at the airport in Lukla to offer their services as porters and guides. In contrast, it can be difficult, even during the tourist season, to hire a porter in Khumbu itself since local residents are not interested in performing that kind of work.

Since most of Nepal is roadless, porters are relied upon to transport goods on foot throughout much of the country.[16] In this regard, Khumbu is little different than other areas of Nepal. With the nearest roadhead at Jiri a 6-day walk from Namche, the inhabitants and tourism businesses of Khumbu rely heavily on portering since airplane and helicopter cargo space is limited and is too expensive for most items. Other than potatoes that are grown locally, nearly all food in Khumbu as well as clothing and other consumer goods have to carried by porters from lowland areas to Namche's weekly market. Thus, tourism work represents only a portion of overall portering employment in the Solu-Khumbu area. Many porters prefer to carry loads for tourists when given the opportunity, since porters can earn a higher wage from tourists (especially when tips are included) and since tourism work may provide an opportunity to learn some English language (a key ingredient to advancement in the lucrative tourism business). Although some porters have complained that the

---

16 According to Karan & Ishii (1994, as cited by Bishop 1998 p.12), Nepal has one the world's lower densities of roads with 4.3 miles of roads per 100 square miles of land. Nearly all of Nepal's roads are in the low lying, southern portion of the country, and only 40 percent are paved. Other means of mechanical transport include rail and air. According to Bishop (1998 pp.12, 24), Nepal has two narrow-gauge railways, both under 30 miles in length, and 42 airfields, most of which are very rudimentary and only accommodate short-take-off-and-landing (STOL) airplanes or helicopters.

higher pay for tourism work disrupts the overall portering market without improving non-tourism portering wages,[17] Jim Duff of the International Porter Protection Group believes that the higher tourism portering wages will eventually lead to higher overall portering wages in Nepal.[18]

The pay for high-altitude porters on mountain climbing expeditions can be as high as US$3,000 for a single two-month expedition to Mount Everest, which is an extraordinary amount when one considers that the average per capita income in Nepal is about US$170 per year[19] and only about US$50 per year in rural areas of Nepal.[20] Despite the high pay, only a small number of Khumbu Sherpas work as high-altitude porters any longer because of the danger involved and because of the well-paying alternative opportunities in trekking tourism that became increasingly available in Khumbu during the 1980s. As a result, high-altitude portering jobs have increasingly been filled by Sherpas from less affluent Khumbu villages that offer fewer opportunities in trekking tourism (e.g. Phortse and Pangboche), by Sherpas from regions outside of Khumbu (e.g. Solu, Pharak, and Rolwaling), and by people of non-Sherpa ethnicity from the surrounding hill regions (e.g. Tamangs). The declining interest of many Khumbu Sherpas in high-altitude portering work during the 1980s is apparent in a comparison that Fisher made of two large climbing expeditions to Mount Everest in 1963 and 1988. The two expeditions hired a similar number of high-altitude porters, and in both cases nearly all of the high-altitude porters were of Sherpa ethnicity. However, the numbers of Khumbu Sherpas employed as high-altitude porters by the two expeditions were greatly different. Of the 32 high-altitude porters hired by the 1963 American expedition, 25 were Khumbu Sherpas (78 percent of the total), while only 7 of the 28 high-altitude porters on the 1988

---

17 Douglas 1997 p.78
18 Jim Duff, personal communication, 1999
19 Moran 1996 p.37. Note: Nepal's per capita income ranked it as the ninth poorest country in the world in 1996.
20 John Mellor, as cited in Odell & Brewer 1998 p.191

French expedition were Sherpas from Khumbu (25 percent of the total).[21] Because of the dangerous nature of the work and the special skills involved, those who have distinguished themselves as successful high-altitude porters are often employed by climbing expeditions outside of Khumbu and even outside of Nepal to such far away mountain ranges as the Karakoram in Pakistan[22] and the Pamir in China.[23]

The highest and most-prized position among Sherpa tourism occupations is that of staff manager (sirdar). A climbing expedition or trekking group sirdar controls every aspect of the operation, from the hiring of staff, porters, and pack animals, to the purchase of supplies and the selection of which shops and lodges to patronize. Because of the level of responsibility it entails, the title of sirdar carries with it a high degree of prestige in the Khumbu Sherpa community. Even though sirdar work is only available for less than half a year during the spring and autumn tourist seasons, annual wages for sirdars have often been at least ten times Nepal's average annual per capita income[24] and more than thirty times the per capita income in rural Nepal. In addition to achieving substantial prestige in his community and earning a high wage, a sirdar has opportunities to supplement his regular income through his discretion over how and where to direct

21 Fisher 1990 p.123. Note: All 32 of the 1963 expedition's high-altitude porters were of Sherpa ethnicity, while 26 of 1988 expedition's 28 high-altitude porters were ethnically Sherpa. In the case of the 1963 expedition, 4 of the high-altitude porters were Sherpas from Darjeeling and three were Sherpas from Solu. The 1988 expedition's high-altitude porters included 1 Gurung, 1 Tamang, and 19 Sherpas from outside of Khumbu.

22 The employment by climbing expeditions of Sherpas from Nepal as porters in Pakistan's Karakoram mountains was common in the past, but the government of Pakistan now requires the exclusive use of Pakistani or Balti porters for this work.

23 I was a member of an international mountain climbing expedition in the Pamir mountains of western China in 1998 that employed two Tamang men from the Solu region of Nepal as high-altitude porters. In addition to their wages, the Tamang men were compensated to travel overland from Nepal to China via India and Pakistan – a distance of over two thousand miles that required nearly four weeks of travel – and were paid for their time and cost of returning home as well.

24 Stevens 1993b p.414

the expenditure of his clients' money. By preferentially employing family members as staff, using family-owned pack animals, directing clients toward relatives' shops and lodges, and purchasing supplies through family connections, sirdars can capture for their families a large portion of the money spent locally by foreign visitors.[25]

In addition to the wages they earn, many porters, staff, guides, and sirdars benefit from keeping the personal equipment with which they are outfitted by the expedition that employs them. Some of the items are kept for their own or their family's use and some are sold to tourists in Namche or in Kathmandu.[26] An additional and sometimes extremely lucrative economic benefit of tourism employment comes from the tips that satisfied visitors often give to their Sherpa staff at the end of a trip. Although 10 percent of total wages is considered a standard tip,[27] considerably higher amounts are not uncommon. Also, it is not uncommon for a visitor to become a long-term benefactor to a Sherpa with whom a close relationship was nurtured while on a trek or climb. Foreign sponsors have provided funds to Sherpas for such things as their children's education abroad, international travel, treatment in Western hospitals, and assistance with the financing of homes, tourist lodges, trekking agencies, and other business ventures.[28] In fact, one Western anthropologist working in Khumbu reported in 1987 that more than one-third of the families in the Khumbu village of Khumjung had received some type of foreign sponsorship, as had nearly all the Khumbu Sherpa families that were living in Kathmandu.[29]

Provision of Goods & Services

Probably more than anything else, the development of shops and especially lodges by local residents has kept a substantial amount of the money spent by tourists in the hands of Khumbu Sherpa families.

---

25   Brower 1991b p.82, Stevens 1993a p.373
26   Fürer-Haimendorf 1974 p.105, Brower 1991b p.81
27   Armington 1997 p.62
28   Brower 1991b p.81; Stevens 1993a pp.373-374, 499; Adams 1996 p.9
29   Adams 1996 p.221

After the first tourist shop in Khumbu was established in 1967, within 25 years the number of shops in the region had grown to about 30.[30] Likewise, 25 years after the first tourist lodge was built in 1971, the number of lodges in Khumbu had grown to over 140. The following graph illustrates the tremendous rate of growth of tourist lodges in the Everest region between 1971 and 1996.[31]

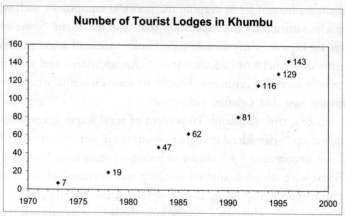

Number of Tourist Lodges in Khumbu

Many lodges have been built just outside of Khumbu as well. Between 1990 and 1997, more than 150 new lodges were built along the approach trek from Lukla to Namche,[32] raising the estimated total number of visitor bed spaces in Pharak and Khumbu to over 5,000.[33]

Although the first Khumbu tourist lodges were simply Sherpa homes and herding huts set up to accommodate a few visitors, modern lodges, especially those along the primary trekking route to Everest basecamp, are today usually specialized structures containing private rooms, indoor toilets, and a large dining area.[34] Building a

---

30 Stevens 1993b p.415
31 1973-1991 data from Stevens 1993a p.365; 1993-1996 data from Rogers & Aitchison 1998 p.71
32 Armington 1997 p.186
33 Rogers & Aitchison 1998 p.69
34 In 1999, there were still several examples of small, simple tourist lodges in Khumbu located in places off of the main trekking routes (e.g. on the eastern side of the Dudh Kosi valley below Gokyo). These small lodges were typically summer grazing shelters 'converted' into a lodge by adding a sign and a simple menu and perhaps a few bunk-style beds.

sizable lodge is a costly undertaking since strategically located land has become expensive and since most of the building materials must be imported from outside of the region. Khumbu Sherpas have utilized interest-bearing bank loans very little to finance lodge construction, and only one lodge in Khumbu has been funded through a government loan. Instead, many lodge owners have financed lodge construction through their savings from tourism work and through assistance from foreign benefactors in the form of gifts and interest-free loans.[35] In 1999, I talked with several Khumbu lodge owners who had operated small, simple lodges for several years (in one case for as long as 20 years) in order to save enough money to construct the larger and more comfortable lodges they were operating now. I also talked to the owner of a bakery and cafe in Khumjung who had received the necessary funds for construction from a foreign sponsor who had befriended the owner during a tourist visit to Khumbu several years earlier.

According to a workforce survey by Kathmandu's Centre for Economic Development and Administration (CEDA), the International Labor Organization (ILO), and the United Nations Development Programme (UNDP), 271 tourist lodges were operating in the Solu-Khumbu area in 1991, and they employed 877 people, over half (55 percent) of whom were female.[36] Lodges are often operated by the women of the owning household and employ a few persons from outside the family to help with such chores as hauling water, cleaning, and cooking. Such lodge employees are normally not from Khumbu since most Khumbu Sherpas are not interested in lodge labor wages, which are low compared to the wages that can be earned from trekking work. With some Khumbu families owning multiple tourism businesses, much of the labor has to come from outside of Khumbu because many Khumbu children are away at

---

35 Stevens 1993a p.499, 1993b pp.415-416. Note: The one Khumbu lodge built with government development funding was the upscale Sherpa Trekking Lodge in Namche, which received a loan in 1979 from the Nepal Industrial Development Corporation.

36 CEDA 1991, as cited in Banskota & Sharma 1995 p.86

school in Kathmandu or abroad.[37] In addition, some of the lodges
located in the more remote, higher elevation areas (e.g. Gokyo, Gorak
Shep, and Chukhung) are operated by hired employees from outside
Khumbu so that the lodge owners themselves do not have to put up
with the cold, harsh conditions in those locations. In 1999, I found
several lodges operated by or at least employing young people of Rai
ethnicity from lower lying villages outside of Khumbu. I also found
one lodge along the main trekking route in Khumbu that had been
sold to a Tibetan businessman living in Kathmandu. The new owner
had renovated and expanded the lodge and hired a couple of young
Rai men to operate it for him.

Khumbu tourist lodges have generally been lucrative business
ventures, with popular lodges grossing over US$10,000 per year and
netting at least US$2,000 in annual profit[38] compared to initial
construction costs of about US$6,000.[39] Such levels of profitability
are even more remarkable when one considers the generally poor
economic situation in Nepal, where, as mentioned already, the
average income is only about US$170 per year, or about US$50 in

---

37 There are a large number of wealthy Khumbu families who have children
   attending school outside of the region and who rely on employees from outside
   of Khumbu to help run their multiple tourism businesses. As an example,
   consider one Namche family that, as of 1999, owned a tourist lodge and
   restaurant, a bakery, a café, and a money exchange in Namche, as well as a
   trekking agency in Kathmandu. The family consisted of a sister and three
   brothers, and one of the brothers was married and had three children. All of the
   children were living and attending school in Kathmandu. The sister ran the café
   with several hired employees, the wife ran the money exchange herself, one of
   the brothers ran the bakery with a couple hired employees, another brother ran
   the trekking agency with a large number of hired employees and also served as
   president of the Nepal Mountaineering Association, and the third brother was
   living and working in America. The lodge and restaurant were operated by two
   hired employees. As another example, consider a Pangboche family that in the
   fall of 1999 had just finished construction of a new tourist lodge adjacent to one
   it had been operating for several years. The family took over operation of the
   new lodge and turned over operation of the older lodge to a young Rai couple
   from outside of Khumbu who had previously been employed seasonally by the
   family to attend to the family's crops. The family was planning to hire
   additional help to attend to their crops the following year.
38 Stevens 1993b p.416
39 Odell & Brewer 1998 p.204

rural areas. The profitability of lodges has been helped by family operation, low wages paid to outside hired help, no taxes, and the establishment of fixed (i.e. non-competitive) prices among Khumbu lodge owners since 1992. In 1999, most Khumbu lodges charged about US$1 for a night's stay in a dormitory and about US$2 for a large but simple meal of rice, lentils, and vegetables. Higher end lodges offering private rooms and a variety of Western style foods charge slightly higher prices depending on the level of accommodation and service they provide.

The enticing profitability of lodge ownership has prompted one wealthy Namche family to build a chain of high-end tourist lodges called Himalayan Chain Resorts. The chain consists of four lodges located in the lower lying villages of Phaplu, Lukla, and Phakding in the Solu and Pharak regions and another five in the Khumbu villages of Namche, Khumjung, Tengboche, and Dingboche. These comfortable, modern lodges are geared toward wealthier trekking tourists who are willing to pay higher prices for amenities not found in normal lodges. The same family who owns Himalayan Chain Resorts also owns the large and well-known Kathmandu-based trekking agency, Asian Trekking.

As the number of Khumbu visitors has grown rapidly over the last couple of years, the lodge infrastructure in the busiest areas of Khumbu (i.e. along the route to Mount Everest) has not been able to keep up with the number of visitors seeking food and shelter. During the peak tourist season the lodges in the popular but remote areas of Lobuche and Gorak Shep, for example, often fill up, and in some cases trekkers have been turned away or forced to find a space to sleep on the dining room floor of a jam-packed lodge. Stories of the overcrowded conditions in Khumbu have even encouraged some trekkers to book their trip to Khumbu with an organized tour group. By offering tent camping or by booking lodge reservations in advance, tour agencies have begun marketing themselves as a way to avoid the problems of overcrowdedness in Khumbu.

In addition to providing food and lodging for tea-house trekkers, many Sherpa landowners also rent ground space for self-contained trekkers to set up their camps. In villages with limited level ground, tents may be set up on terraced fields used to grow potatoes, but this does not necessarily preclude potato growing since the spring and fall tourist seasons occur primarily before and after potato planting and harvesting, respectively. In this way, through tourism, landowners have been able to increase the productivity of the limited flat land in Khumbu. Sherpa families also make money from camping groups by renting a downstairs room in their house or lodge for the group to use as a camp kitchen and as a place for trekking staff and porters to sleep.

Another profitable tourism business opportunity for Khumbu Sherpas is the employment of pack animals to carry loads for mountain climbers and trekkers. Since the mid-1970s, many Sherpa families involved in tourism have purchased male yak-cattle crossbreeds (*zopkio*) from Solu to use as pack stock for this purpose. Yak had historically been the preferred beast of burden for the trans-Himalayan trade conducted by the Khumbu Sherpas[40] and are still used as pack animals within Khumbu, but zopkio are preferred over yak for transporting climbers' and trekkers' loads from the Lukla airstrip up into the Khumbu region because zopkio are more even-tempered and because yak are considered to be susceptible to diseases at lower altitudes such as at Lukla.[41] Although the total number of bovines (including male and female sexes of yak, zopkio, and cattle) remained essentially the same in Khumbu from the 1950s to the 1990s, the proportion of zopkio in Khumbu herds has increased significantly.[42] Because of the popularity of zopkio among Sherpas involved in tourism and the increased amount of cash available among such Sherpas for purchasing them, the number of zopkio in Khumbu increased from about 80 in 1978 to at least 580 in 1991. The number of families owning zopkio in Namche, the Khumbu village most heavily involved in tourism, rose from 5 families in the early 1960s to 51 families by 1991, who collectively owned 171 head

---

40   Fürer-Haimendorf 1975 p.52
41   Brower 1990 p.40, 1991b pp.97-98; Stevens 1993a p.366
42   Brower 1991b pp.109-113; Stevens 1993a pp.366-367, 1993b pp.416, 420

of zopkio. Meanwhile in Phortse, a relatively out-of-the-way village with much less involvement in tourism, only 4 families owned zopkio in 1990, and together they held just 9 head of zopkio.[43]

It is not uncommon during the tourist season in Khumbu to see a pack stock owner driving as many as eight animals along the trail fully burdened with the loads of a trekking or climbing group. Since a yak or zopkio can typically carry twice the load of a human porter, the rate charged per animal is normally twice as much as a porter's wage. Furthermore, an animal owner does not have to pay for food or lodging for the animals along the trail since they can graze and spend the night in the open. Thus, for each animal employed, the owner's daily profit can be four times a human porter's daily profit, since half of the porter's wage may be consumed by food and lodging costs while employed. The financial return of owning pack animals can be inferred from the short time it takes an owner to recover the cost of acquiring an animal. In 1999, the purchase of a zopkio or yak cost about 15,000 Nepali rupees (or about US$225). The rate at which a zopkio or yak could be hired as pack animals in tourism in 1999 was about 1,000 rupees (or about US$15) per day, which equals two times the human porter rate of about 500 rupees per day including food. Thus, in 1999, a pack animal owner could recoup the cost of purchasing a pack animal after about 15 days of employment.[44]

Another example of Sherpa vertical integration along the tourism economic chain comes from Sherpa ownership of Kathmandu-based trekking agencies. The very first trekking agency in Nepal was started in Kathmandu in 1964 by the late Jimmy Roberts, a British expatriate who is commonly referred to as the father of Nepal trekking. A Khumbu Sherpa man from Khumjung who had worked as a sirdar for Roberts was hired to manage the office of Mountain Travel Nepal. He later went on to found another Kathmandu-based

---

43 Stevens 1993a pp.389, 502. Note: The 1978 zopkio number is from Bjønness (1980a p.66, as cited in Stevens 1993a p.389).

44 Stevens (1993a p.390) reported a purchase price of 3,000 Nepali rupees and a hiring rate of 160 rupees per day for zopkio in Khumbu in 1991, which meant that the purchase cost could have been recouped in about 19 days.

trekking agency called Sherpa Cooperative Trekking, which was the first Nepali-owned trekking agency, and his family now owns a Kathmandu-based agency called Arniko Travel and Trekking. A number of other Khumbu Sherpas have also started trekking agencies in Kathmandu, and, as of 1988, 26 of the 56 officially-registered trekking agencies in Nepal were owned by Khumbu Sherpas.[45] Many Sherpa-owned trekking agencies organize and operate treks and climbs not just in Khumbu but throughout Nepal, Tibet, and the Himalaya.

The introduction of various modern technologies such as telephone and internet service to Khumbu has provided additional opportunities for local entrepreneurs to earn money from tourist visitors. When relatively low cost telephone service became available in 1999 in the Khumbu villages of Namche, Kunde, Khumjung, and Syangboche, Sherpa entrepreneurs soon recognized the money-making potential of charging tourist visitors for telephone calls. Wealthy local residents and business people quickly snatched up all of the telephone connections that were allocated to the Khumbu region by the Nepal Telecommunications Corporation (NTC). The new telephone service utilized a microwave dish antenna near Syangboche capable of transmitting signals to and from Kathmandu.[46] Because the new microwave service was considerably less expensive than previously available satellite services, both in terms of the users' telephone equipment and the per minute usage fees, it has been much more widely adopted in Khumbu. Prior to the microwave telephone service, telephone service in Khumbu had been limited to a few satellite telephones in Namche, Tengboche, and the remote trekking destinations of Gokyo and Lobuche where sick or injured trekkers

---

45 Fisher 1990 p.115. Note: Only the larger trekking agencies are typically registered with the Trekking Agents Association of Nepal. According to Armington (1997 p.88), as of 1997 there were 149 registered companies out of a total of 338 trekking agencies in Nepal.

46 According to a newspaper article in the Kathmandu Post (1999), the NTC plans to install over 1,000 telephone communication terminals in remote areas of Nepal. As of December 1999, 74 percent of 3,913 villages in Nepal did not have any means of telephone communication.

were willing to pay the high cost of telephoning Kathmandu to request a medical evacuation by helicopter. With telephone service now less expensive and more widely available, more and more visitors are paying to use it for checking on the availability of and confirming return plane flights, contacting travel and trekking agents in Kathmandu and abroad, calling family and friends while on vacation, and sending and receiving email. In 1999, the NTC was charging 9 rupees (about 13 cents) per minute to call Kathmandu from Namche, while lodge owners were charging tourists 20 rupees (about 30 cents) per minute.

Airline service is yet another example of Sherpa involvement in the tourism business. In 1993, Nepal's government relaxed its monopoly on domestic air transport and began allowing private airlines to operate flights within the country. As of 1999, there were eight private airlines, in addition to the national airline, flying domestically in Nepal. One of these private carriers, Asian Airlines, is owned by the same Khumjung family who started the first Nepali-owned trekking agency as described above. Asian Airlines flies charter and rescue helicopter flights throughout Nepal and provides regular service between Kathmandu, Pokhara, and a number of airstrips in roadless areas of Nepal that are popular with trekking tourists.[47]

Despite the importance of tourism to the Khumbu economy and the large percentage of Sherpas engaged in tourism employment and the provision of goods and services related to tourism, tourism has not completely replaced agriculture and pastoralism in Khumbu. As researcher Stan Stevens pointed out in the early 1990s,

> no Khumbu Sherpa family today relies solely on earnings from tourism. Farming continues to be carried out by all the households and ways are found to compensate for the scheduling problems and occasional labor shortages created by the demands of tourism employment. Even the families which have grown wealthiest from

---

47 Armington 1997 pp.161-162. Note: In 1999, Asian Airlines provided service from Kathmandu and Pokhara to remote airstrips in Phaplu, Lukla, and Syangboche in the Solu-Khumbu region, as well as Jomsom, Manang, Taplejung, and Tumlingtar in other regions of Nepal.

trade and tourism continue to place great importance on maintaining the cultivation of their land and many also keep livestock.[48]

Even with the continuance of the Sherpas' traditional agropastoral economic practices, however, tourism has had deep and pervasive implications on the socioeconomics of life in Khumbu, as discussed in the following sections as well as the next chapter.

Monetization & Multiplier Effect

Money earned from tourism has increased the role of cash in the local economy relative to traditional barter and reciprocal labor arrangements. Noting in the early 1970s that lowland merchants who came to the weekly market at Namche were selling all their goods and grains for cash and not buying anything from the Sherpas, the renowned Himalayan researcher Christoph von Fürer-Haimendorf pronounced that in Khumbu "the era of barter has clearly come to an end."[49] Cash had also replaced the traditional payment of labor wages using butter, potatoes, and grain. However, despite the rise in importance of cash, Stan Stevens claimed in the early 1990s that most agriculture in Khumbu continued to be conducted by reciprocal work groups and that some forms of barter exchange remained important locally.[50]

As wealth among the Khumbu Sherpa community has grown due to tourism, cash expenditures on locally produced goods have increased, further stimulating the local economy and spreading the economic benefits to those not directly involved in tourism. For example, artists and monks in Khumbu have benefited indirectly from tourism through the increased commissioning of artistic and religious works by local residents who have grown wealthy from tourism. In addition, since many Khumbu Sherpas have also increased their purchases of goods and services that are not available

---

48   Stevens 1993a p.85
49   Fürer-Haimendorf 1974 p.107
50   Stevens 1993a pp.380, 423; 1993b pp.418-419

locally, the multiplier effect of tourism earnings has extended to the regional economy as well. For example, while Khumbu Sherpas have increasingly used tourism earnings to purchase locally produced potatoes, hay, and manure, a great deal of tourism-generated money has also been spent on grains, clothing, and consumer products imported from lower altitude regions outside of Khumbu. In addition, most of the laborers hired to help with tourism businesses, household chores, farming, and animal herding have been from outside the region. The same has been true of the majority of the construction workers and materials employed in building lodges and new homes in Khumbu. Similarly, yak-cattle crossbreeds have been acquired in greater numbers from breeders in lower altitude areas of Solu.

Economic Mobility

When foreign mountain climbing expeditions began visiting Khumbu in the 1950s, opportunities to earn money from tourism became available to Sherpas without requiring them to migrate to Darjeeling. Expeditions of the 1950s and 1960s often employed hundreds of lowland porters to transport equipment and supplies to Khumbu, where local residents and their pack stock carried loads up to and above the mountain's basecamp. Among numerous Mount Everest climbing expeditions during this period, the 1952 Swiss expedition hired 163 porters, the 1953 British expedition hired 450 porters, and the 1963 American expedition hired 900 porters.[51] As mentioned already, porters hired by mountaineering expeditions were typically paid much more than the going rate for agricultural day labor in Khumbu. High-altitude porters carrying loads above basecamp were paid much better still, and they also received clothing and equipment provided by the expedition for their use, which they routinely kept or sold for a profit after the expedition was over. A large number of Khumbu residents, including many who had been

---

51 Dittert *et al.* 1954, Hunt 1954, Unsworth 1981 (all as cited in Stevens 1993a p.359)

poor by Khumbu standards, were able to gain work as high-altitude porters and became quite wealthy relative to other residents of the Nepal Himalaya.[52] Fürer-Haimendorf described the opportunity that tourism offered for upward economic mobility among Khumbu residents during this period:

> For the poor but energetic and adventurous young men, expedition work offered unique possibilities. Previously, a Sherpa without land or capital could not hope to attain more than modest prosperity even by a life-time's hard work. The whole structure of Sherpa economics favoured the entrepreneur rather than the wage-earner, and impecunious men had to work many years in the pay of others before they could acquire land or cattle, or venture out as independent traders. But a successful high-altitude porter could, in a single season, earn sufficient cash to engage in some modest trade deals or buy his first plot of land. The sudden affluence of successful porters brought to the fore men of a class which used to live in the shadow of the rich families of inherited wealth.[53]

But jobs as high-altitude porters were limited and opportunities to work for mountain climbing expeditions were only available during a couple of months each year, so during the 1950s and 1960s tourism work was little more than a short-term supplemental activity for most Khumbu Sherpas. In the 1970s, however, after the Nepal government had opened Khumbu to tourists and an airstrip had been constructed in nearby Lukla, trekking tourism began to bring greater numbers of visitors to Khumbu and created additional opportunities for Khumbu residents to engage in tourism. As the number of trekking visitors grew rapidly, the demand for guides and camp staff and for shops and lodges grew along with it, and many Sherpas were able to participate in tourism to a much greater degree.

The widespread involvement of local residents in tourism following the rapid growth of trekking in the early 1970s was reflected in data collected by researchers in the Everest region in 1978, 1985, and 1991, which are summarized in the following table.

---

52 Fürer-Haimendorf 1974 p.108; 1975 pp.86-88, 99; Brower 1991b pp.87, 92
53 Fürer-Haimendorf 1984 p.65

The studies showed that a high percentage of Khumbu households quickly became involved in tourism, and even in Khumbu villages with relatively lower involvement in tourism, a large proportion of households were involved to at least some degree.[54]

Percentage of Khumbu Village Households Involved in Tourism

	1978	1985	1991
Kunde	85%	96%	not avail.
Namche	84%	86%	91%
Khumjung	76%	85%	not avail.
Thame villages	not avail.	81%	not avail.
Pangboche/Milingo	not avail.	66%	77%
Phortse	47%	49%	58%

As mentioned in the earlier section on Employment, the number of Khumbu Sherpas participating in the dangerous profession of high-altitude climbing has diminished as other lucrative, and safer, opportunities in tourism have become available to them. However, high-altitude climbing has continued to provide a means of economic mobility for those Khumbu residents for whom climbing remains an attractive occupation. Many of the Sherpas who have continued to work as high-altitude climbers have been from relatively poor families living in villages that offer little involvement in trekking tourism. The high pay received for successfully climbing Mount Everest under the employment of a Western mountain climbing expedition has, in a considerable number of cases, served as seed capital in enabling relatively poor Sherpas to construct tourist shops and lodges or to acquire land and pack stock. In 1999, I visited several small lodges in

---

54 1978 data from Fisher (1990 p.115). 1985 and 1991 data from Stevens (1993a p.362). Tourism involvement was defined in these studies as receiving income directly from tourism.

the Khumbu villages of Phortse, Samde, and Thamo that, according to their owners, had been started in this way during the past few years. In each of these cases, the owners proudly displayed photos and certificates documenting their climbs of Mount Everest that had paved the way for their investment in a tourism business of their own.

Economic Differentiation

As tourism continued to develop in Khumbu in the 1980s and 1990s, it became an increasingly capital intensive business. Newer, larger, and fancier tourist lodges replaced simple in-home accommodation, while pack animals and helicopters replaced human porters. Labor has remained an important component of trekking and climbing tourism in Khumbu, but wage earnings are small compared to the returns that have been achieved from the ownership of tourism assets such as shops, lodges, pack animals, trekking agencies, and airlines. Although Khumbu Sherpas have rarely had to compete with outsiders in the development of tourism enterprises in Khumbu, they have competed with each other for tourism business, and some Sherpas have fared better than others have. Attributes that have made a real difference in the abilities of Sherpas to engage in and benefit economically from tourism include strategic social and business connections, entrepreneurial confidence, ownership of land along a main trekking route, and available capital to invest in tourism enterprises. Over time, because of variability in the levels of these attributes among Khumbu residents, the degree of tourism involvement between different villages and between different households within villages has been disparate, resulting in accentuated economic differentiation in the region.

Between 1970 and 1982, a period of early tourism enterprise development in Khumbu, researcher Ivan Pawson noted a definite increase in economic differentiation between Khumbu villages that were heavily involved in tourism relative to villages with less involvement. Drawing comparisons between such villages, Pawson observed that "the gap between acculturated [engaged in tourism] and unacculturated [not engaged in tourism] villages, as judged by general levels of affluence, house styles, and other obvious indicators, had widened."[55] Another researcher, Stan Stevens, concluded in the early 1990s that the economic differentiation that had arisen in Khumbu due to different levels of involvement in tourism was significantly greater than the economic differentiation that had existed in the pre-tourism era due to different levels of involvement in trans-Himalayan trade. Furthermore, Stevens noted that local economic differentiation was likely to continue to widen because the amount of capital required to invest and compete in tourism enterprises had grown well beyond the means of poorer families.[56]

Along with the constraint of available capital, Sherpa social and business connections have also played a major role in governing access to opportunities in tourism. As discussed in the earlier section on Employment, the job of trekking staff manager or *sirdar* often brings considerable economic benefits to the sirdar's family and friends. In addition, close relationships with Kathmandu-based trekking agents assure some Sherpas steady and high-level employment with trekking and climbing groups and also help in directing a trekking agents' clientele to a certain family's lodge.

Due to the Everest region's strategic location along an important trade route between Tibet and Nepal and the limited returns available in Khumbu from agropastoral activities alone, nearly all Khumbu Sherpa families had been involved in trade to some degree prior to its decline in the 1960s. It seems very reasonable to surmise that Sherpas developed levels of skill and experience in commercial enterprise that corresponded to the different scales at which they engaged in trade. Of all the Khumbu villages, none were as well positioned to engage in trade as Namche, which because of its location literally served as the gateway between Khumbu and lowland Nepal. Furthermore, because of the lack of agricultural land in Namche relative to other Khumbu villages, Namche residents were practically forced to engage in trade

---

55 Pawson *et al.* 1984a p.74
56 Stevens 1993a pp.371, 376, 379-380

to a larger degree than other Khumbu residents. The resulting general disposition toward business enterprise among Namche villagers was in all likelihood a key factor in the establishment and successful operation of the numerous and wide-ranging tourism businesses that have emerged in Namche and that have made it the center of the Khumbu tourism market. The first tourist shop in Khumbu, which opened in 1967, was located in Namche, as was the first tourist lodge in 1971, as well as the first lodge built specifically to serve tourists, which opened in 1974. Of course it also helped that Namche's geographic location as the gateway village to Khumbu, which had been so important to its involvement in trade, also made it a logical hub for trekking tourists to stop at. As a result of the entrepreneurial spirit of Namche residents and the village's prime location on the Khumbu tourist trail, over 70 percent of all shops in Khumbu in 1991 were located in Namche.[57]

In general, Khumbu residents owning land along the popular trekking route between Namche and Mount Everest have been particularly advantaged to benefit from tourism, especially those who have had sufficient capital to invest in the building of tourist lodges. Since the villages of Namche and Pangboche are located directly on the main trekking route, the residents of those villages have become heavily involved in tourism-related businesses. The residents of Khumjung and Kunde have also become heavily involved in tourism, even though these villages are not located on the main trekking route. The heavy involvement in tourism of Khumjung and Kunde villagers can be attributed to their traditional ownership of numerous seasonal herding huts (yersa) used during the summer while grazing livestock in the high valleys through which the popular trekking routes to Mount Everest and Gokyo pass. Beginning in the 1970s, many of these huts were converted to or rebuilt as tourist lodges. Thus, with the benefit of favorable geography, households in the villages of Namche, Pangboche, Khumjung, and Kunde owned 92 percent of all

---

57 Stevens (1993a p.363) stated that, in 1991, 21 of 29 Khumbu shops were located in Namche and three-fourths of the Namche shops mainly stocked goods aimed at the tourist market.

Khumbu lodges in 1991.[58] But even Sherpas who were not fortunate enough to possess the kind of geographically favored assets described above were still able to gain substantial economic benefit from tourism if they had sufficient capital to invest in other tourism ventures, such as keeping pack stock or running a trekking agency in Kathmandu.

Between 1993 and 1996, two British geographers by the names of Paul Rogers and John Aitchison conducted surveys of 140 households in 33 villages and settlements in the Khumbu, Pharak, and Solu regions (including 69 households in 15 permanent and seasonal settlements in Khumbu) that revealed some striking patterns between household engagement in tourism and household income levels.[59] For a variety of types of engagement in tourism (i.e. different types of employment or enterprise ownership), Rogers and Aitchison determined the number of households of different income levels actually thus engaged. For the purpose of making these comparisons, households were classified as high, middle, or low income according to income thresholds that divided all the households they surveyed into three roughly equally-sized groups. It is difficult to conclusively determine from the data presented whether the type of tourism activity engaged in by households was a cause or an effect of household income level, but Rogers and Aitchison concluded that the type of tourism engagement among households was generally affected by four characteristics of the household: 1) proximity to popular tourist areas, 2) level of education, 3) foreign language skills, and 4) family connections. Of particular relevance were the specific findings among Khumbu households that:

a) Only high income households owned trekking agencies;
b) Only high and middle income households had foreign business contacts;
c) Only high and middle income households owned lodges;

---

58   Stevens 1993a p.378, 1993b p.417
59   Rogers & Aitchison 1998 pp.65-69

d) Only members of high and middle income households were employed as sirdars;

e) Only members of middle income households were employed as trekking guides or cooks;

f) Predominantly middle income households employed yak and zopkio as pack animals for tourists;

g) Only low income households owned small tea shops;

h) Only members of low income households were employed as porters;

i) 69 percent of high income households increased their level of tourism involvement between 1993 and 1996, compared to 49 percent of middle income households and 12 percent of low income households;

j) 25 percent of low income households decreased their level of tourism involvement between 1993 and 1996, compared to 14 percent of middle income households and 0 percent of high income households;

k) 36 percent of all households increased their level of tourism involvement between 1993 and 1996, compared to 18 percent of households who decreased their level of tourism involvement and 46 percent who remained the same;

l) The "vast majority" of tourism employment opportunities were taken by males; and

m) Women were primarily responsible for managing lodge businesses.

Based upon the results of their household surveys, Rogers and Aitchison concluded that "while there have always been [economic] differences between communities in the area, it would appear that inequalities between them are widening [due to differences in tourism involvement]. [If tourism development is] left to market forces, it is probable that income and community inequalities will widen."[60]

---

60 Rogers & Aitchison 1998 pp.88-89

The household surveys by Rogers and Aitchison also revealed various cases of social friction over differences in opportunities resulting from local economic disparities. For example, some poorer Khumbu residents complained that wealthier residents could obtain permits from the national park for felling trees to use in construction or for fuel-wood much more easily than poorer residents could. There were also complaints that wealthier residents were further benefiting from this advantage by turning around and selling the timber permits they received to poorer residents for a profit.[61] Such inequalities and the resulting exploitation of the less privileged – together with rising inflation, limited economic opportunities for the poor, unequal distribution of tourism benefits, and discrimination in employment – have been blamed for aggravating social tensions in Khumbu.[62] The surveys also suggested that tourism had contributed to a furthering of differentiation along gender lines. Because of the rigorous physical nature of trekking and mountaineering tourism work, employment in trekking and climbing has historically been primarily limited to males. Although a small number of females from poor families have worked as porters in the past, only in recent years have females been employed as trekking staff or high-altitude porters, and, as of 1991, only one or two women had held the position of sirdar.[63]

Despite the findings of the surveys, the relative overall differences in the daily wages of porters, trekking staff, and sirdars seem to have become slightly less pronounced over time, as shown in the series of three tables below. The first table shows actual daily wages for porters, trekking staff, and sirdars in 1964, 1978, 1988, and 1999.[64] The second table shows the proportionality of the wages between the different occupations in each of those years. The third table shows the

61   Rogers & Aitchison 1998 p.54
62   Nepal 1997, as cited in Sharma 1998a p.24
63   Stevens 1993b p.414. Note: In 2000, the first all-woman Sherpa expedition succeeded in reaching the summit of Mount Everest, opening the way for more Sherpa women to get involved in mountaineering as a profession.
64   The 1964, 1978, and 1988 data are from Fisher 1990 p.116. The 1999 data are from my own field observations in Khumbu. In 1999, the exchange rate was approximately 67 Nepali rupees per US dollar.

annualized growth rate in the wage for each occupation over each of
the periods, as well as over the entire period. From the second table, it
can be seen that the proportionality of wages between the different
occupations decreased slightly between 1964 and 1978, decreased
more significantly between 1978 and 1988, and then increased
slightly between 1988 and 1999. The third table shows that wages for
all three occupations grew relatively slowly between 1964 and 1978,
then very quickly (especially for porters and staff) between 1978 and
1988, and then continued to grow quickly and somewhat evenly
among the occupations between 1988 and 1999. The third table also
shows that, over the past 35 years between 1964 (the year trekking
tourism began in Nepal) and 1999, the wage for the lowest paid
occupation (porter) has grown the most, and that of the highest paid
occupation (sirdar) has grown the least.

Actual Daily Wages for Trekking Employment
(Nepali rupees)

	1964	1978	1988	1999
Porter	6 ·	10	50	180
Staff	10	15	65	250
Sirdar	16	25	75	300

Proportional Wages for Trekking Employment
(Relative to Porter Wage)

	1964	1978	1988	1999
Porter	100%	100%	100%	100%
Staff	167%	150%	130%	139%
Sirdar	267%	250%	150%	167%

Annualized Growth Rates in Wages for Trekking Employment

	1964-1978	1978-1988	1988-1999	1964-1999
Porter	4%	17%	12%	10.2%
Staff	3%	16%	13%	9.6%
Sirdar	3%	12%	13%	8.7%

The general narrowing of wage differences over the period that Khumbu has been open to trekking tourism suggests that widening economic differentiation in the region has been due more to different levels of involvement in capital intensive tourism enterprises (e.g. ownership of lodges, pack animals, and trekking agencies) than to different opportunities in wage labor occupations. Even so, the ability of wealthier residents to consistently secure higher wage earning jobs would still contribute to economic differentiation. And very significantly, the daily wages compared in the tables above do not reflect the important additional revenue opportunities available to sirdars described in the earlier section on Employment. Furthermore, it should also be pointed out that sirdars and staff typically have greater interaction with tourists than porters do and thus have more frequently benefited from earning large tips, receiving gifts and loans, and entering into long-term relationships with beneficent sponsors.

Inflation

The large numbers of tourists, porters, and trekking staff visiting Khumbu each year have increased the local demand for food and other products and, together with foreign tourists' recognized higher purchasing power, have driven up prices for everyone, causing significant inflation. This has especially been true for items that have to be imported to the region and thus are in more limited supply. An American doctor who had been living and working in Khumbu for the previous four years informed me in 1999 that prices paid by visitors at tourist lodges for goods and services in Khumbu had nearly doubled in the past four years and that prices at the weekly market in

Namche had increased significantly as well.[65] Foreign tourists – all of whom are highly affluent by Nepali standards – are typically willing and able to pay higher prices than local people normally would. For one thing, foreign visitors are usually accustomed to paying higher prices for items of a similar nature in their home countries. Furthermore, they may not be in the habit of bargaining for a lower price (a normal Nepali practice for many things), and they are frequently not aware of the prices paid by local people.[66] These factors, coupled with the increasing local demand for goods as tourist numbers have grown, has caused inflation in the prices of many goods that are purchased by local residents as well, including grains, dairy products, fruits, vegetables, eggs, snack foods, cooking oil, and kerosene. Increased consumption of these items by growing numbers of visitors has also caused shortages, which Stevens claimed had become "one of the most widely cited local complaints [by Sherpas] about the adverse impacts of tourism."[67]

Between 1974 and 1988, the price of potatoes, a locally grown food staple, rose 1.8-fold, while the price of rice, an imported item, increased 3.5-fold. Over the same time period, daily wages for trekking staff rose 4.3-fold and daily wages for sirdars rose 3-fold.[68] From these figures, it seems that a great deal of the nominal economic gains enjoyed by Sherpas employed in tourism during the period from 1974 to 1988 was counteracted by the effect of inflation in the price of food and other goods. This means that only those Khumbu Sherpas who owned highly profitable assets such as tourist lodges, pack animals, and/or trekking agencies were probably able to achieve real economic growth. In other words, tourism seems to have been economically beneficial primarily for those local residents who have been able to invest in non-wage opportunities. Of course, this infers that inflation has made life more difficult economically for those who have not been able to invest in such opportunities, including poorer

65 Dr. Jim Litch, Kunde Hospital physician, personal communication, 1999
66 compare with Bezruchka 1997 pp.85-86
67 Stevens 1993a p.382
68 Fisher 1990 p.116

households in villages away from popular tourist areas, not to mention local teachers, monks, civil authorities, and employees of NGOs and the national park. Indeed, Brower reported in 1991 that residents of the villages of Thame and Phortse, which are located away from the main trekking routes and do not participate as heavily in tourism as other Khumbu villages, "all complain that life has become much more difficult [because of tourism-induced inflation]."[69] Brower went on to illustrate how the prices of certain staples were much higher in areas of Khumbu frequented by tourists than in areas where tourists seldom ventured. For example, potato prices were four times higher in Pheriche, which is located on the main trekking route to Mount Everest, than in Lhahuche, located in an area of the Bhote Kosi valley off limits to tourists. This is even though Pheriche enjoys better conditions for growing potatoes. For families living near the main trekking route but not engaged in tourism, the higher prices for staples could pose quite a burden. Although, as development worker cum researcher Jim Fisher pointed out, inflation in the prices of locally grown staples could benefit those who aren't involved in tourism if they were able to grow enough food for their own use and have a surplus to sell at the higher prices.[70] And the same argument could also be made for those who produced livestock for sale to others, as Fürer-Haimendorf noted that the nominal price of a yak had increased by about 10 times between the 1960s and the 1980s.[71] In addition to the higher price of food and livestock, inflation has also affected the costs of houses and land in Khumbu. For example, Fürer-Haimendorf noted that, in 1983, the cost of a large house in most Khumbu villages had increased by 6 to 9 times what its cost in Nepali rupees had been in the 1960s, while the cost of houses in Namche had increased by an even greater amount. Reasons Fürer-Haimendorf offered included an increase in the cost of wood for construction (which had to be purchased and carried from the Pharak region outside of the national park rather than sourced

69 Brower 1991b pp.88-89
70 Fisher 1990 p.116
71 Fürer-Haimendorf 1984 pp.12, 19-20

locally as in the past), higher wages for carpenters and other craftsmen, and higher purchase prices for land.[72]

Due to the shortage of available farm and hotel labor in Khumbu (as a result of many Khumbu Sherpas working for high wages as trekking guides or migrating to Kathmandu to work in trekking agencies or to attend school), the local cost of labor has increased considerably over the period that tourism has developed in Khumbu. Another factor contributing to the increased cost of labor is the perceived affluence of Khumbu Sherpa employers. As affluence has grown in the Everest region, laborers (including skilled craft workers such as carpenters and masons) hired from regions outside of Khumbu have demanded higher wages from their wealthy Khumbu Sherpa employers. The increased affluence among many local residents due to tourism has also resulted in a higher cost of living in Khumbu. Prices of imported goods have risen as traders from lower altitudes have come to perceive that Khumbu Sherpas are able to pay higher prices.[73] Furthermore, as the level of overall wealth in the Everest region has increased, the degree and frequency of conspicuous displays of wealth have also risen. Indeed, it has become an embarrassment for a Khumbu family not to serve expensive imported foods in social situations. This kind of 'social inflation' has also pressured families to contribute ever-increasing amounts to support community festivals, religious rites, and monastic institutions.[74]

Reliance On & Threats To Tourism

The significance of tourism to the Khumbu economy is unmistakable. So, what if something happened to curtail tourism there? Because many tourists are drawn to Everest by the mountain's iconic fame as the highest point on Earth, a characteristic that is not likely to change, a complete waning of tourist interest seems unlikely.

---

72 Fürer-Haimendorf did not provide data on the change in valuation of Nepal's currency over this time period, but devaluation of the rupee could also have been a factor in increasing nominal prices in Khumbu.

73 Stevens 1993a p.381, 1993b p.418

74 Fisher 1990 p.116

However, there are many potential circumstances that could adversely impact the popularity of Nepal or the Everest region as an international tourism destination and have a serious effect on an economy that has come to depend on a steady flow of foreign visitors. Some of the possibilities expounded upon below include political instability and conflict in Nepal, the threat of international terrorism, border sensitivity with China, a disease epidemic or natural disaster, significant changes in glaciation due to global warming, and something that has already begun to occur in the Everest region – overcrowding.

Overcrowding

The number of tourists visiting Khumbu increased dramatically during the latter 1990s, and many of the trekkers I talked with there in 1999 said that the overcrowding would definitely affect their decision to return to the Everest region in the future. Many said they would prefer to visit other, less crowded regions in Nepal or else other countries. A Western trekking agency owner and guide I spoke with who had visited Khumbu 40 times over the previous 18 years told me that he would stop organizing group treks and climbs in Khumbu if the crowdedness got any worse. According to him, it was "quite obvious that it is getting more and more crowded" in the Everest region. He went on to say that the romance of visiting an exotic place like Khumbu had been considerably diminished by the number of organized tours and the number of visitors.[75] That reports of overcrowding are likely to encourage potential Khumbu visitors to choose other places to travel is evidenced from conversations I had with trekkers in other regions of Nepal in 1999 who said they had intentionally avoided the Everest region because they had heard it was too congested.

---

75   Hooman Aprin, personal communication, 1999

Political Instability & Violence

[Author's note: I originally wrote this section in 2000, just as the conflict in Nepal between Maoist insurgents and government security forces was beginning to increase in intensity and just before it had begun to affect tourist numbers in the country. By the time a peace accord between the Maoists and the government was signed in November 2006, the ten-year long insurgency had claimed more than 13,000 lives, affected millions more, and sent the country's tourism industry into a five-year tailspin. I purposely chose to leave this section as it was written in 2000 in order to illustrate the point that the predicted threat to tourism posed by political instability and violence was in fact a real threat that the residents of Khumbu could do little to counter, and that a return to political instability and violence in the country would likely have the same effect on tourism.]

Since Nepal's monarchy gave up sovereignty to the people following a short but bloody pro-democracy movement in 1990, Nepal's attempt at democratic government has been plagued by political bickering, instability, and corruption. Between 1990 and 1999, Nepal's parliamentary government was dissolved four times. Over the five years from 1994 to 1999, Nepal had seven different governments because no single political party had been able to control a majority position in parliament.[76] Political instability and the resulting turnover of governments have been blamed for slowing the country's economic development and have dissuaded funding agencies such as the World Bank, the Asian Development Bank, and others from funding projects to further develop the country's key tourism asset.[77] While it is difficult to obtain direct evidence that political instability in Nepal has begun undermining the popularity of tourist visits to

---

76 BBC News 1999a
77 BBC News 1998b & 1998c

Khumbu, heightened political turmoil could very well pose a threat to tourism throughout Nepal in the near future. Furthermore, continued political inconstancy could hamper funding for and effective planning and initiation of potential tourism development and promotion programs.

Since 1996, Maoist guerillas in Nepal have waged an insurgency to replace the country's constitutional monarchy with a communist republic. Maoist shootings, bombings, and clashes with police had claimed over 1,400 lives in Nepal as of June 2000.[78] Periodic Maoist calls for nationwide strikes have effectively shut down the country numerous times because workers and business owners have feared violent retribution against anyone who defied the strikes.[79] The Maoist rebels stepped up their violence in the weeks preceding Nepal's national elections in May 1999, including bombings in the capital city of Kathmandu and shootings of politicians and civilians throughout the country. During the elections, which were held during the height of the spring tourist season,[80] over twenty-five thousand police guarded polling stations across the country and the army was on standby in case of terrorist actions. The elections were split into two phases conducted two weeks apart in order to avoid diluting security forces in the face of threatened Maoist attacks on polling stations. On the election days, authorities banned all sales of alcohol and prohibited vehicles from the streets of the capital city of Kathmandu in an effort to limit the movement of potential troublemakers. Despite these precautions, eight people were killed in clashes between guerillas and police on the eve of the first phase of the election.[81]

The U.S. State Department has issued numerous travel advisories warning travelers of the potential for political violence in Nepal. How

---

78 Nepal News 2000, Upadhyaya 1999
79 Associated Press 1998
80 National elections in Nepal can, for practical purposes, only be held in the spring or fall since winter snow renders mountain areas inaccessible and summer monsoon rains cause landslides and floods that wash away roads and bridges.
81 Chalmers 1999a & 1999b

much of an impact the violence, disruptions, and warnings have had on tourist visits to Nepal is not clear, but they have had at least some effect. For example, foreign tourists were not permitted in the Dolpo region in the Spring of 1999 and were redirected to other less sensitive areas in Nepal due to the Nepal government's fear of Maoist violence surrounding the elections in May. In another example, the first reported Maoist rebel attack on a tourist establishment occurred in April 2000, when twenty insurgents carrying rifles robbed an upscale tourist hotel in the heavily visited tourist destination of Pokhara. No one was injured, but if the violence – or even merely foreigners' perceptions of a threat of violence – increases in Nepal, especially in popular tourist areas, then this could have a significant effect on the number of tourists choosing to visit the country.

Terrorism

> [Author's note: Likewise, this section was also originally written in 2000, a year prior to the September 11, 2001 terrorist attacks in the United States that severely impacted international tourism and travel around the world and led to the cancellation of many tourists' travel plans to Nepal.]

On 25 December 1999, an Indian Airlines flight from Kathmandu was hijacked by terrorists seeking the release of Islamic militants imprisoned by the Indian government. In the aftermath of the hijacking, which received a great deal of international media attention, Indian Airlines ceased flying in and out of Nepal for over five months until it was satisfied that the Nepal government had improved security measures at the Kathmandu airport, the sole international airport in Nepal.[82] Since Indian tourists comprised 32 percent of the approximately 440,000 foreign visitors to Nepal in 1999, the stoppage of flights from India caused a significant decline in tourist numbers in Nepal during the first half of 2000.[83] The effect

---

82 *The Hindu* 2000b
83 *The Hindu* 2000a

of the hijacking on tourist numbers from other countries was unclear, but it is likely that some may have decided not to visit Nepal because of the hijacking and some may have changed their plans due to the cancellation of flights. In any case, these events illustrate the vulnerability of Nepal tourism, and hence Khumbu tourism, to terrorism and its aftereffects.

Border Sensitivity with China

Since the occupation of Tibet by communist China began in 1950, thousands of Tibetans have fled across the Nepal border to escape political, ethnic, and religious persecution. Today, there are some 130,000 Tibetan exiles living in more than 30 countries, and about 3,000 additional Tibetans cross into Nepal each year via mountain passes along the Himalayan border.[84] One of the most heavily-used passes by refugees is the Nangpa La, which lies between the Khumbu region and Tibet. Following a brutal Chinese crackdown on Tibetan resistance in 1959, as well as during the tumultuous Chinese 'Cultural Revolution' in the latter 1960s, thousands of Tibetans fled to Khumbu over the Nangpa La pass. Due to the border sensitivities between China and Nepal that followed, the Nepal government refused to permit any mountain climbing expeditions in Nepal from 1966 to 1969. Until restrictions were loosened in 2002, foreign climbers and trekkers were forbidden from visiting the Bhote Kosi valley above Thame, which Nepal's government had designated a military restricted zone because of its proximity to the Nangpa La pass. Although the Nepal side of the Nangpa La is now open to climbers and trekkers, Chinese border patrols continue to shoot and kill Tibetans attempting to escape across the pass to Nepal. Eyewitness reports by foreign climbers of Chinese brutality have caused intense international outrage and deep embarrassment for the Chinese government.[85] In September 2006, a Western climber on Cho Oyu peak near the Nangpa La filmed a Chinese border patrol

84 Associated Press 2000b
85 *Inside China Today* 1999

shooting at an unarmed group of Tibetans attempting to flee via the pass into Nepal. A young Tibetan nun was killed, several Tibetans were wounded, and a large number – including several children – were arrested and held by the Chinese. The release of the film footage to the international media created a huge public outcry, refuting spurious Chinese claims that the border patrol had fired on the Tibetans in self-defense.

The Himalayan highland areas along the Nepal-Tibet border are not the only sensitive places that overlap with tourist destinations. Tens of thousands of Tibetan refugees live in Nepal and India, and refugees have held large demonstrations in those countries protesting the Chinese occupation of Tibet. In March 2000, for example, over one thousand Tibetan protestors gathered at the Buddhist temple of Boudhanath, which is one of the most popular tourist destinations in Nepal's capital of Kathmandu and one that many foreign tourists visit before or after a trek in Khumbu. Nepali police confronted the large group of protestors in order to stop them from heading to the Chinese embassy. After protestors threw rocks at the police, the police swung batons to disperse the crowd and seriously injured at least twenty-five of the protestors. With Nepal's government eager to protect its relationship with China, it has in recent years begun turning refugees back over to Chinese authorities and prohibiting protests against Chinese policies in Tibet. The potential for instances such as those described above to adversely affect tourists' interest in visiting Khumbu or Nepal or to result in restrictions on tourists visiting certain areas near the Nepal-Tibet border should not be underestimated.

Disease Epidemic

Although the presence since the 1960s of a Western-built hospital staffed by Western doctors has significantly raised vaccination rates and overall attention to health-related problems in Khumbu, health care services are poor or nonexistent throughout most of rural Nepal, and disease epidemics have occurred regularly in impoverished areas of the country. Even the relatively developed capital city has not been spared, as an epidemic of meningococcal meningitis occurred in Kathmandu in 1983 that that infected six foreigners, two of whom died. Following this, the U.S. Center for Disease Control issued an alert to travelers to be vaccinated against the disease, which can cause death within 24 hours, and the alert was still in effect as of 1997.[86] In addition, tuberculosis is highly endemic in Nepal and can be transmitted through close contact, although most foreign travelers with healthy immune systems are not considered very susceptible to this risk.[87] Given the country's limited healthcare infrastructure, however, any serious outbreak of infectious disease in Nepal could spread rapidly, discouraging foreign tourists from visiting the country and thereby adversely affecting tourist numbers in Khumbu.

Even disease outbreaks occurring outside of Nepal could negatively affect foreign tourists' plans for traveling to the region. For example, the 2003 outbreak of SARS (Severe Acute Respiratory Syndrome) in China had immediate and severe impacts on tourist travel in Asia, and the closure of the Chinese border in reaction to the outbreak stopped all overland travel to Nepal via Tibet for some time. Similarly, the specter of the Asian bird flu virus hangs uneasily over most of Asia and, even if it weren't to spread appreciably in Nepal, the mere perception of a threat could negatively affect tourist travel to the country.

Natural Disaster

The Himalaya is a young mountain range in a geological sense, only beginning to form about fifty million years ago as the tectonic plate of India rammed into that of Asia. In fact, the mountain range is still being forced upward at an average rate of approximately one centimeter (one-half inch) per year, resulting in frequent earthquakes and landslides and considerable geomorphology.[88] The mountain range is not only rising, it is also being pushed forward by the Indian plate, with global positioning satellite data showing that Mount

---

86   Dr. David Shlim, as cited in Armington 1997 p.122
87   Moran 1996 p.141
88   Moran 1996 pp.9-10, Zhu et al. 2005

Everest is moving northeast at the astonishing rate of nearly two-and-a-half inches (six centimeters) each year.[89] The enormous tectonic forces generating this movement are periodically unleashed in the form of earthquakes, and scientists have warned that the Himalaya region is particularly prone to large catastrophic releases of energy such as the earthquake that devastated Kathmandu in 1934 and the one that killed 75,000 people and left more than three million homeless in the mountains of northern Pakistan in 2005.

In addition to the potential threat of devastating earthquakes and landslides, a considerable threat is also posed throughout the Himalaya by the building up and bursting of ice-dammed and moraine-dammed glacial lakes above villages and routes of travel. The magnitude of this threat in the Khumbu region was realized on August 4, 1985, when the Dig Tsho glacial lake (*tsho* is the Tibetan word for lake) in the Langmoche valley above the village of Thame burst through its glacial moraine dam and the resulting flash flood (*tshoserup*) caused significant downstream destruction. The breaching of the moraine dam was caused by wave action following a large ice avalanche into the lake from the retreating Langmoche glacier. Within hours, five million cubic meters of water had rushed down-valley, carrying along with it huge amounts of debris and resulting in the deaths of at least four people and a large number of livestock. The number of human casualties would undoubtedly have been greater if the flash flood had not occurred during the local *Phangnyi* festival during which residents were congregated in their villages rather than working in their fields alongside the river as normal. The devastating flood destroyed 30 houses, 14 bridges, a newly constructed hydro-electric power plant near Thame, about 20 hectares of valuable pastures and farmland containing unharvested crops, plus extensive forestlands and a large portion of the trail network as far as 25 miles (40 kilometers) downstream. The makeshift trail that replaced the one destroyed by the flood was dangerous to travel and resulted in a

---

89 National Geographic Society & The Associated Press, as cited in *HimalayaNet* 1999

number of accidents during the subsequent tourist season that autumn. Also destroyed or left isolated and useless were a number of tourist lodges, tea shops, and a mountaineering and trekking supply store.[90]

A similar avalanche-induced glacier lake burst occurred in September 1977 from the Nare glacier at the base of Ama Dablam peak. The resulting flash flood swept away part of the village of Jorsale near the entrance to the national park, killing three villagers. It also washed away seven bridges and many sections of trail along the Dudh Kosi river as far as 35 kilometers downstream from the source.[91] According to the recollections of Khumbu residents, several other glacial lake flash floods had occurred within living memory, including a very substantial one in the mid-1950s along the Bhote Kosi river downstream of the Thengpo glacier.[92]

Changes in Glaciation

The above-mentioned huge Dig Tsho glacial lake that burst in 1985 was formed by the retreat of the Langmoche glacier and the trapping of meltwater behind the residual moraine of the receding glacier.[93] Glaciers in the Khumbu region, as well as throughout the Himalaya and the rest of the world, have been receding at rapid rates since the 1960s due to the effects of global warming.[94] Receding Himalayan glaciers have caused the formation of ice-dammed and moraine-dammed glacial lakes to increase significantly in the past few decades,

---

90 Vuichard & Zimmermann 1986 pp.90-94, 1987 pp.91-110; Brower 1991b pp.24-25
91 Armington 1997 p.191, Brower 1991b p.24
92 Brower 1991b p.24
93 Vuichard & Zimmermann 1987 pp.95-96
94 Pearce 1999. Note: A study of Himalayan glaciology by Syed Hasnain of Delhi's Jawaharlal Nehru University was presented in July 1999 at the International Commission on Snow and Ice. In addition to devastating flash floods from glacial lake breaches, Hasnain's study warned that all the glaciers in the central and eastern Himalaya could disappear by the year 2035 at their present rate of decline, causing river flows in South Asia to become less reliable and eventually diminish, resulting in widespread water shortages in the highly populated region.

and numerous lakes have been building up to dangerous levels making it likely that the frequency of glacial lake breaches will increase.[95] Within and around the Khumbu region there are several glacial lakes that pose the threat of catastrophic bursting, with the potential to cause grave destruction and economic hardship for local residents and disrupt the subsistence and tourism economies upon which the local population is dependent.[96] Glacier researchers have predicted imminent breaches in the dams of the Pareshaya Tsho, which is about six times larger than the Dig Tsho was before it burst and which is located above the main trekking route to Mount Everest,[97] and the even larger Rolpa Tsho, which if it were to burst could have a catastrophic effect on the people living downstream in the Rolwaling and Tamba Kosi valleys to the west of Khumbu.[98]

Receding glaciers in the Khumbu region have also made travel over certain passes (e.g. the Tashi Lapcha pass between Khumbu and Rolwaling) and climbing routes on certain mountain peaks (e.g. the standard routes of ascent on Island Peak and Ama Dablam) more difficult and in some cases impractical or unsafe. Researcher Barbara Brower's conversations with elderly local residents in the mid-1980s revealed that receding glaciers had made travel in Khumbu increasingly hazardous over their period of memory.[99] Thus, in addition to posing catastrophic threats and raising objective dangers,

---

95 Vuichard & Zimmermann 1987 pp.106-107
96 While acknowledging there are hundreds of dammed glacial lakes in eastern Nepal alone, Vuichard & Zimmermann (1987 p.107) identified as potential threats the following large dammed glacial lakes in and around the Khumbu region: Tshola Tsho above Pheriche, Pareshaya Tsho above Chukhung, several in the Gokyo valley above Phortse, Rolpa Tsho on the Trakarding glacier above Beding in the Rolwaling valley, Lumding Tsho in the Lumding valley west of Phakding, and several in the Hinku and Arun valleys adjacent to Khumbu.
97 Watanabe, Ives, & Hammond 1994 pp.329-340; Watanabe, Kameyama, & Sato 1995 pp.293-300
98 Yamada & Sharma 1993, as cited in Watanabe, Kameyama, & Sato 1995 pp.293, 299-300; Tribhuvan University hydrologist Bidur Upadhyay, as quoted in Pearce 1999. Note: The government of the Netherlands has funded a multi-million dollar project that was initiated in 1999 to reinforce the Rolpa Tsho glacial moraine dam and drain the lake to reduce the likelihood and catastrophic danger of it bursting.
99 Brower 1991b p.19

climactic changes are also limiting the possibilities available to climbers and trekkers and could perceivably reduce the popularity of visiting certain areas in the Khumbu region.

The credible potential for one or more of the threats described above to adversely affect tourism in the future leads one to wonder how the people of Khumbu would adapt to such a situation. Longtime Khumbu observer Jim Fisher expressed the opinion that local residents would be able to return to their traditional agropastoral livelihoods if there was a decline in tourism since "they have not burned their economic or psychological bridges behind them."[100] While this may be true, it does not acknowledge the fact that Khumbu agropastoralism, by itself, has never supported a population of 3,000 permanent residents, let alone 3,000 residents who have grown accustomed to lifestyles of unprecedented affluence. Supplemental income from tourism replaced that from trans-Himalayan trade, but what would replace tourism? Fisher went on to point out that Khumbu Sherpas, because of their improved educations, would have the option of migrating to Kathmandu to pursue employment opportunities there or abroad. Indeed, I suspect that is exactly what would happen if Khumbu's tourism economy were to decline. As a result, I think it is perfectly reasonable to conclude that the *absence* of tourism, much more so than its presence, would have the greatest economic effect on and pose the gravest threat to the Khumbu Sherpa community.

---

100 Fisher 1990 pp.147-148

CHAPTER 4

Personal Well-Being

Along with the unmistakable boon that tourism has provided to the Khumbu economy over the past few decades, it has also brought some significant improvements to the physical well-being of many local residents. Areas of improvement range from individual household requirements like food, clothing, and shelter to the expansion of local infrastructure and health care benefiting the entire community. While some of the improvements are the result of increased incomes from tourism, others can be traced to local development projects initiated by foreign tourists whose visits led them to take a personal interest in the region and its inhabitants. The positive effects that tourism as a whole has had on local well-being were evident from the surveys conducted among Khumbu households in the mid-1990s by the British researchers Rogers and Aitchison, who noted that "local people emphasized that life is now considerably better, easier and less arduous than before the emergence of tourism."[1]

In a country where half of the population lives below the poverty line, where two-thirds of adults in rural areas are illiterate, and where contaminated water causes four out of every five deaths among children,[2] any positive effects on people's physical well-being are certainly welcome. But while one can argue that the relatively affluent and developed Khumbu region is hardly representative of a nation

---

1   Rogers & Aitchison 1998 p.81
2   Stephens (1998) reported that 46 percent of Nepal's population lives below the poverty line, 65 percent of adults living in rural areas are illiterate, and 80 percent of child deaths are caused by water-borne diseases.

ranked by the United Nations Human Development Index in the bottom 15 percent of the world's countries, the significant improvements to personal well-being that have been accomplished in Khumbu suggest that, with sufficient will, major differences can be made in other areas of the country, too. This chapter explores the diverse ways in which the well-being of local residents has been affected by tourism in Khumbu, along the way revealing some welcome and some not so welcome effects.

Diet, Clothing, & Housing

Increased income from tourism has allowed many Khumbu residents to include a wider variety of foods in their diets, including fruits, vegetables, eggs, meat, and greater quantities of grains like rice, corn, and wheat. The keeping of milk cows has also reportedly risen, enabling an increase in daily household consumption of dairy products.[3] In addition, the increased availability of imported foods targeted at meeting the demands of foreign visitors means that such items have also become more available to local residents. Along with such former luxuries as sugar, chocolate, and coffee, Khumbu Sherpas are now purchasing greater amounts of processed foods such as noodles and breads made from eggs and wheat flour. While some researchers have suggested that dietary changes associated with rising tourism incomes have enriched local diets and improved health,[4] others have argued that the increased consumption of sugary foods, which for the most part had been unobtainable in Khumbu prior to the 1960s, has had deleterious effects on local dental health.[5]

Rising tourism incomes, along with gifts of Western trekking and climbing clothing from visitors, have also enabled many Khumbu Sherpas to improve the quality and warmth of the clothing and shoes

---

3   Stevens (1993a pp.390-391) noted a large increase in the number of Khumbu households owning one or two cows for household milk production since the 1970s, a change he attributed to rising affluence from tourism.
4   Stevens 1991 pp.49, 54
5   Fürer-Haimendorf 1974 p.107, Pawson *et al.* 1984a p.80, Sherpa 2003 pp.123-124

they wear. After the Tibetan border was closed and trans-Himalayan trade came to a virtual halt in the 1960s, Khumbu residents could no longer obtain sufficient wool from Tibet for making clothing. Since the wool produced by Nepali sheep was not fine and soft enough for use in clothing and since efforts to introduce Tibetan sheep were unsuccessful because the Khumbu climate was too humid for sheep accustomed to the arid climate of Tibet, the Sherpas had had to resort to wearing cotton clothing from lowland Nepal, which provided inadequate protection from the cold.[6] Thus, gifts of warm fleece and polypropylene clothing by mountain climbing and trekking tourists were greatly welcomed by local residents. Sunglasses have also become more widely available in Khumbu as tourism has developed there, a definite benefit given the strong effects of the sun at high altitude.

In addition, greater levels of wealth due to tourism have enabled many Khumbu Sherpas to afford building better quality and larger, more comfortable multi-story houses. Fürer-Haimendorf noted an increase in the proportion of double-story houses between 1957 and 1983, a change he "attributed to the fact that poor landless men, who lived in small single-storeyed houses, can now earn cash by working for tourists and are hence in a position to rebuild their houses or abandon an old single-storeyed house and build a new double-storeyed house."[7] In addition to the increased size and quality of housing, construction materials have also changed as the level of Sherpa wealth has grown from tourism. Glass windows, sheet-metal roofs, and concrete foundations and walls, none of which were available in Khumbu before the advent of tourism there, have improved the weatherproofness and livability of Khumbu homes.[8] In recent years, houses made almost entirely of wood have grown in popularity among Sherpas, replacing the traditional houses made of stone around a rough wooden frame. The all-wood houses are warmer

---

6   Fürer-Haimendorf 1974 pp.104, 107; 1975 pp.81-82; 1984 pp.24-25
7   Fürer-Haimendorf 1984 pp.8-9
8   Fürer-Haimendorf (1984 p.10) discussed the new use of glass windows in Khumbu homes in the 1970s and their subsequent wide prevalence in the 1980s.

and more comfortable, but are more expensive and difficult to build than stone houses.[9] An environmental drawback of this trend is the additional quantity of wood required for construction, especially since wood is a limited resource in the region. Along with the change in building materials, contact with outsiders has led to some interesting changes in local architectural styles. For example, Khumbu homes traditionally were built with low doorways, which were believed to prevent stiff-backed evil spirits from entering.[10] Nowadays, because many homes, shops, lodges, and monasteries have been constructed to accommodate Western visitors, it is increasingly rare to find buildings in Khumbu with the traditional low doorways.

Tourism Infrastructure Development

In many cases, Khumbu Sherpas have benefited from local infrastructure developed for tourism purposes. One striking example of tourism infrastructure development that local people have benefited from is the Western medical clinic in the Khumbu village of Pheriche. The clinic, which was constructed with Japanese funds and is located along the popular tourist route to Mount Everest, is staffed by two Western doctors during the tourist season. Although the primary motivation behind establishing the clinic was to provide education and treatment for high-altitude and gastrointestinal illnesses among foreign visitors, local residents are welcome to take advantage of the services offered by the clinic as well. Since the Western doctors who volunteer to work at the clinic are not compensated financially, they are generally drawn to volunteer by their interest in Khumbu's tourism opportunities. The clinic is funded by tourist donations as well as fees charged for the medical services provided to tourists. Local people are charged substantially lower fees according to their ability to pay. The clinic treated approximately 400 patients each year in 1998 and 1999, only about

---

9   Author's personal communication with a carpenter constructing an all-wood house in Pharak in 1999.
10   Kunwar 1989 p.237; Brower 1991b pp.49, 61

half of whom were Western tourists – the other half were local Sherpa residents and Nepali trekking staff.

Local residents have also benefited from the airstrips in Syangboche and Lukla that have been constructed and expanded to serve tourism. The landing strip built at Syangboche (just a 30-minute walk from Namche) by Japanese tourism developers in 1972 is now used primarily for shipments of cargo and supplies to the people of Khumbu.[11] The airstrip in Lukla (just a one-day walk from Namche) was built by Edmund Hillary's Himalayan Trust in 1964 and is today one of the busiest airstrips in Nepal. With multiple flights to and from Lukla each day, Khumbu residents enjoy quick, easy, and relatively inexpensive access to Kathmandu. Fares paid by foreign visitors subsidize the much lower fares available to Nepali citizens, who typically pay only 30 percent of the fare paid by foreigners. Although the Lukla airstrip was originally constructed by the Himalayan Trust to facilitate the construction of a hospital in the Khumbu village of Kunde,[12] the subsequent expansion and maintenance of the airstrip and the frequency of flights to and from Lukla is almost entirely due to tourism. And the Nepal government's paving of the Lukla airstrip in 2000 was primarily motivated by a desire to improve access for tourists.

Development Projects

Khumbu Sherpas have also benefited from many indirect effects of international tourism, such as the development projects sponsored and conducted by foreign visitors and organizations. Compared to other poorer parts of Nepal, Khumbu has received much more than its share of such projects, and it is easy to surmise that the Khumbu region would not have received such attention if it were not as well known internationally. Some of the non-governmental organizations (NGOs) that have contributed assistance to development projects in Khumbu have included Edmund Hillary's Himalayan Trust, the

---

11 Armington 1997 p.173
12 Fisher 1990 pp.xxii

Canadian Sir Edmund Hillary Foundation, the World Wildlife Fund, the United States Peace Corps, British Water Aid, the American Himalayan Foundation, the Japanese Himalayan Adventure Trust, the French Association Environment Insertion Economic, the Austrian Eco-Himal, the United Nations Education, Scientific, and Cultural Organization (UNESCO), the International Union for the Conservation of Nature (IUCN), Cultural Survival, and many, many others.[13]

A clear example of how Khumbu development projects have often been facilitated by tourism comes from the long-term involvement of Edmund Hillary's Himalayan Trust in the Everest region. Researcher Vincanne Adams made the point that all the Himalayan Trust's development projects in Khumbu "were carried out on expeditions that attracted economic support from Western volunteers because of their dual orientation. The volunteers aimed to help the Sherpas [but] they also intended to climb mountains."[14] One of the largest projects sponsored by the Himalayan Trust was the construction in 1966 of a hospital in the Khumbu village of Kunde, which to this day is financed and run by the Sir Edmund Hillary Foundation. The Kunde Hospital is staffed year-round by a pair of Western physicians serving two-year stints. As the physicians are paid only US$80 per month, most are obviously drawn to the post by the tourism opportunities Khumbu affords. In 1998, the hospital received nearly 9,000 patient visits, the vast majority (over 96 percent) of whom were local residents of Khumbu and surrounding areas.[15] According to hospital staff, many Nepali people walk for several days to see the Western physicians in Kunde even if there are other healthposts closer to where they live. The reasons for this, according to hospital staff, are that Nepali patients trust Western physicians more than Nepali physicians and because Nepali physicians are seldom found in remote clinics because they generally

---

13   Lachapelle 1998 p.56, Brower 1991b p.78, Sherpa & Höivik 2003 pp.21-30
14   Adams 1996 p.90
15   Litch & Bishop 1999, as cited by Dr. Jim Litch, Kunde Hospital physician, personal communication, 1999

prefer staying in Kathmandu or the district headquarters. Like the healthpost in Pheriche discussed earlier, the Kunde Hospital charges Nepali people considerably lower fees for service than it charges Western tourists. As a result, the hospital's services to Nepali people are partially subsidized by payments from tourists with the balance covered by donations received by the Hillary Foundation.

The Himalayan Trust was also responsible for building the first school in Khumbu, located in Khumjung, in 1961. Since then, the Himalayan Trust has financed, built, provided books for, and trained teachers for some forty additional schools in the Solu-Khumbu district, including several elementary schools and a high school in the Khumbu region itself. Other Himalayan Trust sponsored projects in Khumbu include bridge construction, trail building and repairs, tree planting, and village water supply systems.[16]

In 1999, a drinking water and sewage system project was completed in the Khumbu village of Namche by Eco-Himal, an NGO funded by the Austrian government. With electrical power from the hydro-electric plant near Thame (another Eco-Himal project, which will be described later in the section on Alternative Energy and Fuel Efficiency), water from the natural spring at the bottom of Namche village is pumped to a holding tank above the village. Water from the holding tank feeds by gravity through a system of pipes and valves that provide water on demand to individual homes and lodges in the village. End users are billed according to their metered water usage. Responsibility for operating and maintaining the system, as well as billing and collecting revenues from customers, was handed over to the local electric company, the Khumbu Bijuli Company or KBC (which had been established by Eco-Himal to take over the operation of the Thame hydro-electric plant). Since the Thame hydro-electric scheme had not been profitable, Eco-Himal hoped that additional revenues from the drinking water and sewage project would allow the KBC to be

---

16 Fisher 1990 pp.71-73, Sherpa & Höivik 2003 pp.21-30

financially self-sustainable and thus not require continued financial subsidy from the Austrian government.[17]

Eco-Himal is also sponsoring a number of other development projects in the Thame area as well. The NGO has stated that its motivation for active involvement in the Thame area comes from the fact that, compared to other villages in Khumbu, Thame area residents have not grown as affluent from tourism since their valley is less visited by tourists. Eco-Himal plans to provide electricity to all of the villages in the Thame valley, as well as building trails and bridges, supporting agriculture and education, and constructing water supply systems and composting toilets.[18] Other than its projects in the Thame area, Eco-Himal has decided to phase out its involvement with aid projects in other parts of Khumbu. According to an Eco-Himal representative I talked with in Khumbu in 1999, the Austrian government is no longer as interested in funding aid projects in Khumbu as it once was. The reason cited was that many Khumbu residents have grown rich over the years and it is difficult to justify continued aid for them when there are people in other regions of Nepal who have a much greater need for aid. The Eco-Himal representative noted that there were numerous Khumbu Sherpas who had become millionaires (as measured in US dollars) as a result of their involvement in tourism.

Along with the direct assistance that foreign visitors and international NGOs provide to residents of Khumbu, it is also worth mentioning that the Nepali government's budget for local development projects in areas such as Khumbu is bolstered by the revenues the government collects from tourist visas, trekking and climbing permits, and national park entrance fees (totaling about US$10 million in 1998).[19] Even more importantly, approximately 50 percent of Nepal's national budget is provided by foreign aid in the form of grants and loans, the availability of which has undoubtedly been influenced by the attention the country receives as a result of

---

17   Eco-Himal 1999
18   Eco-Himal 1999
19   Gurung 1998, Nepal Ministry of Finance 1999

foreign visitors' awareness of the poverty and lack of development there. A portion of the government's overall budget is allocated to village development committees (VDCs) throughout the country to spend on local community development projects. For example, in 1999 the Namche/Thame VDC used government-allocated funding to improve a section of the trail between Namche and Thame. The project employed eleven laborers, all of whom were from outside Khumbu, for one month at a wage of about US$5 per day. The improved trail was not only of benefit to local residents but also to tourists visiting Thame and its monastery.

Health Care, Infant Mortality, & Family Planning

The construction, funding, and staffing of the Kunde Hospital discussed in the previous section brought Western-style health care, vaccinations, and family planning methods to the residents of Khumbu for the first time. Before the hospital was built in 1966, the closest medical facilities were in Kathmandu or Darjeeling, either way at least a ten-day walk from Khumbu.[20] Not only did the tourism-influenced Himalayan Trust project bring Western medical care closer for the residents and visitors of Khumbu, but, as Vincanne Adams pointed out, it brought better equipment, better staff, and better funding than what was available at the time in the entire country of Nepal.[21] Local health problems that the hospital attended to included vaccinations against smallpox and polio, an extremely high prevalence of thyroid diseases such as goiter and cretinism resulting from a lack of dietary iodine, skin lesions and impetigo caused by poor hygienic conditions, a high incidence of gastrointestinal illnesses due to unclean water, a 25-percent prevalence of respiratory infections among children and an emerging presence of tuberculosis among adults, and extremely high infant

---

20 Fisher 1990 p.190
21 Adams 1996 pp.89, 271

mortality rates estimated at 25 to 50 percent of children under the age of thirteen.[22]

In the midst of a smallpox epidemic in 1961, which claimed the lives of twenty-five Sherpas and scarred many others, a vaccination program administered by the Himalayan Trust was credited with saving many lives in Khumbu. According to an American physician I spoke with at the Kunde Hospital in 1999, vaccination coverage among children in Khumbu is now higher than areas in the United States, a situation he attributed to the effective outreach by and confidence in the hospital among the local population.[23] After the Kunde Hospital began an iodine distribution program for local residents, cretinism and goiter, which previously had an incidence rate of 92 percent in Khumbu, were virtually eliminated.[24] In the first two years of the hospital's operation, nearly 4,000 patients were treated at the hospital, and another 2,000 were treated at outlying clinics by the hospital's doctors. Treatments included eye surgery for cataracts, amputations for damaged limbs, tooth extractions, prenatal and natal care for mothers, and drug therapy for respiratory, gastrointestinal, skin, eye, and ear infections and arthritis.[25] Diagnosis of tuberculosis among local residents, as well as adherence to and compliance with treatment protocols, benefited from the nearby presence of the hospital. Infant mortality rates decreased sharply in Khumbu after the hospital was built, which was attributed to the gradual acceptance of the hospital's outreach programs.[26]

The use of contraceptives, including intrauterine devices and Depo-Provera injections, has become quite prevalent in Khumbu, especially in villages more heavily involved in tourism and thus more influenced by Western acceptance of contraception. Between 1970 and 1982, the number of births as well as the reported number of

---

22 Hillary 1964, Pearl 1965, Lang and Lang 1971, Fisher 1990, all as cited in Adams 1996 pp.91-92; McKinnon 2003
23 Dr. Jim Litch, Kunde Hospital physician, personal communication, 1999
24 Pawson et al. 1984a p.80; Fisher 1990 pp.66, 165; McKinnon 2003 pp.119-120
25 Adams 1996 p.95, McKinnon 2003 p.120
26 Pawson et al. 1984a pp.75, 77, 79, 80

desired children decreased in Khumbu, the latter being attributed to the decreasing economic importance of a large family in Khumbu since most households have come to rely more on income from tourism than on subsistence agropastoralism.[27]

Although tourism seems to have contributed positively to components of Sherpa physical well-being such as diet, clothing, housing, infrastructure, clean drinking water, education, and health care, this has not come without a price. As the following sections attest, some Sherpas have suffered from increased stress associated with the responsibilities and worries that go along with high-pressure tourism businesses. In addition, those who have been employed by mountain climbing expeditions have often experienced life-threatening dangers, while those working as porters for tourist groups have suffered under difficult and exploitative working conditions.

Stress, Competitiveness, & Unhappiness

> The price of material progress is too often to replace a smile with a worried frown, the god being money instead of inner peace.
> (Tom Weir, 1955, *East of Katmandu*)

The stress that has arisen from the responsibilities of high-level tourism occupations such as sirdar has reportedly caused an increase in problems such as ulcers and alcohol abuse among Khumbu Sherpas.[28] As one example of this, climbing expedition leader Arlene Blum recounted that the Sherpa sirdar of her 1978 expedition to Annapurna suffered from stomach problems and high blood pressure due to the stress of managing their 300 porters and worrying about the logistics of providing pay and food rations to them.[29] According to Fisher, in the late 1980s the hospital in Kunde saw "an increase in such stress-related conditions as mental illness, ulcers, alcoholism, and depression."[30] Furthermore, Adams noted in 1987 that Western

---

27 Pawson *et al.* 1984a pp.75, 77, 79, 80; Fisher 1990 pp.146-147
28 Stevens 1991 p.47, 1993a p.500
29 Blum 1980 p.63
30 Fisher 1990 pp.165-166. Note: Fisher credited John Draper for collecting this medical information.

physicians working in Khumbu "began to attribute ulcers to overwork on expeditions by Sherpas who did not handle stress well," with physicians estimating that 10 to 15 percent of Khumbu Sherpa men suffered from ulcers.[31]

In the early 1980s, Fürer-Haimendorf noted a general decrease in the happiness of the Khumbu Sherpas relative to what he had observed there before tourism had developed in Khumbu, writing: "Happiness is a phenomenon difficult to measure, but my subjective impression is that the Sherpas I knew in the 1950s were happier than they and their descendants are in the 1980s."[32] Fürer-Haimendorf opined that the Sherpas' society and lifestyle had been "transformed by the impact of outside forces which disrupted the delicately balanced social fabric and undermined the traditional ideology that had dominated Sherpa thinking and conduct for countless generations."[33] He attributed much of the disruption to the long absences from home of men engaged in tourism work, which he believed implied that Sherpas were placing a higher priority on tourism earnings than on their family lives. Indeed, many of the Sherpas I spoke with in Khumbu in 1999 were women operating lodges by themselves or with hired helpers while their husbands and children were either away in Kathmandu or on a trekking or climbing expedition. Some of the women complained of loneliness and said that they looked forward to the end of the tourist season so that they would get to see their families.

Fürer-Haimendorf also ascribed the decreased happiness he perceived among Khumbu Sherpas to a change in their traditional moral values, a circumstance he associated with their full-blown economic engagement in tourism. In a passage seemingly full of idyllic nostalgia, Fürer-Haimendorf described what he considered to

---

31   Adams 1996 pp.96, 210
32   Fürer-Haimendorf 1984 p.xi
33   Fürer-Haimendorf 1984 p.18. Note: Although Fürer-Haimendorf made these comments upon returning to Khumbu in the early 1980s after a long absence from the region, he had opined as early as 1963 that "long years of work for expeditions tend to develop egocentric attitudes in the individual [Sherpa] which accord ill with Sherpa ideals of behaviour"(Hornbein 1965 p.74).

be an unprecedented competitiveness between villagers and a new obsession with wealth:

The moral values which characterized the traditional Sherpa society undoubtedly developed in small communities whose well-being depended on the peaceful and willing cooperation of all the families inhabiting a village. There was little competition for scarce resources, for pastures were adequate for as many yak as the inhabitants of a village were able to look after, and it seems that land-disputes were also extremely rare. Success in trade resulted from individual skill and energy, and the magnitude of the volume of trade with Tibet of one merchant did not affect the chances of other traders. Hence there was little scope for rivalry in the sphere of economic enterprises [and] there were few occasions for acrimonious disputes disrupting the peace of village life.

This situation changed with tourism. Today the Sherpas are no longer alone in Khumbu and the old values of a society virtually free of competition and rivalry no longer fit an economic system which encourages individuals to consider acquisition of money their first priority. Previously, a congenial domestic atmosphere was regarded an essential element of the good life, and wealth was not desired for its own sake, but as a means of running a household in which all members were provided with adequate food and clothing, and there was sufficient surplus to entertain guests as often and lavishly as possible. Wealth was also valued because it enabled a man or woman to dispense charity and give donations to religious institutions, and thereby acquire merit.

Though many men frequently went on trading trips, they normally spent the greater part of their time with their family. The present absence of the majority of young and middle-aged men on tourist-treks and mountaineering expeditions places the traditional ideal of the good life out of reach of many families, particularly if the husband has a second establishment in Kathmandu. While the successful yak-breeder and agriculturalist did not have to sacrifice any part of his domestic life to these activities, a mountaineering or trekking sirdar can only sustain the competition of the other Sherpas in the same business if he gives his professional duties priority over his family life.

The competition for lucrative jobs comes also into the picture. The system of sirdar who command the loyalty of other

Sherpas and control the allocation of jobs on expeditions and tours inevitably leads to the emergence of factions.[34]

Nostalgia aside, there are reasons to suggest that some Sherpas have indeed undergone tumultuous changes in their personal priorities and social relations as they have grown affluent from tourism. A so-called ratcheting effect of accumulation among some Sherpas – a vicious cycle of increasing wealth fueling the desire for greater wealth and so on – has led at least two non-Sherpa observers, who have had intimate insights into everyday life in Khumbu over several years, to characterize some Sherpas as obsessed with the pursuit of wealth. In the opinion of Kunde Hospital physician Dr. Jim Litch, who lived and worked in Khumbu for four years in the latter 1990s, obsessions with wealth and the dissolution of families and traditional values have contributed to deep unhappiness and a decline in aspects of the quality of life for some Sherpas. Litch noted that some Sherpas have become "quietly desperate" with their situations and that this has been manifested in the overuse of alcohol and related violence. As a result, according to Litch, depression, psychotic disorders, alcohol abuse, and domestic violence (notably spouse and elder abuse) have become much more prevalent in Khumbu.[35] These observations were echoed by a representative of the Austrian NGO Eco-Himal, who has worked closely with a number of Khumbu families over the past decade and with whom I also spoke in 1999.

Danger

Even more tragic than the stress and unhappiness created by tourism jobs, wealth, and declining traditional values is the number of Sherpas who have died or been injured while working for foreign mountain climbing expeditions. The dangerous nature of their work has been a harsh reality for Sherpa high-altitude porters since Western expeditions first began climbing in the Himalaya in the early part of

---

34   Fürer-Haimendorf 1984 pp.112-113
35   Dr. Jim Litch, Kunde Hospital physician, personal communication, 1999

the 20th century. The first deaths on Mount Everest occurred in 1922 when seven Sherpas were killed in an avalanche triggered by their British employers. Over the years, employment by mountain climbing expeditions has exacted a heavy toll on the Sherpas. Fisher reported that between 1950 and 1989, 84 Sherpas were killed on mountaineering expeditions in Nepal.[36] This figure does not include the many Sherpas killed before 1950, after 1989, or on mountaineering expeditions outside of Nepal. By the mid 1990s, more than 134 Khumbu Sherpas had died on mountain climbing expeditions throughout the Himalaya.[37] To get a sense of the high risks faced by Sherpas while working on mountain climbing expeditions, consider that of the 148 people who had died on Mount Everest through 1996, 55 were Sherpas.[38] Nepal's government has done little to discourage dangerous activities on the mountain,[39] leaving foreign climbers and trekking agencies employing Sherpa and other Nepali staff to their own recognizance.

Working Conditions

Injuries and deaths have not been limited to Sherpa climbers. Porters employed by both trekking and climbing groups in Khumbu have died due to altitude illness, exposure to extreme weather, and falls on treacherous terrain. Most porter fatalities and injuries could be avoided if trekking agencies, guides, and the trekkers and climbers themselves took greater responsibility for their porters' welfare. It is very rare to see porters given the clothing, footwear, safety equipment, or shelter appropriate for the harsh mountain environment in which they work. With the paltry wages porters receive and their low economic status (otherwise they would not seek

---

36 Fisher 1990 pp.146
37 Adams 1996 p.211
38 Coburn 1997, as cited in Arnold 1998. Note: According to Travers and Kelly (1999), the total number of deaths on Mount Everest had grown to 161 people (156 men and 5 women) as of March 1999, and Douglas (1999b p.78) put the number of Sherpa deaths at 60.
39 compare with Kauder 1996

such grueling work), it is obvious that porters cannot afford to buy such items themselves. It is all too common to see porters walking in cheap flip-flop sandals and wearing tattered cotton clothing, with no hat, gloves, or socks to protect them from the cold. Nor are many porters given sunglasses, and an early snowfall in Khumbu during the autumn tourist season of 1999 resulted in several cases of porters being stricken with snow blindness.

Despite their poor clothing, porters are often expected to sleep outside at night rather than sharing the same shelter as tourists and their staff and guides. It gets extremely cold at night at Khumbu's high altitude, especially for porters who do not have shoes, socks, hats, or warm clothing. And since most porters hail from lower altitude areas outside of Khumbu, they are much more susceptible to altitude-related illnesses than Sherpas accustomed to living at higher elevations. According to Abrahm Lustgarten, who studied porter conditions in Nepal in the mid-1990s, each year in the Everest region an average of five to six fatalities occur among porters, and in 1995 there were ten porter fatalities in the just the first half of the year.[40] Indeed, while in Khumbu in 1999, I learned of a porter who had recently died due to a combination of altitude illness, exposure, and exhaustion, all of which were entirely preventable. Apparently, the porter was carrying an extremely heavy load[41] to the high-altitude trekking destination of Gokyo (4,800 meters or 15,600 feet above sea level) when he complained of exhaustion and showed signs of altitude sickness. Despite the commonly understood seriousness of altitude sickness and the urgency of immediate and rapid descent under such

---

40 Lustgarten 1996 p.183
41 Porters can sometimes earn an extra wage by carrying a double-sized load, but not always. According to Ken McDonald (personal communication, 1999), a geographer studying portering labor in the Himalaya and Karakoram mountains, trekking agencies often try to cut their costs by forcing porters to carry heavier loads than the maximum 30-kilogram weight limit allowed under Nepali law (a law which is rarely enforced) while only compensating the porters for a normal load. Due to the high demand for work among porters and the plentiful supply of inexpensive labor in Nepal, the power relations between employers and portering laborers are greatly unbalanced in favor of the employer.

circumstances, the porter was not allowed (under the implied threat of losing his job)[42] to descend. When his condition became unbearable, he attempted to go down in the night by himself. He was found dead the next morning.

Because of the high rates of injury and mortality among people employed in trekking and mountain climbing, Nepal's government now requires trekkers and climbers to purchase insurance on behalf of their Nepali employees.[43] Unfortunately, few porters are actually insured unless they are hired through a reputable trekking agency that has an insurance policy covering its staff, and, even in some cases where insurance was provided, porters or their families have had to resort to lawsuits to receive insurance benefits for injuries or death.[44]

---

42 According to Jim Duff (personal communication, 1999) of the International Porter Protection Group, when sirdars hire porters for trekking or mountaineering groups, it is not uncommon for a sirdar to keep 50 percent of the porters' wages as compensation for hiring them and to readily dismiss porters without pay if they become sick or injured.

43 According to Armington (1997 p.107), approximately US$2,000 in accidental death insurance is required for each porter and staff member, at a cost of approximately US$20 for 30 days of coverage. Insurance costs are higher for staff engaged in climbing.

44 Ortner 1998 p.20

CHAPTER 5

The Environment

Nowhere in the Great Himalaya is concern for the environment more intense than in the Khumbu area. Processes of change have brought a plethora of environmental disruption to this formerly remote, unspoiled region. A major factor is tourism and the hordes of overseas tourists and trekkers.

(P.P. Karan & Cotton Mather, 1985, *The Geographical Review*)

The impact of tourism on the environment in Khumbu is a subject that has drawn an amazing amount of international attention over the past three decades. Paradoxically, while the popularity of the Khumbu region among tourists has been considered an important factor in the degradation of the Khumbu environment, the same popularity has also led to great local, national, and international awareness of and attentiveness to the area's problems. Reports by Westerners who visited the Everest region during the period of rapid tourism growth in the early 1970s promulgated the notion that environmental degradation had reached crisis proportions in Khumbu.[1] This prompted influential foreign aid organizations to hurriedly recommend to Nepal's government that it designate the region as a national park so that strict environmental protection regulations could be instituted to stem the damage.[2] The management policies of the national park that was created reflected the conservation ideology of its Western sponsors and the popularly

---

1   Blower 1971; Mishra 1973; Fürer-Haimendorf 1975, 1984; Bjønness 1979, 1980a, 1980b, 1983; Hinrichsen *et al.* 1983
2   Lucas *et al.* 1974

held view of widespread human-caused deterioration of the Himalayan environment.[3]

In response to the proclamations of crisis heralded by these early reports, numerous researchers conducted what has come to be considered more scientifically thorough and less emotionally biased fieldwork over longer durations of time to assess the actual degree and extent of environmental degradation that had occurred.[4] The results almost universally indicated that human impact on the Himalayan environment in general, and tourism impact on the Khumbu environment in particular, had been more subtle and localized than previously thought. At the same time, the findings generally pointed out that significant threats of degradation did exist, especially in situations where human uses of resources and impacts on the environment were left unmanaged. What follows is a summary of some of the major effects on the Khumbu environment that have been associated with or influenced by tourism.

Traditional Resource Management Systems

> Ruin is the destination toward which all men rush, each pursuing his own best interest in a society that believes in the freedom of the commons. Freedom in a commons brings ruin to all [...]. The individual benefits as an individual from his ability to deny the truth even though his society as a whole, of which he is a part, suffers.
>
> (Garrett Hardin, 1968, "The Tragedy of the Commons," *Science*)

According to Fürer-Haimendorf, the Sherpas of Khumbu traditionally had a "high sense of civic responsibility and a remarkable degree of discipline regarding matters affecting the common good," characteristics that the anthropologist attributed to the Sherpas' traditional resource management systems through which the

---

3   Eckholm 1975 & 1976 were notable works among many that promulgated such a view.
4   Summaries of the research are provided by Brower (1991a) and Guthman (1997), while Ives & Messerli (1989) and Thompson & Warburton (1988) provide more detailed accounts.

responsibility for facilitating and enforcing rules of common resource use rotated among households.[5] Fürer-Haimendorf considered the Sherpas' traditional forest, pasture, and agricultural management systems an indication of a local awareness of the fragility and scarceness of available natural resources and a willingness to conserve those resources and utilize them in a cooperative fashion.

After the first Western visitors began traveling to Khumbu in the 1950s, and especially as the number of tourist visitors expanded rapidly in the 1970s and thereafter, the demands placed upon local natural resources and the environment in Khumbu increased dramatically. To cater to growing numbers of visitors, trees were cut down to build tourist lodges and to provide fuel-wood, as will be described later in the section on Deforestation and Soil Erosion. To take advantage of visitors' demands for pack stock, additional livestock were purchased and pastures near villages were heavily grazed, as will described in the section below on Overgrazing. Such effects of tourism have been blamed for contributing to the demise of the Khumbu Sherpas' traditional resource management systems. The idea that tourism was connected to the demise was further advanced by observations that the Sherpas' traditional pastoral management systems declined in the late 1970s and the 1980s in villages that were heavily grazed by pack animals used in tourism, while the systems were less affected in villages that were not heavily involved in tourism. For example, the *di* pastoral management system and its *osho nawa* enforcement mechanism faltered in the heavily visited villages of Namche and Dingboche, while they remained active in the less visited villages of Phortse and Thame.[6]

---

5 Fürer-Haimendorf 1984 pp.50-51
6 Fisher 1990 p.142; Brower 1991b p.168; Basnet 1992 pp.123-124; Stevens 1993a pp.285, 327-331. Note: The traditional pastoral management system faltered in Namche in 1979 and in Dingboche in 1987. It also faltered in Thame in 1984, but Thame villagers re-established the system in 1986. Fisher suggested that even if the traditional nawa system had continued functioning in all of the villages, nawa only regulated land and forest use near the villages and the penalty for breaking the regulations was negligible as fines were paid in homemade beer (*chang*). Therefore, Fisher felt it was unlikely that the Khumbu

On the other hand, several researchers have claimed that the demise of traditional forest management systems in Khumbu was not due to tourism, but rather to the imposition of national institutions and regulations governing forest use in Khumbu. While tourism obviously put pressure on Khumbu forests, the failure of the Sherpas' traditional forest management systems was ultimately due to their being undermined by the nationalization of Khumbu forests in the 1960s and the designation of Khumbu as a national park in the 1970s. As forests were nationalized throughout Nepal, all unregistered forestlands in the country began to be administered by the national government, and tree felling required authorization from a forest management office set up in each district. Because there were only a few negligible areas of privately registered forestland in Khumbu, all tree felling in the region required a permit from the district forest office established in 1965 for the Solu-Khumbu area.

From the start, the focus of the district forest office, which was staffed by government employees from outside the region, seems to have been more on revenue collection than on forest management or conservation. According to Stevens, the office readily issued tree-felling permits with little regard for the quantity or location of trees to be felled, as long as the appropriate fees were paid.[7] The district forest office was originally located in Namche, but in 1970 it was moved to Salleri, a four-day walk from Namche. After the office was moved, few Khumbu Sherpas bothered to go to Salleri to seek permits. In addition to the inconvenience of at least an 8-day round-trip journey, there was little incentive to adhere to the government regulations after the district forest office no longer had an enforcement presence in Khumbu.[8]

Since the authority to regulate forests was now in the hands of the national government, the Sherpas' traditional forest management

Sherpas' traditional nawa system would have been able to keep the extensive demand for resources in check throughout the region.

7   Stevens 1993a pp.298-299
8   Fürer-Haimendorf 1975 pp.97-98; Rowell 1980, as cited in Stevens 1988 p.75; Stevens 1993a p.493

systems lost their power to control forest use and the systems fell out of use in several villages.[9] Stevens noted that the traditional forest management systems faltered at this time in Namche, Kunde, and Khumjung, although they continued to be observed in Phortse and Pangboche until these villages' forestlands were gazetted for the establishment of Sagarmatha National Park in 1976. Even in those villages where the traditional forest management systems were not abandoned initially, their authority was effectively undermined and circumvented by the granting of tree-felling permits by the district forest office and subsequently by the national park.[10]

Today, some of the healthier forests in Khumbu are those that were historically declared sacred and protected by religious tradition.[11] Striking examples I found of this in 1999 include the forests near Tengboche, Phortse, and Pangboche. In the case of the forest near Tengboche, felling of trees had been prohibited by local tradition since the forest was placed under the protection of local monks following the construction of the Tengboche monastery in 1916. However, as with other forests in Khumbu where local management has been undermined, forest nationalization followed by national park designation has officially taken away the monks' actual authority to protect the forest here as well.

Deforestation & Soil Erosion

Only about two percent of the total area of Khumbu is forested,[12] but forest resources have long been an integral part of the Khumbu environment and of Sherpa subsistence. The growth of tourism in the Everest region has placed heavy demands on local forests and has been suspected by Western scientists and land managers to be the cause of widespread Khumbu deforestation, which in turn posed a significant threat of soil erosion. These suspicions, however, have been mostly refuted by actual research. Studies by American researcher Alton

---

9   Fürer-Haimendorf 1975 pp.97-98, 1984 pp.57-61
10 Stevens 1993a pp.299-302, 314
11 Stevens 1993a pp.196-202
12 Stevens 1993a p.187

Byers of repeat photographs taken of the Khumbu landscape between 1955 and 1995 showed that the extent of forest cover had remained essentially unchanged (with a few exceptions described below), thereby suggesting that regional deforestation had been the result of historic action by local populations rather than an effect of tourism.[13] These findings were supported by the published testimony of Dr. Charles Houston, a member of the first Western party to visit Khumbu in 1950, who returned to the area in 1981 and noticed little change in forest cover.[14] A study of regional tourism impacts conducted by Nepal's government in 1977 concluded that annual fuel-wood use by seasonal tourists, who numbered about 4,000 per year then, was approximately 10 percent above the normal fuel-wood requirements of the roughly 3,000 local residents. The government study concluded that tourism fuel-wood use had not been a primary cause of the region's widespread historical deforestation, even taking into account tourism prior to the national park's forest protection regulations.[15]

While tourism does not appear to have caused extensive widespread deforestation in Khumbu, significant removal of trees outside the boundary of the national park, where there are fewer restrictions on forest use, has been reported and linked directly to the demands of tourism growth and structural development.[16] The Pharak region adjacent to Khumbu has been the main source of lumber and fuel-wood for the Everest region since national park policies were implemented to protect Khumbu forests in the 1970s. Increased demand for and reliance on wood from Pharak, due to the growth of tourism in both Pharak and Khumbu and national park protection of Khumbu forests, has led to the overuse of forests outside of the national park. Large mature trees have been felled for use as

---

13   Byers 1987a, 1987b, 1997, 2003
14   Houston 1987 p.76
15   His Majesty's Government of Nepal 1977, as cited in Pawson *et al.* 1984b
      p.242. Note: Brower (1991b pp.153-154) offered as a possible explanation for
      historical deforestation in Khumbu the deliberate burning of forests by Sherpas
      in the past to clear land for grazing.
16   Stevens 1993a pp.396, 503

beams and planks in the construction of tourist lodges as well as the new larger homes of Sherpas who have grown wealthy from tourism. The use of wood for cooking and heating by trekking and climbing groups, commercial porters, and the region's many tourist lodges has also increased regional demands for wood. Fuel-wood is carried by porters into the national park and stockpiled by every home and lodge in Khumbu. In fact, during the one-year period from July 1996 through June 1997, over 125,000 kilograms of fuel-wood were transported from Pharak into Khumbu.[17]

Byers' repeat photography studies showed that little change in surface geomorphology had occurred over the previous several decades, suggesting that the region's slopes were generally stable and had not suffered from the significant widespread erosion that had been predicted in earlier reports. In addition to the photographic studies, a detailed field study by Byers of soil erosion throughout the Khumbu region before, during, and after the monsoon season of 1984 showed that soil loss was low within most areas. However, in the region's summer settlement alpine areas above 13,000 feet soil loss was high. The high soil loss was considered the result of seasonally bare soils due to grazing pressures and continued shrub harvesting for firewood in remote alpine areas where national park regulations prohibiting these actions were difficult to enforce. Since similar surface conditions were observed in summer settlement alpine areas regardless of their proximity to popular tourist routes, tourism did not appear to have played a role.[18]

However, a follow-up study by Byers in 1995 showed that approximately 60 percent of the juniper shrub cover near the village of Dingboche had been lost since 1962, with the majority of the change occurring during the period of high tourism growth from 1984 to 1995, during which annual tourist numbers in the region increased from about 5,000 to 14,000. During his 1995 study, Byers noted stockpiles of juniper shrub fuel-wood near lodges and

---

17 Sagarmatha Pollution Control Committee 1998
18 Byers 1986, 1987b

restaurants in the vicinity of Dingboche. Another area of thinned woodlands noted by Byers' repeat photographic studies was the slope above Kunde and Khumjung villages, where an estimated 36 percent of juniper shrub cover had been removed between 1962 and 1984.[19] Because juniper at high elevations such as Khumbu takes 60 or more years to grow to one foot in height, any measurable loss of shrub cover over a short time frame could be considered unsustainable.[20]

Tourism-Related Built Environment

Byers' repeat photography studies also documented the noticeable degree of infrastructure development that had occurred in the region between the 1960s and the 1990s. The modifications, nearly all of which were primarily related to tourism, included an airstrip and luxury hotel at Syangboche, an expansive administrative headquarters for the national park at Namche, and numerous tourist lodges in Namche and elsewhere along the main trekking routes. The visible increase in lodges had been particularly high during the period between repeat photographs in 1984 and 1995.[21] During this period of extensive lodge construction, the number of lodges in Khumbu increased from roughly 50 to over 125, as shown in the graph that appeared in Chapter Three.

Overgrazing

As part of the above-mentioned warnings of environmental crisis issued by Khumbu visitors in the 1970s, overgrazing was cited as a severe problem that required immediate regulation by the new national park. Early observers recommended that grazing be regulated and that limits be established on the size of livestock herds to limit the continued degradation of rangeland resources and the resulting erosion of soils.[22] However, more thorough research in the 1980s by

---

19 Byers 1997
20 Bjønness 1980b, as cited in Rogers & Aitchison 1998 p.54
21 Byers 1987a, 1987b, 1997
22 Blower 1971, Lucas et al. 1974, Bjønness 1980a

Alton Byers and Barbara Brower refuted the commonly held beliefs that Khumbu rangelands were severely overgrazed and that soil erosion was substantial and caused explicitly by grazing.[23]

While historical grazing practices had apparently not caused serious degradation of the Khumbu environment, the growth of tourism over the past few decades has led to changes in Khumbu pastoralism that may have important implications for the region's rangeland resources. Starting in the mid-1970s, many Khumbu Sherpa families began increasing their ownership of pack stock to take advantage of the growing popularity of using pack animals to carry loads for trekking and climbing groups. Male yak-cattle crossbreeds (zopkio) have been particularly popular for use as pack animals because of their docile nature and their resistance to low elevation diseases, which allows them to also be used at lower elevations such as the airstrip in Lukla. The lack of available labor to tend livestock (described in more detail in Chapter Seven) and the changing composition of Khumbu herds due to the popularity of zopkio (described earlier in Chapter Three) have caused considerable changes in Khumbu animal husbandry practices and important ramifications for the Khumbu environment.[24]

The engagement of many Sherpas in tourism work has resulted in a shortage of available labor for herding and looking after animals in remote high pastures, and thus more grazing is occurring in the lower pastures closer to villages. Furthermore, prior to and during the tourist seasons, local stockowners prefer to keep their animals near their village so that the animals will be readily available when portering opportunities turn up. New stockowners, especially those whose families had not previously kept livestock and therefore did not own private grazing lands, have relied heavily on common-land grazing resources but have often paid little attention to the traditional controls regulating use of those lands. Together, these cumulative effects have disrupted the normal seasonal grazing patterns in

23   Byers 1987a, 1987b; Brower 1990, 1991a, 1991b
24   Brower 1990 pp.40-41, 1991a p.158, 1991b pp.165-168

Khumbu, led to uncontrolled overgrazing of the lower pastures close
to villages, and undermined the Sherpas' traditional *osho nawa* and *di*
pasture management systems that had served to regulate livestock
transhumance practices. The increasing proportion of zopkio in
Khumbu herds has further exacerbated the problem. Since zopkio do
not tolerate high altitude as well as yaks, the zopkio tend not to graze
the higher pastures. As a result, the lower pastures are being
overgrazed outside of the tourist season as well.

As the number of zopkio increased significantly during the
period of high tourism growth in the latter 1990s, the animals have
put more and more pressure on the limited rangeland resources of
Khumbu. According to national park staff with whom I spoke in
1999, this is not just a problem for domestic livestock but also for
park wildlife such as Himalayan tahr and musk deer, which also rely
on the region's rangeland resources for sustenance. The park staff
added that the increased number of Tibetan traders crossing the
Nangpa La pass from Tibet and bringing their pack stock into the
park in the past few years has also contributed to the burden on park
rangelands.[25]

Pollution & Sanitation

The discarding of food wrappers, bottles, and other waste has become
such a problem in the heavily visited areas of Khumbu that the main
tourist route has been nicknamed 'the garbage trail.' A study
conducted in 1984 of solid waste pollution in Sagarmatha National
Park revealed that tourism was responsible for 90 percent of the trash
generated in the area, and the worst offenders were found to be
mountain climbers, tourist lodges, and trekkers.[26] In addition to the
rubbish left by visitors, the growing consumption of packaged goods
by local residents has increased the amount of nonbiodegradable
waste generated in Khumbu.

25 Sagarmatha National Park rangers Uddhab Dhungana and Shyam Krishna
    Shrestha, personal communication, 1999
26 Basnet 1993 pp.131-139

The growing number of tourists and their accompanying staff has also resulted in a significant increase in the generation of human waste in the region relative to pre-tourism levels. Self-contained trekking groups typically dig shallow (about 6 inches in depth) pits in the ground at each camping location and erect a small 'toilet tent' over the pit for privacy. Tea-house trekkers typically utilize deeper and more permanent 'out-house' style pit toilets provided by lodges. Approximately one-half of the lodges in the village of Namche have begun using septic tanks rather than mere earthen holes, although since there are no uniform criteria for septic tank design or installation they are often simply lined with stones.[27] Thus, whether temporary or more permanent, most toilet pits lack an effective barrier lining and thus often leak fecal material and coliform bacteria into surrounding water sources. In some cases, out-house toilets have even been constructed directly over the edge of streams so that the waste will be carried away by the water. And for decades in the Everest region, mountain climbers simply threw their human waste in the snow or in glacier crevasses. Human waste disposed of in this way also eventually finds its way into local water sources as the snow and ice on the mountain melts.

As early as 1981, a national park study reported coliform bacteria in every sampled stream and spring in Khumbu and high levels of coliform bacteria (11,000 organisms per liter of water) in the Dudh Kosi river directly below Namche. The study concluded that the "maintenance of drinking water quality within the park is a significant problem."[28] In addition, an environmental impact assessment of tourism in the Everest region conducted in 1990 found that drinking water in the region contained high levels of coliform

---

27 Sonam Gyalzin Sherpa and Wendy Brewer Lama, personal communications, as cited in Lachapelle 1998 p.54. Note: National park regulations regarding sanitation standards do not apply in the villages or temporary seasonal settlements of Khumbu, which are where most lodges are located, because these areas were excluded as private enclaves within the park when the park was created.

28 Garratt 1981, as quoted in Lachapelle 1998 p.54

bacteria (4,000 organisms per liter of water).[29] And a 1993 national park working paper reported that "streams and rivers in the main tourist areas [...] are contaminated. Many more streams and rivers are at grave risk of contamination."[30] The implications of the region's poor sanitary conditions were highlighted by a 1998 study of school children in the Khumbu village of Khumjung, which revealed that 37 percent of the children sampled were suffering from parasitic infections resulting from unclean water supplies.[31]

National Park Protection & Restoration

While tourism has routinely been blamed for negatively impacting the Khumbu environment, it has also played a significant role in positive efforts that have been made on the environment's behalf. The concerns of foreign visitors and the international community about the degradation of the Khumbu environment from overuse of natural resources and from pollution were the driving forces behind the designation of the area as a national park in the mid 1970s. The resulting regulations and programs instituted by the national park staff along with the continued concern of foreign visitors have led to an increase in environmental awareness and constructive actions among both local residents and visitors. For example, national park regulations have played a crucial role in protecting the forests of Khumbu by restricting the felling of trees in the region. Local residents may still collect fallen wood and may seek permission to cut a limited amount of standing wood to use as beams in house or lodge construction, but all other cutting, including the lopping of live branches, is prohibited. And, since 1979, the national park has also prohibited the purchase of fuel-wood by trekking groups in Khumbu. In 1999, the park's regulations were enforced by 37 national park

29   Khadka 1990, as cited in Lachapelle 1998 p.54
30   Sherpa 1993 p.44, as quoted in Lachapelle 1998 p.54
31   Ramesh Basnet, personal communication, as cited in Lachapelle 1998 p.54

staff and about 250 army personnel,[32] and infractions were punishable by fines.

The park's forest protection policies and restoration efforts seem to be paying off. Byers noted in a 1995 study that natural forest cover had increased in many areas of Khumbu, a change he attributed to nearly two decades of national park protective policies. Byers also characterized as effective the combined efforts of the national park and the Himalayan Trust to restore forests around Namche, Kunde, and Khumjung, noting that, through a program utilizing local nurseries and enclosed plantations, tree seedlings planted in the 1980s had by 1995 reached between 3 and 9 feet in height.[33]

In addition to the park's reforesting efforts, park restrictions on hunting and poaching (particularly a threat for musk deer and snow leopards, which are valued for their scent glands and furs, respectively) have led to a noticeable increase in Khumbu wildlife populations. According to Barbara Brower, the numbers of Himalayan tahr (similar to mountain goats) and Impeyan pheasant (the iridescently colorful national bird of Nepal) "increased spectacularly" under national park protection.[34] However, as has been the case in other Nepal national parks where local people living inside or near the park have been prohibited from hunting,[35] the growing numbers of wildlife in Khumbu have become a nuisance for residents due to increased crop depredation.[36]

The efforts of national park staff have extended beyond forests and wildlife to the protection of local aesthetic qualities as well. For example, when hydro-electric projects were developed to introduce

---

32 Numbers provided by Sagarmatha National Park ranger Uddhab Dhungana, personal communication, 1999
33 Byers 1997 p.38. Note: Nurseries were established in 1979 to supply tree seedlings of indigenous conifer trees for the park's reforestation program. In 1999, I observed forest plantations in Khumbu with trees between approximately 2 and 12 feet in height.
34 Brower 1991b p.36
35 Kharel (1997 pp. 127-134) discussed this issue in Langtang National Park in the Nepal Himalaya.
36 Fürer-Haimendorf 1984 p.60, Brower 1991b p.36, Stevens 1993a p.502, Byers 1997 p.38

electricity to Khumbu, national park authorities were wary of the effect that aboveground transmission wires would have on the sensitivities of tourist visitors. As a result of such concerns, the national park has required power lines to be placed underground in most places within the park, especially within villages and along popular trekking trails. This requirement effectively caused the abandonment of a proposal for extending the Khumbu power grid to Pharak, since laying underground lines would have been too difficult and costly in the rocky gorge of the Dudh Kosi below Namche.

The national park has also played a small role in regulating tourism development in Khumbu. For example, national park authorities have restricted the building of tourist lodges in certain areas, and in one case park authorities ordered the removal of a tea house located on a hillside in an area near Namche that the park authorities wished to preserve.[37] The national park has also promoted the construction of composting toilets by tourist lodges to help reduce the growing problem of disposal of human waste generated by rising numbers of visitors. Composting has the added benefit of producing fertilizer for local residents' potato fields, although composting toilets are only prevalent in the lower altitude Khumbu villages where temperatures are warm enough for composting to be effective and where most Khumbu agriculture occurs.[38] The national park has also created regulations that require trekking and climbing groups to carry out their trash, although this has proven somewhat difficult to enforce. Perhaps the most important tourism policy set forth by the park has been the requirement since 1979 that trekking groups use kerosene instead of wood fires for cooking. To help trekking groups adhere to this requirement, the national park

---

37 Armington 1997 p.103
38 Although a national park ranger (Uddhab Dhungana, personal communication, 1999) attributed credit for an increase in composting toilets in Khumbu to the park's promotional efforts, this seems to contrast with Brower's (1991b pp.50-51) observation that composting toilets were already standard among Khumbu Sherpas in the 1980s and attributed their use in Khumbu to the relaxed Buddhist attitudes toward handling human waste, which is in marked contrast to Hindu proscriptions against it.

established a kerosene depot at the entrance to the park, and several additional kerosene depots have subsequently been established throughout the Solu-Khumbu district.

Despite the park's prohibition on wood fires, however, some trekking group staff and porters have continued to burn wood for cooking and warmth. While in Khumbu in 1999, I observed several instances of trekking group staff and porters using wood fires. The park has had a hard time enforcing the ban because the use of wood fires is an age-old practice among porters throughout Nepal, as the following excerpt from a guidebook on climbing in Nepal points out: "lighting fires is now frowned upon, although it is difficult to enforce this amongst [Nepali] people who are used to sitting around fires and for whom Western ideas of conservation, during a cold night, are of little relevance."[39] Brower also commented on the difficulty of enforcing the park's restrictions against fires:

> despite national park regulations which forbid camp and cooking fires for trekking groups and expeditions, many groups continue to violate these rules, which are a relatively recent innovation and follow many years of unregulated use of fire by tourists. Often the fires of trekking groups burn with impunity, either because the camp kitchen is sufficiently remote to elude scrutiny, or because of special under-the-table arrangements made with park personnel (once quite common, according to local reports, but increasingly rare). Cooks prefer to use wood fuel to the dirty, recalcitrant kerosene stoves that are the primary alternative. Treks and expeditions may have a kerosene budget that can be turned to meet other expenses [or pocketed by the staff] if the trek staff gathers its own fuel-wood. Trekking agency offices in Kathmandu may claim that their policy is to use stoves in accordance with national park regulations and good conservation practice, but even the most closely supervised kitchens of the most committed and conscientious group leaders are likely to use wood fires at some times.[40]

---

39   O'Connor 1989 pp.181-182
40   Brower 1991b p.159

After considerable criticism of trekking groups' continued use of wood fires, the Trekking Agents Association of Nepal (TAAN) established responsible guidelines for trekking agencies in the hope of discouraging environmentally destructive practices. However, according to Nepali researcher Hari Upreti:

> trekking agencies do not seem to have been taking any responsibility for managing the members of the group except tourists. [Trekking group staff] were found to use kerosene in and around the vicinity of authority, from whom they were likely to be accused. [...] they depend on forest resources for their requirement elsewhere in the absence of conservation authority. [...] thus guidelines, management plans, and environmental codes of conduct are covering only the pages of the book [and not the actual practices of trekking agencies].[41]

Alternative Energy and Fuel Efficiency

Several projects have been implemented within the national park in the hope of reducing local reliance on wood fuel. According to a brochure describing one of these projects, "new [house and lodge] construction and increased demand for fuel-wood to satisfy the needs of tourists made the utilization of new energy resources necessary to avoid intolerable environmental stress and the eradication of the forests in the region."[42] Projects aimed at increasing alternative energy use and fuel efficiency in Khumbu have included hydro-electric power schemes, solar water heaters, back-boiler water heating stoves, low wattage electric stoves, and increasing the availability of kerosene.

The intense focus that international non-governmental organizations (NGOs) have placed on electrification projects in the Everest region have been promoted with claims that electric lights and stoves would reduce the burning of wood in local homes and lodges. Ironically, it has since been suggested that electric lighting may be enticing Khumbu residents and tourists to stay up later at night and

---

41 Upreti 1998 p.60
42 Eco-Himal 1995

thus burn more wood to stay warm.[43] This idea was refuted by a study conducted in 1997 by the Austrian NGO Eco-Himal, the organization responsible for building the Thame hydro-electric plant, which showed that firewood consumption within the area provided with electricity "was reduced by one-third in the two years after the completion of the power plant [in 1995]."[44] Surveys of households and tourist lodges in Khumbu conducted by the British researchers Rogers and Aitchison confirmed that wood consumption in the electrified area had been reduced between 1993 and 1996, with surveyed households reporting more than a two-thirds reduction and tourist lodges reporting a one-half reduction in fuel-wood use.[45]

All the hydro-electric projects that have been constructed in Khumbu have been financed and completed with international assistance. These have included a small hydro-electric scheme in Namche, which was completed in 1983 with a US$78,000 grant from UNESCO,[46] and another in Tengboche, which was completed in 1989 with a grant from the American Himalayan Foundation. In 1999, the American Himalayan Foundation began work to replace the Tengboche hydro-electric system's damaged turbine and improve the water intake to reduce future damage from glacial sediments. The new turbine is expected to boost power generation from 5.5 kilowatts to 30 kilowatts, which, according to Tengboche residents, would allow for the use of electric hot water heaters to "help meet the unstoppable demand from tourists for hot showers without causing further deforestation."[47]

The largest and most elaborate of the Khumbu hydro-electric plants, located near Thame, was a multi-million dollar project

---

43   According to Fisher (1990 p.157), "instead of going to bed soon after dark, as they traditionally did, [Khumbu] Sherpas now stay up as long as the lights are on (until 10:00pm) and thus burn even more wood to keep warm and to cook." The use of electric lighting versus the primary alternative of burning kerosene lamps was also mentioned by Pye-Smith (1988 p.32).

44   Eco-Himal 1999

45   Rogers & Aitchison 1998 p.54

46   Pye-Smith 1988 p.32

47   Tengboche Monastery internet website, http://www.tengboche.com, 1999

undertaken by the Austrian government to provide electricity to the villages of Thame, Namche, Syangboche, Kunde, and Khumjung. The project was initiated in 1976, with a planned completion date of 1982. However, due to a series of delays and a devastating flash flood that swept away the plant in 1985 (the Dig Tsho glacial lake outburst discussed in Chapter Three), the project was not completed until 1994. The plant now provides 600 kilowatts of electricity 24 hours a day to 645 paying customers (as of October 1998), including residences, government offices, tourist lodges, and other businesses. With the goal of turning the plant's operation over to the local community, the Khumbu Bijuli Company (*bijuli* is Nepali for electricity) or KBC was created in 1994, and its staff of thirteen local residents were trained by Austrian technicians to operate and maintain the plant and conduct customer billing. The KBC is 85 percent owned by its customers and 15 percent owned by Nepal's national electric utility, and it is managed by a board elected by its local customers.

To keep billing rates down for less affluent household users (particularly those in Thame, which is less involved in tourism), a graduated pricing system was adopted based on power usage. To achieve economic self-sustainability and fund future plant maintenance costs, the KBC raised electric prices by 40 percent in 1999 and anticipated an additional rate increase in the near future.[48] Billing revenues were initially limited by low electric usage since local residents owned few electrical appliances, with only half of the plant's capacity utilized in 1999. However, with more affluent Khumbu residents and lodge owners purchasing a growing number of electrical appliances, the local usage of electricity was expected to soon match the plant's output. Demand was also expected to increase after the planned extension of the power grid north of Thame, and possibly to Phortse as well.

---

48 KBC Finance and Administration Chief Ang Danu Sherpa, personal communication, 1999

By the early 1980s, many Khumbu households had modified their traditional open-fire hearths with a tin enclosure intended to concentrate the fire's flame on the cooking vessel and thus economize on fuel-wood use.[49] For its part, the national park installed several experimental solar energy cells and back-boiler water heaters in Khumbu households and lodges during the 1980s to assess the effectiveness of these technologies in minimizing the use of fuel-wood.[50] Due to Khumbu's high-altitude and frequently clear morning skies, it was thought that solar power held considerable potential as an alternative energy source if photovoltaic cells and storage batteries could be procured cheaply enough for general use. Back-boiler water heater stoves were designed to meet the growing demand for heated water created by tourists' desire for hot showers. Back-boiler water heater stoves conserve fuel by routing water pipes through the stove to heat water while the stove is being used for cooking. By 1999, rooftop solar panels, along with their associated storage batteries and low wattage fluorescent lights, were becoming common in lodges in areas without hydro-electric power. Back-boiler water heater stoves were less common, however, perhaps due to the same technical limitations that slowed their initial adoption in Nepal's Annapurna region. In 1999, the Austrian NGO Eco-Himal installed two large, Austrian-made, electric water heaters in Namche lodges to demonstrate their efficient electricity use in the hope of influencing other lodge owners to purchase similar water heaters.[51] Also in 1999, an experimental low wattage electric cooking stove

---

49   Fürer-Haimendorf 1984 pp.10-11. Note: As Stevens (1993a pp.308-309) and Fisher (1990 p.64) pointed out, in the 1960s some Khumbu Sherpa households had adopted Tibetan-style enclosed stoves made of stone and mud, which were more fuel-efficient than the Sherpas' traditional open-fires hearths for cooking. Stevens also mentioned other fuel saving measures adopted by Khumbu Sherpas such as Chinese-made thermoses in the 1960s and pressure cookers in the 1970s.

50   Byers 1987b p.214

51   In addition to using less electricity to heat water, the new hot water heaters could heat water late at night when electricity rates in Namche are 50 percent less than in the daytime and evening due to lower demand for electricity late at night.

developed by an Austrian technical college was being tested by Eco-Himal in several Khumbu lodges.

In a study of firewood use by Khumbu tourists in the mid-1970s, Bjønness found that only a very small fraction (7 percent) of trekking groups carried kerosene fuel with them for cooking, instead relying on fuel-wood purchased in Khumbu.[52] As the number of people trekking in Khumbu grew several-fold during the 1970s, supplying them with fuel-wood became a profitable business for local residents. For example, Bjønness noted that Pangboche villagers sold an incredible US$16,800 worth of fuel-wood to trekkers in 1976. To reduce the use of fuel-wood in the region, the German Alpine Club helped the national park to establish a kerosene depot at the park entrance, and the national park began requiring trekking groups and climbing expeditions to use kerosene instead of wood for cooking within the park. As of 1999, this requirement had not been extended to tourist lodges, although the national park warden had convened a meeting of Khumbu lodge owners in 1994 that resulted in a voluntary offer by several lodge owners to use kerosene for cooking.[53] Because kerosene must be carried in from the Jiri trailhead by porters, its use costs more than fuel-wood in Khumbu. For example, in 1997 a liter of kerosene cost about US$1.00 in Namche, compared to US$0.15 in Kathmandu.[54] As a result, wood burning stoves were still the norm in most Khumbu lodges in 1999, with kerosene stoves typically used only during busy times when a lodge's kitchen had more food orders than it could quickly prepare using a wood burning stove alone. Due to cost and practicality, the preferential order of fuel use for cooking was wood, then kerosene, and then electricity.

Another source of energy that forms an alternative to wood use is the burning of yak dung for cooking and warmth. Dung is primarily used for fuel in higher altitude, seasonal herding settlements and lodges located above tree-line where wood is not available and the cost of having it carried in from lower elevations is prohibitive.

---

52 Bjønness 1980b p.126, as cited in Stevens 1988 p.75 & 1993a p.393
53 Stevens 1997 p.76
54 Armington 1997 p.172

Several Sherpa lodge owners with whom I talked in 1999 about dung burning considered it to be just as good a fuel as wood, and some even suggested that properly dried dung produces a hotter flame than wood.[55] Indeed, in areas that serve as summer pastures for yak, most lodges have large stockpiles of dung that has been collected for use as fuel.

Community-Based Conservation

Although Khumbu Sherpas historically developed and utilized a number of traditional systems for managing access to communal resources such as forests and pasturelands, researcher Stan Stevens criticized romantic Western notions attributing the Sherpas with admirable altruistic motives of conserving their natural environment. Stevens argued that the Sherpas' traditional resource management systems were not based upon environmental conservation ethics, but rather were driven by the importance the Sherpas placed on individual economic freedoms and the practicalities of convenience. It seems that the Sherpas' traditional resource management systems were conceived primarily to ensure that individual households could gain access to communal resources when needed, with such access tempered only by religious veneration of spirits inhabiting the natural world as well as an awareness of the seasonal availability of certain natural resources.[56] According to Stevens:

> the power of the community to intrude into household economic behavior was limited by cultural and social beliefs about the limits of communal management and the community's right to influence household economic decisions.
>
> No Khumbu resource-management institution was charged with monitoring the scale and intensity of use in particular places and associated environmental change, much less was given the power to respond to these observations by adjusting resource-use policy and regulations. Nor should it be assumed that the goals of Khumbu Sherpa traditional resource-management institutions

---

55 compare with Stevens 1993a p.475
56 Stevens 1993a pp.268-294, 419-420

were foremost and centrally concerned with environmental conservation. These institutions addressed a broad range of local concerns, not all of them by any means concerned with moderating the environmental impact of subsistence.

[The Sherpas' traditional resource management systems] certainly had important ramifications for environmental quality and resource conservation. But these were by-products of economic and spiritual concerns, not the result of either core beliefs in preserving biological diversity or native vegetation communities or a desire to place regional resource use in general on an environmentally sustainable basis. Such cultural values were not translated into Khumbu-wide environmental and land-use policies nor coordinated into community or regional planning as explicit goals of local resource-management institutions.[57]

Thus, Stevens claimed that in Khumbu the concept of environmental conservation was largely a Western-conceived notion that had little precedent among the Sherpas prior to the influx of tourists and the raising of concerns about the local environment by foreign visitors. The same was true for litter and pollution. For Khumbu residents, the accumulation of trash and other solid waste was historically of little concern since the region's limited resources did not support a very large population and, more importantly, since paper, cardboard, plastic, glass, and metal packaging were practically non-existent in the region prior to the arrival of the first foreign visitors in the 1950s.

Beginning in the 1970s, environmental education programs by the national park and by local employees of the Himalayan Trust and the World Wildlife Fund (all of which were based on the rhetoric of the international conservation organizations that provided funding) promoted an increased awareness among Khumbu residents of the fragile nature of the local landscape and natural resources.[58] Initially, environmental conservation ideologies and policies were simply imposed upon local residents, but in the early 1990s, perhaps spurred by the recent democratic revolution in Nepal, local residents were

57   Stevens 1993a pp.290-291
58   Byers 1987b p.214

encouraged by international non-governmental organizations (NGOs) and the national park to participate in conservation at a grass-roots, community level. Since then, Khumbu residents have shown initiative in dealing with local environmental issues such as pollution that others have been unable or unwilling to address. For example, the monks of the Tengboche monastery have become quite active in community-based conservation. With donations from tourist visitors and from NGOs such as the Himalayan Trust and the American Himalayan Foundation, a trash incinerator has been installed in Tengboche and workers have been employed by the monastery to clean up trash in the area on a daily basis. The monastery also plans to establish an 'Eco-Center' where visitors can receive education on responsible tourism behavior.[59]

But the most significant example of community-based conservation in Khumbu was the establishment by local residents of a locally based and locally staffed NGO focused on conservation issues. In the 1980s and early 1990s, as visiting tourists voiced their displeasure with the growing pollution in the Everest region and as reports of the pollution were published around the world, Khumbu residents recognized the threat that unchecked pollution posed to the popularity of tourism there. As the locally influential head monk of the Tengboche monastery stated in the early 1990s, "if tourist numbers declined because of the talk of garbage, Khumbu's economy would be devastated."[60] In response to this threat, approximately eighty local residents volunteered to remove garbage from popular trekking areas and, with funding from the World Wildlife Fund, formed the Sagarmatha Pollution Control Committee (SPCC) in 1991. The SPCC's stated purpose was to engage in conservation and community development projects "to preserve both the natural and cultural heritage of the Sagarmatha (Mt. Everest) region."[61] The

---

59 Tengboche Monastery internet website, http://www.tengboche.com, 1999
60 Rinpoche Ngwang Tenzin Jangpo, as quoted in Douglas 1997 p.103
61 Sagarmatha Pollution Control Committee 1998. Note: According to Armington (1997 p.194), the SPCC was considering changing its name to the Khumbu Environmental Conservation Committee, although this still has not happened.

SPCC executive board has been chaired by the head monk of the Tengboche monastery, and other members of the eleven-member board have included the warden of Sagarmatha National Park, local residents holding democratically-elected positions on local village development committees in the Khumbu and Pharak regions, and several Sherpas who have been prominent in Nepal conservation and development circles.[62] As of 1999, the SPCC employed a staff of 16 people. The SPCC's main source of funding has been Nepal's Ministry of Tourism, which provided the SPCC with a small fraction of the climbing permit fees collected from climbing expeditions to Mount Everest between 1994 and 1998, and the SPCC has also received funds from international conservation and development organizations as well as from the national park.[63]

The SPCC's efforts to reduce pollution in the region have included collecting trash and disposing of burnables by incineration,[64] transporting recyclable aluminum and glass to Kathmandu, and burying other trash in garbage pits constructed at more than 35 locations throughout the Everest region. During the five years from 1994 to 1999, the SPCC disposed of over 980,000 kilograms of trash and transported over 60,000 kilograms of glass bottles to Kathmandu for recycling.[65] In addition to trash removal and recycling, the SPCC has also tried to promote greater understanding of the pressures on the local environment and the importance of conservation programs. The SPCC has produced brochures, posters, and slide shows on the

---

62 Stevens (1997 pp.91, 310) reported that in 1994 the national park warden resigned from the SPCC board but continued to serve as an advisor.

63 Stevens 1997 p.91. Note: According to the SPCC's 1998 annual progress report, Nepal's Ministry of Tourism provided the SPCC with operating funds of approximately US$34,000 in the 1993-1994 fiscal year, US$37,000 in 1994-1995, US$25,000 in 1995-1996, US$25,000 in 1996-1997, and US$15,000 in 1997-1998. According to Stan Stevens (personal communication, 2000), Nepal's Ministry of Tourism ceased providing funds to the SPCC in 1999, and continued funding for the SPCC was uncertain.

64 Four trash incinerators have been provided by the Japanese Himalayan Adventure Trust and the French Association Environment Insertion Economic and are in use at Lukla, Namche, Tengboche, and Lobuche.

65 SPCC 1998 & the SPCC's Nima Nuru Sherpa, personal communication, 1999

negative effects of pollution, conducted public awareness campaigns for both visitors and local residents, established environmental education programs in local schools, and created tourist information centers in the heavily visited villages of Lukla and Namche. In 1999, the SPCC information center in Namche featured detailed and up-to-date displays on the local environment and the clean-up achievements of the SPCC, and the information center staff were encouraging visitors and local residents to provide feedback on conditions in the region. That the SPCC had become the Khumbu clearinghouse for visitor feedback was supported by the large number of complaints the SPCC information center staff had been receiving from trekkers in 1999 about the numerous commercial advertisements for tourist lodges painted on rocks along the trail leading up to Namche. The SPCC's efforts on behalf of the local environment have prompted praise from foreign observers, journalists, and writers such as Ed Douglas, who claimed in a book about the Everest region that "the SPCC's work has made a profound difference to the superficial environmental quality of the Khumbu."[66] A number of foreign researchers have also praised the SPCC's efforts, with the British geographers Rogers and Aitchison claiming that "there can be little doubt that the SPCC has been highly effective in improving waste management throughout Pharak and Khumbu."[67]

The SPCC's initiatives have extended beyond pollution as well. With funding from the World Wildlife Fund and a private Dutch individual, the SPCC has also collaborated with local community forest user groups in developing tree nurseries and agroforestry programs (including apple tree plantations) in the heavily impacted forests of the Pharak region. The Pharak region, because it is adjacent to Khumbu but outside the national park, has borne the brunt of the increased local demand for forest products that has resulted from the regional growth in tourism, as described earlier in the section on Deforestation and Soil Erosion. To help reduce the import of

---

66 Douglas 1997 pp.103-104
67 Rogers & Aitchison 1998 p.59

firewood from Pharak to Khumbu, the SPCC has established kerosene depots along the main trekking route in Syangboche, Pheriche, and Dole.

Taking advantage of the enthusiasm engendered by its success, the SPCC has expanded its efforts beyond the environment to coordinate and take the lead on a number of community service, cultural conservation, and tourism development projects in the Everest region. Examples of community service projects the SPCC has been involved with include village water supply systems, health education programs, maintenance of trails and bridges, construction and maintenance of public toilets along trekking routes, enlarging the area for Namche's busy weekly market, and providing vegetable seeds at subsidized prices. In the area of cultural conservation, the SPCC has funded the repair and maintenance of religious prayer wheels and mani walls and provided financial assistance to a number of monasteries in the region. And in the area of tourism development, the SPCC helped organize a lodge owners' association and, with support from the United Nations Development Programme, the International Labor Organization, and Nepal's Hotel Management and Tourism Training Centre, conducted basic training courses in lodge operation that emphasized vegetable farming, food preparation, hygiene, fuel efficiency, and kerosene use.[68]

Government Efforts to Control Pollution

In an effort to attract more foreign visitors while minimizing the negative impacts often associated with large-scale tourism, Nepal's government has tried to promote the country as a destination for

---

68 Although the SPCC has accomplished a great deal, Stevens (1997 pp.93-94) argued that the organization had not been a model of grass-roots conservation. According to Stevens, following the 1991 volunteer clean-up effort, the SPCC had "not been able to mobilize much local participation in clean-up campaigns, tree-planting, or other basic activities, which instead have to be carried out mainly by paid labor or by foreign volunteers. Although young trekking Sherpas are hired to help with base camp cleanups, the year-round employees who are charged with collecting and incinerating trash and recycling bottles are mainly non-Sherpa workers from outside the region."

'eco-tourism,' a concept of environmentally and socially responsible tourism that has grown in popularity among Western travelers in recent years. As part of this effort, Nepal's Ministry of Tourism has adapted its rhetoric to the times, employing the popular term 'sustainable' not once but twice in its official public motto: 'A sustainable habitat through sustainable tourism.'

In keeping with its new rhetoric, in 1993 Nepal's government began requiring foreign mountain climbing expeditions to post a US$4,000 bond, which is refundable only if an expedition removes all of its trash.[69] Furthermore, climbing expeditions in the Everest region are now required to collect and transport their basecamp human feces to disposal sites designated by the SPCC. In the 1996-1997 fiscal year, climbing expeditions in the Khumbu region brought down over 2,000 kilograms of human waste from their basecamps on Mount Everest, Lhotse, and Pumori.[70] To help monitor adherence to environmental and other regulations, the government requires climbing expeditions to hire and be accompanied by a government-appointed liaison officer.

In an effort to halt the growing amount of glass waste in the Everest region, Nepal's Ministry of Tourism banned the transport and sale of drinks in glass bottles in Sagarmatha National Park beginning in August 1998. National park staff now refuse to allow glass bottles into the park, and compliance with the ban is monitored by the SPCC. The new policy has effectively stopped the supply of new glass bottles into the park, but large stocks of beer, liquor, and soft drinks in glass bottles that had been brought into the park prior to the ban still remained available for sale in Khumbu lodges in 1999. Thus, the stacks of empty glass bottles have continued to pile up beside many lodges because most visitors do not think or bother to

---

69 The bond program has been widely lauded, but Bishop & Naumann (1996 p.324) suggested that the US$4,000 deposit amount may not be sufficient incentive for expeditions to remove all of their trash since the cost of removing all garbage, transporting it to Kathmandu, and shipping it back to the country of origin may cost more than US$4,000.

70 Sagarmatha Pollution Control Committee 1998

carry their empty bottles back with them to Kathmandu where they can be recycled.

The reason so many empty glass bottles have accumulated in Khumbu is because the cost of transporting to Kathmandu the estimated 300,000 empty bottles in the Everest region is higher than the recycle value of US$0.04 per bottle. Although tourists themselves have been responsible for the most of the glass waste, the resulting piles of bottles have been such a source of displeasure among tourists that local residents realized that if the piles had continued to grow unabated it could have hurt tourism business in the area. A Sherpa restaurant owner in Tengboche commented that "foreign trekkers have always complained about beer bottles that are scattered all over the area. The ban should take care of that problem."[71] Indeed, local residents have generally been very supportive of the ban and have expressed desires to see the ban extended outside the park to the main tourist entry point of Lukla. Others have called for the ban to be expanded to include plastic bottles as well in order to stem the growing volume of plastic mineral water bottles discarded by foreign visitors who do not bother to bring filters or iodine to purify their drinking water. But although they present an eyesore, the accumulation of empty plastic bottles is not considered as serious a problem as glass since the lightweight empty plastic bottles can be transported to one of the SPCC incinerators and burned.

In addition to stopping the import of glass bottles to the Khumbu region, the ban has had other positive local effects as well. Since the ban has reduced the availability of imported beer, which in Nepal comes mostly in bottles, local residents seem to be making and selling more of their traditional homemade beer (chang). In addition, drinks packaged in aluminum cans provide more profit to local merchants since they cost less to transport into the region than the heavier bottled drinks and since the merchants can receive money for empty cans sold to recyclers. Empty aluminum cans, because they are lighter in weight and can be flattened to reduce their bulk, can be

---

71 Dawa Tshering Sherpa, as quoted in Gurubacharya 1999

transported much more economically than glass bottles to recycling facilities in Kathmandu, which pay an average of US$0.80 per kilogram for aluminum.[72] Thus, the substitution of glass bottles with aluminum cans has not only lowered the accumulation of waste in the Everest region, it has also created an additional source of revenue for those who collect and transport empty aluminum cans for recycling.[73]

Environmental Clean-up Expeditions

In addition to the community and government pollution programs described above, numerous foreign climbing expeditions have made efforts to remove accumulated trash and waste from the basecamps and slopes of mountains in Khumbu. Because it has attracted more climbers than any other mountain in the area, Mount Everest has also accumulated the most waste. Over the years the mountain has become littered with trash, used equipment, fecal waste, and even the bodies of an estimated 120 climbers who have died and been left on the mountain. According to one estimate, 700 tons of garbage were left in the basecamp areas of Mount Everest between 1979 and 1988 alone.[74] As early as 1963, Mount Everest had already been dubbed "the world's highest junk yard" by an article in *National Geographic* magazine,[75] and the poor waste management practices of climbing expeditions and growing build-up of trash on the mountain have continued to earn a great deal of international media attention ever since.

Spurred by the shameful reputation and sordid condition of Mount Everest, an American volunteer group conducted a clean-up campaign of the mountain's basecamp area in 1975, collecting 1.5 tons of trash.[76] In 1990, a New Zealand climbing expedition led by Rob Hall and Gary Ball removed approximately 9,000 pounds of

---

72 BBC News 1998a
73 Gurubacharya 1999
74 McConnell 1996 p.21
75 Bishop 1963 p.489
76 Gray 1980, as cited in Stevens 1988 p.74

garbage from the basecamp area.[77] The same year, an American expedition removed nearly 3,000 pounds of garbage from the basecamp area on the Tibetan side of Mount Everest and transported the garbage to a landfill constructed 110 kilometers away near the Tibetan village of Shegar. In conjunction with an American NGO working in the area (The Mountain Institute) and with a donation from the Dow Chemical Company, the leader of the American clean-up expedition, Bob McConnell, established the Everest Environmental Project, which among other things donated a Chinese five-ton truck to the Tibetan Chomolungma Nature Preserve for continued use in transporting garbage from the mountain to the landfill.[78]

The popularity of such clean-ups really picked up in the mid-1990s as numerous foreign climbing expeditions eagerly began billing themselves as 'environmental expeditions' in order to obtain funding from sponsors on the basis of their intentions to remove trash. Between 1994 and 1997, a series of such expeditions removed over 17,000 pounds of trash from the Nepal side of Mount Everest and other areas in the Khumbu region, and their example established a new standard of environmental responsibility for other expeditions to emulate.[79] A member of the 1994 American Sagarmatha Environmental Expedition, Brent Bishop (son of Barry Bishop, the first American to summit Everest), originated what has since become a popular scheme for paying high-altitude porters to help clean up the mountain. The porters, who were already working for climbing expeditions on Mount Everest, were paid an incentive bonus for removing trash on their way down from the mountain's upper slopes. Not only did the scheme result in the removal of hundreds of discarded oxygen cylinders and thousands of pounds of other garbage, it also provided welcome earnings for the porters who participated, and it did not make the mountain any more crowded or subject

---

77   Bishop & Naumann 1996 p.324
78   McConnell 1991 pp.359-366, 1999 p.32
79   Bishop & Naumann 1998 pp.177-178

additional people to risk.[80] The success of the scheme garnered a lot of international attention and helped bolster the marketability of the 'clean-up expedition' concept in the eyes of corporate sponsors.

The accomplishments of the clean-up expeditions and the establishment of new standards among climbing expeditions for dealing with garbage led Bishop and colleague Chris Naumann to claim in a 1996 article that "further accumulation of trash on the Nepalese side of Everest has generally halted due to a change in both attitudes and economics. Most importantly, climbers have become more environmentally conscious and the norms of behavior have changed. No longer is it acceptable to leave any waste behind on a mountain."[81] In the spring climbing season of 1998, three separate Mount Everest climbing expeditions engaged in clean-up efforts on the mountain. Between them, the expeditions and their hired porters removed 173 discarded oxygen cylinders (in addition to the ones the expeditions used themselves), 4200 pounds of garbage, 211 discarded fuel canisters, and 546 used batteries. The expeditions also utilized a fecal waste collection system to collect, compost, and dispose of human waste.[82]

Despite the seeming good deeds of the expeditions endeavoring to clean up Mount Everest and the Khumbu region, it should also be pointed out that the use of clean-up intentions as a promotional tool has helped provide numerous foreign mountaineers with the financial backing necessary to pursue their personal climbing ambitions. The appeal among expedition sponsors of generating positive public relations via their association with heavily advertised Mount Everest clean-up expeditions has been aggressively exploited by many expedition organizers regardless of whether their priorities may lie more with the climb or clean-up. As climbing writer Ed Douglas pointed out, "the name Everest sells everything from mineral water to double glazing. And while there are thousands of unclimbed mountains and difficult routes still to be explored, finding news ways

---

80 Bishop & Naumann 1996 pp.323-327
81 Bishop & Naumann 1996 pp.326-327
82 Bishop & Naumann 1999 pp.182-183

of reaching the summit of Everest captures the interest of sponsors ahead of any other project."[83] Climbing activist Armando Menocal denounced what he called an exploitative "cashing in on trash" and observed that "although they may label themselves 'clean-up' expeditions, the main objective of these big-budget operations has always been to climb the mountain. This means that almost all of the money is spent on permits, guiding, equipment, and so on, with only a tiny percentage really needed to meet the modest clean-up achievements."[84] Indeed, Bishop quantified the percentage of a typical Mount Everest clean-up expedition's budget actually going toward clean-up activities as a mere one percent of the total budget.[85] Others have chimed in as well against the use of clean-up plans to finance climbers' hopes of reaching the summit of Everest. Lhakpa Norbu Sherpa, a highly educated Khumbu native who served as warden of Sagarmatha National Park in the 1980s, suggested as early as 1992 that the issue of trash on Mount Everest was receiving more attention than it deserved and was serving merely as an opportunity for fundraising by Western climbing expeditions.[86] Mountain climber and author David Roberts referred to money raising campaigns by climbing expeditions to clean up trash on Mount Everest as "something of a boondoggle [...] to finance an expensive [climbing] outing."[87] As an example, the American Everest 2000 Environmental Expedition received a whopping US$500,000 in funding from sponsors based upon the expedition's stated intention of removing garbage, while the expedition members admitted that their primary goal was to climb the mountain.[88]

Regardless of clean-up expeditions' ulterior motives or even their success in removing trash, some people have questioned the value of

---

83   Douglas 1997 p.4
84   Menocal 1999 p.54
85   Bishop (1999 p.56) calculated typical clean up related costs of US$2,200 for a typical expedition with a total budget of US$200,000.
86   Sherpa 1992 p.28
87   Anker & Roberts 1999 p.29
88   Guido 2000, Van Slambrouck 2000, and the Everest 2000 Environmental Expedition internet website http://www.everestcleanup.com

all the focus on cleaning up Mount Everest and suggested that attention should instead be directed toward other, more pressing problems in Nepal. For example, Menocal suggested that "all this concentration on climbers' waste and garbage diverts attention from Nepal's real problems [...] of human waste, lack of potable water, poverty, child labor, and trafficking in humans."[89] Paul Lachapelle, who has studied sanitation problems in both Khumbu and Kathmandu, also offered that the money involved in clean-up programs could be better spent, writing that "the perceived issues the climbers see are not that important at all. They are [only] important from a Western standpoint. They pale in comparison to the real issues [in Nepal]. You fly into Kathmandu and see the sewage, solid waste issues, infant and maternal mortality – the issues are so much grander in scale than a couple hundred oxygen bottles at the top of this mountain."[90] Even climbing writer Ed Douglas expressed an opinion that "there seems to be an Everest-sized mountain of hypocrisy over the issue of garbage [on and near Mount Everest]. Trekkers and mountaineers want the advantages of a western lifestyle in an environment that can't deal with its detritus and then they feel guilty about the consequences. Because of the media coverage the subject has generated and the guilt it has provoked, garbage in the mountains is considered a huge problem. But compared to the ruination of the environment in Kathmandu it is trivial."[91] And longtime Khumbu observer Barbara Brower (the daughter of renowned conservationist David Brower) argued that removing garbage from a relatively inert position on the uninhabited slopes of Mount Everest and transporting it to Kathmandu moves rather than solves the problem, and, worse yet, moves the garbage to a place with a much worse pollution management problem that affects considerably more people.[92]

---

89 Menocal 1999 p.54
90 Paul Lachapelle, as quoted in Kauder 1999 pp.2, 8
91 Douglas 1997 pp.104, 107
92 Barbara Brower, as cited in Kauder 1999 p.2

CHAPTER 6

Self-Determination

A departure from the institutions of equal liberty [...] cannot be justified by or compensated for by greater social or economic advantage.

(John Rawls, 1971, *Theory of Justice*)

No matter what improvements tourism may have brought to the economy and the well-being of Khumbu residents, I would argue that if it has impinged upon their freedom to determine their own fate and to pursue their own aspirations, then tourism has been a devil's bargain and its true benefit is questionable. In terms of the Khumbu Sherpas' degree of self-determination, tourism has had a multitude of effects, several examples of which are presented and discussed in this chapter.

Liberation from Historical Subservient Relations

As described by anthropologist Robert Miller, who conducted research in Khumbu in the 1960s, involvement in tourism helped to free some poorer Khumbu families from subservient relationships with wealthier and more powerful outsiders to whom they had historically been indebted. Because the harsh environmental conditions in Khumbu placed constraints on local farming and herding, the poorer members of the community struggled just to eke out a subsistence livelihood. Particularly for those with little land, few livestock, and minimal involvement in trade, life was very hard in Khumbu prior to the advent of tourism there. Due to their home region's advantageous location along a trans-Himalayan trade route, a considerable number of Khumbu residents were able to supplement their limited local agropastoral production by engaging in trade, bartering salt and wool from Tibet for grains grown in lowland Nepal. But the ability to engage in trade to any considerable degree required capital and available free time, both of which poorer residents generally lacked. According to Miller, "there were a few rich families, but most of the [Khumbu Sherpas] were tenants working the lands of landlords. Many were in debt to richer families"[1] from the Solu region to the south of Khumbu.

Miller claimed that Sherpas and members of other ethnic groups living in the Solu region were much better off economically than Khumbu Sherpas with limited involvement in trade because Solu enjoyed much greater agricultural productivity due to its lower elevation. Solu's greater proximity to the lowlands also enabled its residents to forge closer relations with the Nepal government than was the case among Khumbu residents, who historically had closer ties with Tibet.[2] Because of their closer relations with government officials in Kathmandu, influential village officials from Solu were appointed by the national government to collect taxes and settle disputes among the residents of the entire Solu-Khumbu area. Poorer families who were hard-pressed to make ends meet were often forced to go into debt to wealthy Solu residents in return for mortgaging their land and providing free labor to their debtors. Thus, through tax collection, jural authority, and debt relations, wealthy Solu residents traditionally enjoyed considerable power over the poorer villagers of Khumbu.

As Sherpas from Khumbu began migrating to Darjeeling in the latter 19th century to work for British colonial enterprises there, the tax collectors of Solu required payments from Khumbu residents to allow them to return home to their villages with their earnings. However, as the number of Khumbu Sherpas traveling to Darjeeling increased in the 1920s due to opportunities available with British

---

1   Miller 1965 (1997 reprint p.18)
2   compare with Brower 1996 pp.249-255

mountaineering expeditions, it became more difficult for the Solu tax collectors to enforce their demands. By the time Fürer-Haimendorf began studying the Sherpas in the 1950s, the job of collecting taxes from the residents of Khumbu was held by Sherpas living in Khumbu itself rather than Solu.[3] In addition, the incomes Khumbu Sherpas earned from their work with mountain climbing expeditions enabled them to pay off their debtors and lessened their need to take on additional debts. Miller noted that, due to their engagement with tourism,

> few [Khumbu] men remained [home] to work the land of the wealthier landlords, who in consequence lost one of their lines of control over the less favored population. Fewer poor families were forced to mortgage their small holdings to the rich, and the reduction of many families to tenant-status was slowed. In short, tenants and debtors became fewer, and the preeminent economic role of the rich declined.[4]

Control Over Tourism Development & Operation

In the book, *Tourism and Indigenous Peoples*, Richard Butler and Thomas Hinch defined indigenous tourism as "tourism activity in which the indigenous people are directly involved either through control and/or by having their culture serve as the essence of the attraction."[5] In the case of tourism in Nepal's Everest region, the indigenous Sherpa people fit both aspects of this definition. While there are many cases around the world where an indigenous people's culture has attracted tourists, there are far fewer cases in which the indigenous people have actually exercised a great deal of control over the development and operation of tourism. While many factors have contributed to the high level of control the Sherpas have had over tourism in Khumbu, two of the more fundamental factors have been the Sherpas' enthusiastic welcoming of tourism as a supplemental

---

3   Fürer-Haimendorf 1964 pp.117-125
4   Miller 1965 (1997 reprint p.19)
5   Butler & Hinch 1996 p.9

economic activity replacing trans-Himalayan trade and their self-confident, aggressive engagement in its development and operation.

As Butler and Hinch pointed out, "whoever has control [of tourism development] can generally determine such critical factors as the scale, speed and nature of development."[6] Up to now, tourism development in Khumbu has for the most part been on Sherpa terms rather than according to the impersonal, large-scale designs of outside interests such as transnational corporations, international development agencies, or the national government. Despite some interest in Khumbu tourism development by outside agencies (including the World Bank in the 1970s), a variety of regional characteristics that limited the perceived prospects for rapid growth have discouraged nearly all of them from investing heavily in the region, leaving tourism development to local entrepreneurs.

One notable exception to this was the construction of the luxury Everest View Hotel and its private airstrip at Syangboche by Japanese developers in the early 1970s. The villagers of nearby Khumjung, on whose land the development occurred, not only did not have control over the project, they were split between support for the jobs created by the project and resentment of the destruction of forests it involved.[7] In the end, these contentions made little difference because the developers went forward with the project anyway and were able to recruit enough paid labor to finish the work. The project catered to wealthy tourists willing to pay high prices for the readily accessible and comfortable views of Mount Everest afforded by the site of the hotel. But the twelve-room hotel was plagued by problems related to high altitude, limited demand, and prohibitive costs and eventually closed down in the early 1980s. After pressurized Gamow Bag chambers became available to treat altitude sickness and chartered helicopter service made arriving and departing flights more reliable, the hotel reopened in 1990, although it still suffers from high vacancy rates.

---

6   Butler & Hinch 1996 p.9
7   Fürer-Haimendorf 1974 p.109-110

With the exception of the Everest View Hotel described above, Khumbu Sherpas have generally maintained a great degree of control over local tourism infrastructure (e.g. shops and lodges), wage labor opportunities (e.g. sirdar and guide occupations), and business development (e.g. Kathmandu-based trekking agencies). This high level of control over local tourism development has been crucial to the correspondingly high level of self-determination many Sherpas have been able to achieve. And it is very reasonable to suspect that control over tourism development will play a crucial role in many Sherpas' level of self-determination in the future as well. Increased empowerment throughout the entire Khumbu population, however, will depend on the extent to which the benefits from tourism can be more equally distributed and shared with those who have not been as heavily involved. As things stand now, differences in the level of involvement in tourism among the wealthy and the poor are reflected in graphically different levels of self-determination and empowerment. As Khumbu researchers Paul Rogers and John Aitchison pointed out, "increasingly marked variations in the social distribution of [tourism] benefits […] has certainly contributed to a widening of the gap between the rich and the poor; and […] has had the effect of marginalizing many of the least wealthy from both the social benefits of tourism development and local decision-making processes."[8]

Respect & Recognition

The traditional roles that Sherpas have played for trekking and mountain climbing expeditions has been to break trail, set up camps, and carry loads, even when, particularly in the case of climbing expeditions, dangerous conditions kept their Western clients waiting below. As one Sherpa working as a climbing guide put it: "We push, we pull climbers, up, down, we set the path, carry and pitch their tents, cook their food, and sometimes have to go places we know are

---

8   Rogers & Aitchison 1998 pp.94-95

dangerous. [It's] crazy."[9] Regardless of their invaluable contributions
to the success of expeditions they have worked for, Sherpa climbers
have often remained in the shadow of their Western clients. As
another Sherpa climbing guide bemoaned: "We're not noticed
sometimes. An expedition ends, the Sherpa is paid, then leaves. The
[Western] people take the victory photograph without us."[10]

In recent years, however, Sherpa climbers have been earning
greater respect and recognition from foreigners, enabling them to
transcend their traditional subservient background role on the
mountain. In 1991, the first all-Sherpa climbing expedition reached
the summit of Mount Everest, receiving international acclaim for
their accomplishment including a full-length story in *National
Geographic* magazine.[11] Expedition member Sonam Dendu Sherpa,
who had climbed Mount Everest twice previously with foreign
expeditions, summed up the feeling of the Sherpa climbers when he
said: "This is *our* expedition. It is for all the Sherpas."[12] Another team
member, Lopsang Sherpa, who had worked as a servant before
becoming a mountain guide, reflected on the significance of the climb
to Sherpas: "We want to take pride as a people apart."[13]

Since the success and attention gained by the all-Sherpa
expedition, Sherpa climbers have been increasingly recognized for
their own accomplishments rather than taking a back seat to foreign
climbers as they had in the past. For example, in 1998, Kaji Sherpa
received international media attention for climbing from the
basecamp to the summit of Mount Everest in a record 20 hours 24
minutes, bettering by more than two hours a record that had been
held for nearly a decade by a well-known Western climber.[14]

---

9   Chuldin Norbu Sherpa, as quoted in Arnold 1998
10 Kami Sherpa, as quoted in Arnold 1998
11 Carrier 1992 pp.70-89
12 Sonam Dendu Sherpa, as quoted in Carrier 1992 p.70
13 Lopsang Sherpa, as quoted in Carrier 1992 p.74
14 The previous record for the fastest ascent of Mount Everest via the standard
    'South Col' route had been set by French climber Marc Batard in 1989. The
    climb from basecamp to the summit normally takes about 4 days for climbers
    who have already spent weeks acclimatizing to the high altitude.

Following his accomplishment, Kaji became a hero in Nepal, and his image appeared on billboards across the country. Kaji claimed he stepped into the limelight to advance Sherpa pride and fame and to move Sherpas out from behind the shadow of foreigners: "I did this for Sherpas, for Sherpa pride. It is important for Sherpas to be known."[15] In another example of the increasing recognition afforded to Sherpa climbers, Babu Chhiri Sherpa earned international acclaim in 1999 – as well as a bevy of international advertising opportunities – for remaining on the summit of Mount Everest for a record 21 hours without bottled oxygen.[16] Of the few climbers who manage to make it to the summit of Mount Everest, most spend only minutes on the top because of their fatigue and because of the extremely cold and rarefied air at that high altitude. The following year, in May 2000, Babu Chhiri Sherpa again made international headlines when he broke the record for the fastest ascent of Mount Everest, bettering by more than 3 hours the above-mentioned record set by Kaji Sherpa two years earlier.[17]

Perceptions of gender equality in Sherpa society have also been affected by climbing achievements on Mount Everest. When Pasang Lhamu Sherpa became the first Nepali woman to reach the summit of Mount Everest in 1993, Sherpa women were afforded greater respect by both foreign and Sherpa male climbers. However, some felt the impact of Pasang Lhamu's accomplishment was lessened by the fact that she climbed with a male Sherpa team and because she died on the way down from the summit. In 2000, a group of five Sherpa women set out to advance the cause of women in Khumbu and in Nepal by trying to become the first team of Nepali women to scale the world's highest peak. The expedition leader, Mingma Yangje Sherpa from Tengboche, complained that Sherpa women working for mountain climbing expeditions have been limited to cooking, cleaning, and carrying loads to lower camps on the mountain.

15 Kaji Sherpa, as quoted in Arnold 1998
16 Associated Press 1999a
17 Babu Chhiri Sherpa's record ascent took 16 hours 56 minutes from the basecamp to the summit of Mount Everest via the 'South Col' route.

Mingma Yangje added that Sherpa men "have always discouraged us from climbing, telling us we are not good enough to face the harsh conditions on the mountain. We are tired of being in the shadow of our men. I am doing this for [my daughters'] future and for the womenfolk [of Khumbu]."[18] Under the spotlight of considerable media attention that included the making of a documentary film, the all-woman Sherpa team achieved success when one of its members, Lhakpa Sherpa, reached and safely descended from the summit of Mount Everest.[19] And, she returned again the following year to climb Everest a second time.

With their self-confidence bolstered by their accomplishments in the mountains and their success in the tourism business, many Sherpas have stopped seeing themselves as subservient to visitors. One indication of this is the fact that Sherpas no longer use the master-servant term 'sahib' to address foreign visitors, as they had in the earlier days of Western mountaineering and tourism.[20] According to anthropologist Sherry Ortner, Khumbu Sherpas have managed to transcend their historical subservient relations with Westerners and have gained the respect and hierarchical acceptance of visitors.[21] As a result, Khumbu Sherpas have been able to enjoy a much greater level of self-determination in their dealings with Westerners than that which has been achieved by many other indigenous peoples.

---

18 Mingma Yangje Sherpa, as quoted in Associated Press 2000a
19 According to a news report in *USA Today* (19 May 2000), the all-woman Sherpa team was criticized by some male Sherpas who claimed that the women's presence on the mountain was offensive to Chomolungma, the goddess of Mount Everest, and was to blame for particularly bad weather during the spring 2000 climbing season.
20 Fisher 1990 p.137, Ortner 1990 p. 5. Note: The term 'sahib' is a carry over from British colonial rule in India, where it was used by servants to address their 'master.' Fisher noted that Westerners are still sometimes addressed as sahib by Nepali household and hotel servants, as well as by some Nepali tour guides in Kathmandu.
21 Ortner 1990 p.8

Role Relations with Visitors

An interesting paradox seems to have developed in regard to the effect that tourism has had on the Sherpas' level of self-determination in their relations with visitors. While, as suggested by the preceding section, the Sherpas' success in tourism has allowed them greater latitude in their relations with outsiders, it also seems that, for at least some Sherpas, the roles they play in tourism and the relations they enter into with visitors are dictated by visitors' expectations of them. In fact, some Western anthropologists have suggested that many Sherpas willingly and deliberately play the roles expected of them by visitors, and in doing so actually exploit visitors for the Sherpas' own benefit. Referring to such role-playing Sherpas as "tourist Sherpas," Jim Fisher suggested that "successful trekking Sherpas realize that they are, in part, paid professional actors and entertainers" delivering what their paying clients want.[22] Vincanne Adams took this notion further, claiming that the Sherpas' very sense of identity has been heavily influenced by Western tourist impressions of what Sherpas are *supposed to be*, as described in the following excerpts from her book about "virtual" Sherpas.[23]

> Accommodating Western interests for a particular sort of Sherpa is part of who Sherpas are, [making it] unclear where the boundary is between who Westerners would have the Sherpas be and who they truly are. (p.12)

> Becoming what Westerners desire is built into the ways in which Sherpas are expected to be similar to Westerners [...] but becoming what Westerners desire also demands that Sherpas remain different from them [and therefore remain 'authentic' Sherpas]. (p.9)

> [...] despite [Western] desires to make Sherpas into 'moderns' through development, Western discourse about Sherpas has never enabled them to be 'wholly' the same because of concurrent Western desires for cultural Otherness in Sherpas, whether as innately gifted climbers, highly spiritual Buddhists, or villagers

---

22 Fisher 1990 p.119
23 Adams 1996

familiar with more intimate and 'seductive' ways of life than Westerners believe are available in the West. (p.19)

According to Adams, Sherpas, by playing roles to be who visitors want them to be, have exploited the propensity and desire of Western visitors to sponsor 'needy' Sherpas. Dr. Jim Litch, a Western physician who resided in Khumbu while working at the Kunde hospital from 1995 to 1999, told me that he even knew of instances where Sherpa recipients of financial aid were actually wealthier than their unsuspecting Western sponsors.[24] Both Adams and Litch noted how Sherpas often maintained multiple Western sponsors, each of whom was kept unaware of the existence of other sponsors. From an early age (and for well over a generation now) Sherpas have learned to play foreign visitors for financial gain. Adams claimed that Sherpas "recruit" and "seduce" Westerners to be their sponsors and to provide them with gifts, money, employment, and more by constructing and reinforcing an image of themselves in the Westerners' eyes as being in need and being deserving of aid.[25] This has become increasingly difficult for some Sherpas, however, as signs of their affluence have grown more obvious. Such role-playing in exploiting the desire of beneficent visitors to assist needy villagers has taken on a much more subtle and complex form among Khumbu Sherpas than the overt begging that parents teach their children to do in some tourist areas in Nepal.[26] Indeed, begging children are practically nonexistent in Khumbu, perhaps because Sherpas are very much in tune with Westerners' perceptions of them and therefore realize that begging is not looked upon favorably.

Dependency on External Benefactors

According to some outside observers with intimate knowledge of Khumbu community life, a large number of Sherpas have become

---

24 Dr. Jim Litch, Kunde Hospital physician, personal communication, 1999
25 Adams 1996 pp.9, 16, 111
26 I have on numerous occasions watched parents and/or older siblings teaching and encouraging young children to beg from passing trekkers in some tourist areas of Nepal.

SELF-DETERMINATION 179

spoiled and developed a 'hand-out' mentality as a result of the myriad generous donations and development projects that have rained down upon the people of Khumbu over the past few decades. An American aid worker summed up the situation in the 1980s as follows:

> Perhaps no other rural, mountainous region in the world has experienced the levels of free commodity, monetary service, and technical gifts as the Khumbu, with the result that these items have become more or less expected and perceived as a fact of life by the corresponding generation of Sherpa villagers. Trekkers provide down coats, sleeping bags, and scholarships; climbing expeditions do not climb without the guaranteed provision of an average of $3,000 of technical climbing gear and related goods to the sirdar and climbing Sherpas; schools and hospitals are simply built and often staffed by foreigners; and the installation of major hydro-electric projects is provided with no required investment [from Sherpas].[27]

Similarly, a Western doctor living in Khumbu while working at the Kunde Hospital in the late 1980s voiced concern over what anthropologist Vincanne Adams referred to as a rising 'welfarism' among the Sherpas of Khumbu:

> It irritates me when a young [Sherpa woman] from Namche comes into the clinic asking for baby bottles which she can get from us for only one rupee [the equivalent of a couple cents in U.S. currency]. It is obvious that she can get them herself from Kathmandu. Her husband is a sirdar and earns a good living. He could easily bring them to her.[28]

In Namche in 1999, I spoke with an Austrian employee of the NGO, Eco-Himal, who had been working in Khumbu for several years and had established close relations with a number of Khumbu families. The representative made clear to me his general disgust with many of the residents of Namche, claiming that the wealthier they grew the greater their obsession with wealth became. He described them as greedy, selfish, rich people spoiled by the free handouts they

27   as quoted in Pye-Smith 1988 p.31
28   as quoted in Adams 1996 p.93

had become accustomed to receiving from foreign NGOs, development agencies, governments, and individual visitors. He described the handout mentality that had developed among many Namche villagers whereby they expected to be given free services and complained about having to fend for themselves or to pay for services such as electricity and water that had been provided by outside organizations such as Eco-Himal. He contrasted Namche residents with Sherpas from other Khumbu villages who had not grown as wealthy from tourism or received as much aid from abroad, stating that Sherpas in the poorer villages were not as greedy or spoiled as the Sherpas from Namche. He expressed an opinion that the attitude of dependence that had developed among Namche villagers was the fault of those (including Eco-Himal staff) who had freely given so much to the people of Khumbu. He thought it was natural for the people of Namche to have eagerly accepted the aid they were offered and to have selfishly pursued the economic opportunities available to them through tourism.

Along the same lines, in writing about sanitation projects funded by foreign development agencies in Namche and Tengboche (the two Khumbu villages that have received the most outside attention and aid), development worker Paul Lachapelle claimed that the projects had eventually fallen into disrepair because, rather than taking any initiative themselves, local residents expected the foreign agencies to continue to fund and maintain the projects.[29] Indeed, while traveling through Khumbu, despite the great wealth of many of the area's residents, one cannot help but notice the plethora of donation boxes and signs along trails asking foreign visitors to give money for monasteries, schools, and a variety of local projects. Even the Everest region's single greatest benefactor, Edmund Hillary, has expressed reservations about the dependency situation fostered by his and so many other foreigners' generosity to the Sherpas. Remarking on his Himalayan Trust's long-standing support for development projects in the region (running about US$500,000 per year as of the late 1990s),

---

29   Lachapelle 1998 p.56

Hillary said: "the Sherpas regard me as someone who is prepared to assist them with what they want to do. So far I don't believe we have ever let them down."[30] I witnessed this type of expectation of assistance myself in Khumbu in 1999 when, in the village of Dingboche, I suggested that trekking group guides should take responsibility for ensuring that group trash is handled responsibly. The response I received from two local Sherpa guides was that, instead, foreigners should raise money in their own countries and organize clean-up expeditions to remove the trash that accumulates in Khumbu.

Education

A key contributor to the high level of self-determination among Khumbu Sherpas has been the availability and quality of education in Khumbu, as well as the large number of Khumbu children attending schools in Kathmandu and pursuing higher education abroad. Tourism has been both directly and indirectly responsible for these improvements through the support foreign visitors have provided for schools in Khumbu and through the increased ability of families engaged in tourism to afford the costs of private education. A clear example of the former is the support provided by Edmund Hillary's Himalayan Trust, which since the early 1960s has built, maintained, supplied books for, and trained school teachers in every Khumbu village as well as villages in other nearby areas.[31] In addition, the Himalayan Trust and the American Himalayan Foundation have supported the education of Sherpa children through subsidies to induce them to stay in school rather than drop out to pursue jobs in tourism, as well as by providing scholarships for attending college. Surveys of Sherpa households in the mid-1990s by Paul Rogers and John Aitchison confirmed that donations from visiting tourists have directly funded the building and maintenance of several schools in

---

30   as quoted in Gray 1999
31   Fürer-Haimendorf 1984 pp.61-62, Fisher 1990 pp.71-73, Sherpa & Höivik
      2003 pp.21-30

Khumbu as well as the provision of books and educational supplies. Furthermore, Rogers and Aitchison noted that "the majority of survey households recognized [...] that the changing nature and complexity of the local economy meant that a good education for their children was an increasingly important priority."[32]

Reflecting in 1991 on the importance of the educational opportunities made available to Khumbu Sherpas through the previous thirty years of support by the Himalayan Trust, Edmund Hillary commented: "It was absolutely vital that the local people obtain schooling so that an influx of tourists not overwhelm them. That they not just become peons but instead can take advantage of the economic possibilities [of tourism]."[33] Jim Fisher also pointed out the significance of education to local self-determination, arguing that education enabled Khumbu Sherpas "to exploit the change [brought by tourism and other external forces], control it, and confront it on their own terms rather than be exploited and victimized by it. At least [Sherpas] will be in a far stronger position to affect their destiny than without [education]."[34] Nepali anthropologist Ramesh Kunwar also noted the effect education was having on increasing the choices available to Sherpas, stating that "due to the impact of modern education, educated Sherpas are gradually leaving their traditional jobs like herding, farming, trading, and trekking and have become school masters, pilots, medical doctors, veterinary doctors, professors, national park managers, overseers, district forest officers, and other government officials."[35]

National Park

Tourism has also contributed significantly to arguably the single largest negative effect on Khumbu Sherpas' degree of self-determination – the designation of their home region as a national park. With the double objectives of attracting more tourists to Nepal

---

32   Rogers & Aitchison 1998 pp.79-81
33   as quoted in Carrier 1992 pp.87-88
34   Fisher 1990 pp.162-163
35   Kunwar 1989 p.118

to increase the country's foreign exchange earnings[36] and protecting the environment of the Everest region to appease international organizations controlling the purse strings of foreign aid,[37] the government of Nepal gazetted the entire Khumbu region and designated it as Sagarmatha National Park in 1976. Khumbu residents were initially concerned that they would be forced to leave their homes, facing the same fate as over twenty thousand people in the Chitwan, Bardia, and Rara regions of Nepal who had been displaced when their homelands were turned into protected areas. In each of those cases the resident population had been moved from their homes by the Nepali army in deference to new strict nature preservation principles.[38] In the case of Sagarmatha National Park, however, the Khumbu Sherpas were allowed to continue living in their villages, which along with their private fields became legal enclaves within the park. However, all communal lands outside of villages, which the Sherpas had traditionally used for obtaining forest products and for grazing their animals, came under the strict control of the park administration, backed up by a company of armed soldiers.

After the authority for regulating natural resource use was handed over to the park, the Sherpas' traditional systems of resource management were undermined and, as described in Chapter Five, fell

---

36   compare with Brower 1991b p.73

37   Stevens (1997 pp.67, 308) pointed out for Sagarmatha and other national parks in Nepal the heavy involvement, influence, and funding of international organizations such as the United Nations Food and Agriculture Organization (UN FAO), the United Nations Development Programme (UNDP), the World Wildlife Fund (WWF), and the International Union for the Conservation of Nature (IUCN).

38   According to Stevens (1997 pp.32, 67, 77, 308-309), twenty-two thousand residents were forced to move from Chitwan when it was designated a wildlife sanctuary in 1964. Chitwan later became a national park in 1973. Two villages in Bardia were evacuated when it was declared a hunting reserve in 1969, and a third village was displaced when Bardia was redesignated a wildlife reserve in 1976. In the case of Rara, which became a national park in 1976, 650 indigenous residents from two highland villages were relocated to lowland areas where many were reported to have died of malaria, to which they had no resistance.

out of use in many villages. The restrictions placed by the park on cultivation, keeping livestock, felling trees, and killing wildlife, which have been enforced by army patrols and punishable by fines, have been a continual source of conflict between the park staff and local residents, who viewed the park's policies as an unwelcome intrusion in their affairs.[39] As Fisher noted, "Sagarmatha National Park was established with neither the advice nor the consent of those who live within its boundaries. Because it was not so much established as imposed, it has faced an uphill battle to restore the confidence of the villagers."[40]

The national park's environmental protection regulations and restoration programs have affected Khumbu residents in a number of ways. Restrictions on tree felling and branch lopping in Khumbu have made the collection of fuel-wood and animal fodder more difficult, time-consuming, and expensive and forced Khumbu residents to purchase firewood and lumber from the neighboring region of Pharak. This has added considerably to the cost of house and lodge construction, especially for residents living in the more remote reaches of Khumbu, who have to pay a great deal for the transport of timber from Pharak. The higher cost of lumber has prompted residents to utilize other types of construction materials, such as the now ubiquitous sheet-metal roofs that previously had been considered too expensive.[41]

As part of its attempts to increase forest cover in the region, the national park has established forest plantations on several areas of bare slopes and restricted livestock grazing in these areas. As Stevens noted, "the forest plantations are extremely unpopular with some local herders, who complain that the government is taking away some of their most important grazing land."[42] And Brower has called the park's restrictions against grazing in the plantations unnecessary and

---

39 Fisher 1990 pp.141-142; Brower 1991a pp.156-158, 1991b pp.76-77, 173; Stevens 1993a pp.312-315, 1997 pp.80-84
40 Fisher 1990 p.161
41 Stevens 1993a pp.313, 492
42 Stevens 1993a p.488

misinformed, since established silver fir trees are tolerant to grazing animals.[43] Sherpa livestock owners were further incensed when, in 1983, park authorities persuaded the local government to outlaw goats in Khumbu because their grazing was thought to be destructive to the park's alpine grasses.[44] National park authorities have also restricted residents from expanding cultivated land holdings within the park, which a number of Khumbu Sherpas were interested in doing in the mid-1980s. There have even been instances where army patrols employed by the park uprooted crops and destroyed fields that had been planted in areas regarded as off-limits by the park's policies.[45] Further contributing to the Sherpas' resentment of the national park's interference in their lives has been the fact that the national park staff and the army personnel who patrol the park have been almost exclusively lowlanders from outside of Khumbu who speak Nepali rather than Sherpa and practice Hinduism rather than Buddhism. According to Fürer-Haimendorf, "the Sherpas consider them as outsiders and resent being subjected to their supervision in their own territory where until recently they had been free to do whatever they chose."[46]

Despite the severe negative implications the park's creation and management have had on the level of self-determination among Khumbu Sherpas, it should be noted that Sagarmatha National Park was one of the first national protected areas in the world to allow significant indigenous settlement and resource use.[47] International attention and concern for the Sherpa inhabitants of the new park had a great deal to do with the progressive and accommodating nature of the park's administrative policies.[48] The New Zealand natural

43 Barbara Brower, as cited in Butt & Price 2000 pp.17-18
44 Stevens 1997 pp.82-83
45 Stevens 1997 p.83
46 Fürer-Haimendorf 1984 pp.60-61
47 Stevens 1997 p.79
48 According to Stevens (1997 p.69), the "innovative initiatives" implemented in Sagarmatha National Park to respect and accommodate the subsistence needs and culture of the indigenous residents were the result of "world concern for the welfare of the high-altitude Sherpas."

resource managers and Nepali ecologist involved in recommending and planning the new park in the 1970s endeavored to include local residents in the process of planning and operating the park.[49] The planning and creation of the park were discussed with the indigenous Sherpas, 63 legal enclaves were created to allow continued Sherpa control over village lands and private fields, a formal Sherpa advisory committee was created to meet with the park administration, Sherpas were formally trained (in New Zealand land management institutions) to hold park staff positions, and Sherpas were eventually given significant roles in the park's administration including senior positions such as park warden.[50]

But although a number of Khumbu Sherpas have held the positions of chief park warden or assistant park warden, some observers have complained that the management of the park has still suffered from a lack of open consultation with the local population. According to Stevens, "Village meetings were seldom held after the establishment of the national park. The local advisory committee failed to become a significant institution, and during some periods was not convened for years at a time. [...] There have also been strong local complaints that too much of the consultation between both Sherpa and non-Sherpa national park officials and villagers takes place in closed-door meetings between park staff and local politicians and other local elite. The arrangements agreed to often do not reflect the concerns of other Khumbu residents."[51]

Despite these criticisms, two successive Sherpa park wardens in the 1980s, Mingma Norbu Sherpa and Lhakpa Norbu Sherpa, made efforts to re-establish the Sherpas' traditional forest guardian system (*shingo nawa*) in order to help patrol forests and enforce the park's restrictions on forest use. Furthermore, in 1990 a new park warden, Surya Bahadur Pandey, relaxed some of the park's restrictions on forest use and established a regional forest management committee

---

49 Lucas *et al.* 1974 p.15, as cited in Brower 1991b p.75; Mishra 1973 pp.3, 14, as cited in Stevens 1997 p.78
50 Brower 1991b p.75; Stevens 1993a pp.310-313, 1997 pp.78-79
51 Stevens 1997 pp.83-84

that gave Khumbu villages more control over local forest use and gave greater authority to the Sherpas' shingo nawa forest guardians. Pandey even allowed local communities to keep the revenues obtained from tree-felling permits, which the national park had previously forwarded to government authorities in Kathmandu. This arrangement only lasted for two years, however, as Pandey's superiors did not approve of the loss of revenue.[52] The following year, however, Nepal's government (working with the United Nations Development Programme's Parks and People Project) passed the 1993 Buffer Zone Amendment to Nepal's National Parks and Wildlife Conservation Act, which provided that up to 50 percent of national park entrance fees (which up to that point had gone entirely to the national government) could be allocated to local communities within and around national parks for conservation and development related activities.[53] Surveys conducted in the mid-1990s of 69 households in 15 Khumbu villages and settlements, as well as surveys of national park staff, led Rogers and Aitchison to conclude that "following initial reservations, Khumbu residents now fully appreciate the benefits of a strict Park policy."[54] And in 1999, a park official told me during an interview that relations between local residents and park staff had improved immensely over the past decade and had become very good.[55]

---

52   Brower 1991a p.158, 1991b p.77; Stevens 1993a pp.196, 317-320, 1997 pp.85-90
53   Stevens 1997 p.95; Lhakpa Sherpa, as cited in Butt & Price 2000 p.18
54   Rogers & Aitchison 1998 p.53
55   Sagarmatha National Park ranger Uddhab Dhungana, personal communication, 1999

CHAPTER 7

Cultural & Societal Continuity

A s one might imagine when tens of thousands of foreign visitors converge each year on a relatively confined area inhabited by a numerically smaller indigenous population, tourism has had and continues to have significant effects on Khumbu Sherpa society and culture. Although researchers like Fürer-Haimendorf and Bjønness reported in the 1980s that tourism was causing profound and pervasive changes in the Sherpas' culture and society,[1] more recent observations and perspectives of researchers such as Fisher and Stevens have suggested that the effects have been more subtle than what had been reported earlier.[2] In this chapter, I explore the manifold ways in which Khumbu Sherpa society and culture have been affected by tourism. For the reader, one thing should become abundantly clear – things are not static in Khumbu. But surprisingly it's not all as bad as one might expect. For, as well as the disruptive influences that the intrusion of thousands of outsiders has had on local life, there are also examples of Khumbu Sherpa society and culture having been strengthened as a result of tourism.

Tradition of Change

After years of close observation of Khumbu society, geographer Stan Stevens concluded that most of the cultural changes that had occurred since the arrival of tourism were "relatively superficial [and] do not signify an abandonment of local values for the consumer

---

1   Fürer-Haimendorf 1984, Bjønness 1983
2   Fisher 1990; Stevens 1991, 1993a, 1993b

culture of the West."[3] Stevens went on to claim that Sherpas who became adults during the era of tourism had not given up the traditional practices of reciprocity and communal cooperation that continue to permeate daily social experiences ranging from working in fields to building houses to organizing village festivals. And no significant generational gap had developed in terms of lifestyles or cultural values either. Indeed, Stevens suggested that "if Sherpa culture is changing in some dimensions it is primarily because Sherpas are choosing to change it, adopting what they choose from the ideas, values, and material goods which tourism and their own travels have introduced them to and integrating new concepts and goods into long-valued cultural frameworks."[4] Journalist Jim Carrier drew a very similar conclusion about the active roles Sherpas themselves were playing in consciously adapting to the manifold changes that have occurred in Khumbu, writing that "Sherpas have been resilient, managing to blend wisely with the modern world, partly because they have been needed and respected for their skills, rather than exploited. Much of traditional Sherpa life is intact, and many Sherpas, thoroughly cosmopolitan, are choosing to keep it that way."[5]

To me, such observations raise some fundamental questions about Western value judgments associated with the notions of cultural change and continuity. Just how is it that cultural change has come to be characterized so negatively and cultural continuity painted in such a positive light? From where and from whose perspective do such value judgments arise? After all, aren't all cultures essentially defined and distinguished by change and differentiation? Anthropologist Sherry Ortner has taken the position that culture is a product of change, with history providing the major source of cultural meaning. According to her, as a result of social, economic, and political shifts, "cultural symbols, styles, and practices acquire

---

3   Stevens 1991 pp.49-50
4   Stevens 1991 p.54
5   Carrier 1992 p.89

and lose their meanings over time."[6] Likewise, Stevens, in writing about the Sherpas, argued that "it is necessary to keep in mind that peoples continually redefine their cultures and their identities, and that cultural change has to be evaluated from a local perspective rather than from an outside assumption that any departure from 'tradition' represents cultural erosion. The concept of tradition itself must be re-examined, for the cultural past of many peoples has often been as dynamic or nearly as dynamic as their present."[7]

Indeed, well before tourism took off in Khumbu in the 1970s, Sherpa history had been dynamic and wrought with change. As examples, consider the Sherpas' emigration from the Tibetan region of Kham in the 1400s, settlement in Khumbu in the 1500s, founding of Buddhist institutions in the 1600s, political acquiescence to Hindu forces in the 1700s, monopolization of the Nangpa La trade route in the 1800s, increased population growth following the introduction of the potato in the latter 1800s, large-scale seasonal migration to Darjeeling and unprecedented level of support for local monastic institutions in the early 1900s, employment by Western mountaineering expeditions beginning in the 1920s, and the curtailment of Tibetan trade and the nationalization of forests and local government in the 1960s. In the context of these tumultuous changes, anthropologist Jim Fisher concluded that "the customary commonsense distinction between *tradition* and *change* is therefore ultimately untenable. Rather there is, and always has been in Sherpa society, a *tradition of change*."[8] Stevens took this argument even further in claiming that Sherpas have benefited from, and fashioned a survival strategy out of, their ability to adapt to change and to find new opportunities from it.[9]

While multiple generations of Khumbu Sherpas have been embracing change and making the most of it, the challenges the community has faced also seem to have bolstered certain traditional

---

6   Ortner 1990 p.19
7   Stevens 1991 p.43
8   Fisher 1990 p.64 (emphasis added by Fisher)
9   Stevens 1993a

aspects of the Sherpas' unique cultural identity. Along these lines, mountain writer Ed Douglas suggested that "the old way of life in the Khumbu was never so hard that the Sherpas abandoned it altogether when an alternative came along, but was hard enough to make them create a robust and supportive culture."[10] And after a span of three decades studying the Khumbu Sherpas and their response to the onslaught of Western tourists and Nepali officials, Fürer-Haimendorf concluded that the Sherpas "remain a people proud and conscious of their identity, and determined to preserve the basic features of their traditional style of life within the framework of a modernized society."[11]

Acknowledging such perspectives on cultural continuity has made it quite difficult for me to ascribe positive or negative connotations to societal and cultural changes that have occurred among the Khumbu Sherpas as a result of tourism. Perhaps the best that an outsider (especially one heavily dependent upon the observations of other outsiders, as I am) can hope to do is to attempt to identify the ways in which tourism has served to encourage or reinforce continuity in Sherpa society and culture and contrast this with the ways in which tourism has caused or shown the potential to cause societal and cultural change.

Community Continuity & Leadership

With the staging of mountaineering expeditions from Nepal rather than Darjeeling beginning in the 1950s and the growth of tourism that followed in Khumbu, the economic opportunities that arose in tourism allowed Sherpas to continue living in Khumbu after the decline of trans-Himalayan trade in the 1960s rather than migrate elsewhere as some other highland peoples were forced to do. Today, Sherpa involvement in tourism is so lucrative that some men can earn an entire year's income without requiring them to leave home for more than a couple of trips each year of a few weeks duration.

---

10 Douglas 1997 p.141
11 Fürer-Haimendorf 1975 p.105

Although some Sherpas who are heavily involved in tourism may spend larger amounts of time away from home, especially young people early in their careers or owners of trekking agencies based in Kathmandu, those who own or work in local lodges and shops can pursue rewarding economic opportunities in tourism without having to leave the Everest region at all. The continued ability of Sherpas involved in tourism to maintain close ties to Khumbu has been an important factor in enabling many of the brighter and more talented individuals to fulfill leadership roles in their communities.[12]

In the early 1960s, Fürer-Haimendorf observed that Sherpas from historically wealthy families, who traditionally held the region's political clout, were suspicious of those Sherpas who had achieved newfound affluence from tourism.[13] By the early 1970s, however, Fürer-Haimendorf noted that economic and political power in Khumbu had "shifted from the older men of long established Sherpa families to young and middle-aged men [involved in tourism] who are not necessarily of families enjoying inherited high status."[14] While traditionally wealthy families may have had early advantages investing in tourism ventures such as building lodges and starting Kathmandu-based trekking agencies, these capital-intensive types of tourism ventures initially developed slowly in Khumbu. Meanwhile, mountaineering and trekking employment opportunities enabled young men even from traditionally poor families to attain considerable economic success in tourism. Nowadays, it is those who have achieved success in tourism who enjoy the most influence among their peers and prestige in their communities. Along these lines, Kunwar noted that "in Khumbu there are many traditionally rich people but nowadays they are not as respected as the trekking guides who can offer job opportunities to those who want to join in trekking and mountaineering."[15] Likewise, Stevens pointed out that, during the 1980s, the two highest elected positions in the Khumbu

---

12 Stevens 1991 pp.52-53
13 Fürer-Haimendorf 1963 (reprinted in Hornbein 1965 p.74)
14 Fürer-Haimendorf 1974 p.108
15 Kunwar 1989 p.106

region were held by a trekking sirdar and a tourist lodge owner.[16] Fisher also observed that success in tourism served to enhance social status among Khumbu Sherpas, and that such success transcended the importance of local presence, as exemplified by the case of a prominent Khumbu civil-religious position (*chorimba*) being held by a Sherpa man who had been spending 10 months a year in Kathmandu for the past 15 years running a successful trekking agency.[17]

Cultural Encouragement & Religious Continuity

Although it may seem counterintuitive, there is ample evidence suggesting that in some cases tourism has actually served to strengthen and intensify Sherpa identity and pride and to encourage the practice of traditional culture and religion. One explanation of this is Fisher's assertion that "Sherpas are so massively reinforced at every point [by visitors] for being Sherpas that they have every reason not only to 'stay' Sherpa but even to flaunt their Sherpahood."[18] An example of such reinforcement is the construction and financial support of a Sherpa cultural center in Tengboche by the American Himalayan Foundation and Cultural Survival, a pair of international NGOs whose priorities lay with the preservation of indigenous cultures. Another example is the production of a compact disk recording of traditional Sherpa songs sponsored by Eco-Himal, another international NGO. These and many other similar externally supported projects over the years have provided the type of cultural encouragement that led Fisher to suggest that "Sherpas have come to value some of their traditions even more than they did prior to the advent of tourism."[19] Adams took this idea even further, questioning the very construction of Sherpa authenticity and claiming that Western produced representations of Sherpa culture have become the

---

16   Stevens 1991 p.53
17   Fisher 1987 pp.19-20, 1990 pp.138-139
18   Fisher 1990 pp.136-137
19   Fisher 1990 p.139

essence of what Sherpas now reproduce for the 'gaze' of Western
tourists:

> The authorities Sherpas often cited in describing themselves were
> those representations of Sherpas found in the writings of
> Westerners. The qualities of Sherpas depicted in representations of
> expedition work, in folklore about trekking and tourism, and even
> in anthropology are the distillation of perceived differences
> between Sherpas and Westerners. But the exoticism of their
> religion, hospitality, and even traditional medicine is perceived by
> Sherpas as important to their economic and cultural survival. The
> versions of 'Sherpa-ness' mirrored by Westerners for Sherpas have
> consequently become indistinguishable from those that Sherpas
> themselves now reproduce for Westerners. To say in their own
> voices who they are, Sherpas consult Others' representations of
> them. Moreover, to establish the *authority* to say who they are,
> Sherpas turn to accounts and discourses of identity in which their
> stories are already told by Westerners.[20]

Adams even found that when she asked Sherpa villagers about their
culture, she was repeatedly told that if she wanted the correct answer
she should consult the ethnography of the Sherpas written in 1964 by
Christoph von Fürer-Haimendorf, a Western anthropologist.

Offering a somewhat different perspective, Stevens attributed a
good deal of what he characterized as a continuity and strengthening
of Khumbu Sherpa cultural practices to the Sherpas' increased
discretionary income from tourism,[21] noting that a similar
phenomenon had occurred in the early 1900s when increased
prosperity due to potato cultivation and employment opportunities in
Darjeeling facilitated the establishment of the first monasteries and
nunneries in Khumbu. A correspondence between economic
prosperity and support for material culture was also pointed out by
Fürer-Haimendorf, who noted a significant falling off of Sherpa
support for local religious institutions between 1957 and 1971,[22]
which he attributed to the declining economic fortunes of formerly

---

20 Adams 1996 pp.65-66 (emphasis added by Adams)
21 Stevens 1991
22 Fürer-Haimendorf 1974 pp.110-111, 1975 pp.102-103, 1984 pp.89-91

affluent Khumbu Sherpas hit hard by the curtailment of trans-Himalayan trade in the 1960s. The number of monks in the main Khumbu monastery at Tengboche, which Fürer-Haimendorf used as a proxy to gauge the level of Sherpa economic support for local religious institutions, had fallen from 32 in 1957 to only 14 in 1971. However, as many Sherpas grew wealthy due to their involvement in a tourism economy that expanded greatly during the 1980s, there was a resurgence in financial support for local monasteries, religious rites, festivals, temples, and shrines.[23] According to Stevens, by 1987 the number of monks at the Tengboche monastery had risen to 40, more than at any time since the monastery was founded in the early 1900s. When I visited Tengboche in 1999, the number of monks had grown to 50, and, according to the monastery's internet website, numbers were expected to grow even further due to "an increase in the availability of funds."[24]

The Tengboche monastery's increased funding is the result of generous donations both from foreign visitors and from increasingly wealthy (thanks to tourism) local residents, as well as handsome profits that the monastery itself has made from the tourist lodges it owns. In addition to providing financial support for local monasteries, a number of Sherpa households have also joined together to donate labor for the renovation of several Khumbu temples as well as the building of a new religious shrine in the village of Khumjung. According to Stevens, the Khumjung shrine was the first new shrine built in Khumbu since at least the 1930s and was built with labor

---

23   Fürer-Haimendorf 1984 pp.91-92; Fisher 1990 pp.94, 139, 149, 167; Stevens 1991 pp. 50-52, 1993a p.424

24   Tengboche Monastery internet website, http://www.tengboche.com, 1999. Note: The growth of monastery funds has spurred not only an increase in the number of monks but also a broadening of the demographics of the monastery's students. According to the monastery's internet website, "it used to be that students were supported by their families, but now many poorer students, some without any family support at all, are asking to be enrolled." In addition to expanding the monastery's enrollment, the monks want to establish a college in Tengboche for higher Buddhist education in philosophy, medicine, and arts "so that monks won't have to move away to Kathmandu and India [to study] and so the local [Khumbu Sherpa] culture can be strengthened and preserved."

donated by people of all ages and from every household in the villages of Kunde and Khumjung. Other recently commissioned religious works in Khumbu include the building of new prayer walls at Kunde and the carving of Buddhist mantras in boulders above Namche and along the main tourist route.

As local affluence from tourism grows, Sherpas are also spending more money on religious ceremonies, festivals, and pilgrimages, as well as on household rituals and the purchase of lavish religious books and paintings.[25] And, rather paradoxically, it is generally the case that the more successful and seemingly 'Westernized' Sherpas are observed to be the most religiously devout.[26] By way of explanation, Fürer-Haimendorf noted that according to Sherpa social norms, the liberal "expenditure of material wealth for religious ends [...] gives rise to admiration. Not the accumulation, but the proper utilization of wealth, lends a person prestige" as well as religious merit (sonam).[27] Indeed, Alton Byers and Lhakpa Sherpa have expressed the opinion that financial offerings to monasteries by affluent Sherpas are motivated more by the personal prestige to be gained than by religious devotion per se. Byers and Sherpa pointed out that while displays of personal wealth have become more extravagant and more visible in recent years, the less conspicuous tradition of providing monks with food to live on has declined and individual monks have suffered. As a result of this shift, Byers and Sherpa suggested that monasteries in Khumbu had become increasingly dependent on external financial support rather than the support of the local population.[28] As Rogers and Aitchison pointed out, the Sherpas "have become a celebrated people and received a great deal of international exposure. The Sherpas themselves are very much aware of this

---

25 Sherpa households throughout Khumbu maintain religious shrines in their homes and conduct household rituals to replace the prayer flags on their roofs four times a year.

26 Fisher 1990 p.139

27 Fürer-Haimendorf 1963 (reprinted in Hornbein 1965 p.76)

28 Byers and Sherpa 1991 p.171. Note: Tourists have also provided a major source of support for local monasteries through their purchases of religious paintings (thangka) created by local artists (compare with Stevens 1991 pp.45-46).

fascination with their culture and have been able to direct this interest towards the building and repair of local monasteries," which have enjoyed considerable financial support from foreign sponsors in recent years.[29] This last point is exemplified by the considerable amounts of money that have been generated from tourists who come to watch the masked dances of the Mani Rimdu ritual each spring and autumn.[30] But probably the single most illustrative example of the increased reliance on foreign support was the rebuilding of Tengboche monastery in the early 1990s. After the monastery was destroyed by a fire in 1989, a host of international donors led by the Himalayan Trust and the American Himalayan Foundation immediately stepped up to provide the funds to reconstruct the monastery and replace some five hundred religious books that had been lost in the blaze.[31]

It is important to point out, however, that regardless of the actual motives underlying local spending on religious rituals or the increased dependency of local religious institutions on external funding, tourism and the resulting affluence of Khumbu Sherpas do not seem to have changed the observance of traditional Sherpa life cycle rites ranging from naming ceremonies to marriages to funerals. According to Stevens, not only have the rites themselves not changed in recent years, they continue to be observed by the younger generation of Khumbu Sherpas.[32]

Intrusion

Many tourist visitors are simply not aware of the intrusive effect their presence can have on local residents. Other visitors seemingly do not care and self-righteously justify their holiday activities, intrusive or not, as being a reward for their hard work back home, as if the price of a plane ticket and a national park entrance fee entitles them to do

29   Rogers & Aitchison 1998 p.87
30   compare with Stevens 1991 p.46
31   National Geographic Society 1989; Adams 1996 pp.129-130; Tengboche Monastery internet website, http://www.tengboche.com, 1999
32   Stevens 1991 p.50, 1993a p.424

anything they please. For example, most tourists are eager to take photographs of local people and do not bother to ask permission before doing so. Understandably, local residents can't help but resent their loss of privacy to thousands of camera-toting tourists, with some elderly Sherpas feeling threatened by a traditional fear of being photographed.[33] A small number of Sherpas even hold that the climbing of Mount Everest, which they consider a sacred mountain that should not be tread upon, is an intrusion by visitors and by Nepal's government, which profits from the issuance of climbing permits.[34]

Tourist attendance of Sherpa religious ceremonies, such as the Mani Rimdu festival held in Thame and Tengboche during the spring and autumn each year, is also considered an intrusion by some local residents. The masked dances of the Mani Rimdu festival have become a very popular tourist attraction, with tourists and their cameras often outnumbering locals. Some Sherpas have expressed dismay at what they consider an interference in one of their more important community events. Despite the unfortunate disruptions caused by tourists, however, it is worth noting that the rites for the festival have not been changed as a result of tourist attendance, and the festival has remained well attended by Sherpas from throughout the region.[35]

Monks at the Tengboche monastery, which constitutes a popular stop on the main tourist trail, have grumbled about disturbances from tourists at times outside of the Mani Rimdu festival as well. For example, monks have complained that tourist groups' drinking and singing late into the night disrupt the peace and solitude of the monastery environs. Other tourist disturbances reported by the monks include wearing revealing clothing while sunbathing on the

---

33   compare with Stevens 1991 p.45, 1993b pp.424-425
34   Surveys of 140 households in 33 villages or settlements within the Solu, Pharak, and Khumbu regions (including 69 households in 15 villages or settlements in Khumbu) conducted between 1993 and 1996 enabled Rogers & Aitchison (1998 p.44) to conclude that only 'a small number' of local Sherpa residents held the belief that Mount Everest should not be climbed.
35   Stevens 1991 p.46, 1993b p.425

monastery steps, playing soccer on the grounds in front of the
monastery, bathing half-naked at public water sources, and taking
disruptive flash photographs of the monks during their daily
meditations.[36]

Despite the intrusive nature of tourism, especially given the
recently rapid growth of Khumbu visitor numbers, not a single one of
the many Sherpa lodge owners or trekking employees with whom I
spoke in 1999 expressed a desire to see fewer tourists in Khumbu.
Time and again Sherpas told me that they wished even more tourists
would visit so that they could make more money during the tourist
season. While making more money may be a priority for most
Sherpas, there are few who do not value the reprieve of the summer
and winter seasons when tourism dies down in Khumbu and local life
resumes a less hectic and chaotic state. Stevens attributed the Sherpas'
off-season return to normalcy as having had great importance for the
continuity of Sherpa culture and society.[37] In recent years, as
Khumbu has grown more and more crowded during the tourist
season, many trekking guide authors and travel club newsletters have
begun promoting off-season trekking as a way for visitors to avoid
crowds and experience closer, more personal insights into local
traditional culture. But off-season trekkers, though still relatively few
in number, may actually be considered more intrusive by local
residents than the masses of people who visit during the normal
trekking season. Indeed, one off-season trekker remarked later that
"many lodge owners [...] viewed the off-season as a time to relax and
treated our stay in their teahouses as an intrusion."[38]

Conflict & Hospitality

In addition to its intrusive effects, tourism, like other situations that
bring together people from diverse backgrounds and cultures, can
sometimes result in instances of offense, friction, and conflict. Such

36   Tengboche Monastery internet website, http://www.tengboche.com, 1999
37   Stevens 1991 p.55
38   Cravitz 1999 p.3

instances can often be traced to tourists' ignorance of or insensitivity toward local customs and conventions. In the case of tourism in the Everest region, visitors are often unfamiliar with local cultural practices and etiquette, such as keeping religious shrines on the right when passing, not burning trash in the household hearth, and not cleaning clothes or dishes in natural springs or other drinking water sources. For the most part, Sherpas quietly tolerate such transgressions when they are the result of visitors' ignorance. It is obviously harder to look the other way, however, when tourists blatantly abuse their hosts' hospitality. Indeed, Ortner has attributed most cases of conflict between visitors and Sherpas to visitors' uncompromising demeanors.[39] The impact of such negative interactions on the general relations between visitors and Sherpas is difficult to measure, but Fisher suggested that the early image Sherpas had of Western visitors as generous, egalitarian, and well-intentioned people, has more recently "given way to a less clearly focused one that has emerged out of the Sherpas' experiences with thousands upon thousands of tourists."[40]

As the annual number of visitors has grown, the hospitality of local residents seems to have diminished. Ang Rita Sherpa, a distinguished Khumbu native who works for Edmund Hillary's Himalayan Trust, has pointed out that, for Khumbu residents, "Life has changed somewhat with all the tourists. Earlier, we felt we should extend our hospitality to foreigners, without receiving any payment. But now that there are so many foreigners, we have become less hospitable and charge for firewood and food, for example."[41] Edmund Hillary himself has acknowledged the diminished hospitality of Khumbu residents, noting that "there's been a change from the very great generosity and warmth of welcome that we used to receive forty years ago."[42] And a pair of trekkers with whom I talked in Phortse in 1999, who had previously visited Khumbu in 1986 and

---

39   Ortner 1990 p. 12
40   Fisher 1990 p.125
41   Ang Rita Sherpa, as quoted in Fisher 1990 p.105
42   Sir Edmund Hillary, as quoted in Gray 1999

1996, told me that that the hospitality of lodge owners, especially in the busier areas of Khumbu, had decreased over the years and that "now they are just busy taking care of thousands of nameless and faceless consumers instead of talking and joking with guests."

A change in the general demeanor of Khumbu Sherpas toward outsiders has also been noticed by many Nepali people, including some Sherpas from outside of Khumbu. For example, a Nepali national park official living in Namche told me in 1999 that the hospitality of the Khumbu residents toward tourists had decreased over the past several years as the number of tourists had increased. And a Sherpa man from Lukla with whom I spoke in 1999 told me that, after working in Khumbu as a porter and then as a cook for trekking groups for the past ten years, he preferred not to work there anymore. He said that he would rather seek work on treks to other regions of Nepal because, as he put it, Khumbu Sherpas were "not nice people." He said they had become rich elitists who treated Sherpas and other Nepalis from outside Khumbu very poorly and as lesser people. These kinds of testimonials contrast starkly with and suggest a major change from the kindhearted disposition Khumbu Sherpas had grown famous for prior to the rapid growth of Khumbu tourism in the 1990s. For example, Fürer-Haimendorf, who spent considerable time in Khumbu in 1953, 1957, and 1971, remarked that "relations between [Khumbu Sherpa] employers and hired workers [from outside Khumbu] are usually very amicable, and no dispute over wages or conditions of work has ever come to my notice."[43] And Ramesh Kunwar, a Nepali anthropologist who conducted research in the Everest region in the late 1970s and early 1980s, noted that Khumbu Sherpa employers treated workers hired from regions outside of Khumbu very well and did not discriminate between themselves and their servants.[44]

---

43   Fürer-Haimendorf 1975 p.40
44   Kunwar 1989 p.95

Absence, Labor Distribution, & Agropastoral Practices

Involvement in climbing and trekking tourism has taken many Sherpa men and boys away from home, especially during Nepal's popular spring and fall tourist seasons. In a 1982 survey, 172 Khumbu males who reported their primary occupation as 'expedition guide or sirdar' had spent an average of about 5 of the preceding 12 months away from home. In contrast, 104 Khumbu males who reported their primary occupation as 'farmer' had only been absent for an average of 0.2 of the preceding 12 months.[45] From the survey, it was evident that the long periods that many Sherpa males were spending away from home was causing disruptions in family life and child-raising, household labor practices, and community leadership. Even religious life has been interrupted as monks have taken temporary, and in some cases permanent, leaves from Khumbu monasteries to pursue economic opportunities in tourism.[46]

One result of the absence of so many Sherpa males due to tourism is that many females have had to take on a larger share of their households' agropastoral subsistence activities. Since Sherpa women have traditionally been responsible for the majority of domestic and farming chores anyway, the periodic absence of males from the household labor pool does not pose a significant issue except during those times of the year when males traditionally helped with farming, such as the plowing of fields in late spring and the harvest in early autumn.[47] During such periods, and increasingly throughout the rest of the year as well, money earned from tourism has been more than sufficient to allow many Khumbu families to hire laborers from outside the region to help with household farming and domestic work.[48]

Although more of the work has shifted to women and hired laborers, agricultural practices among Khumbu Sherpa households have not changed appreciably compared to the past, and most

45   Pawson *et al.* 1984a p.79
46   Nepal 1997, as cited in Sharma 1998a p.24
47   Brower 1991b p.88; Stevens 1991 p.55, 1993a pp.384-385
48   Brower 1991b pp.85-86; Stevens 1993a p.385, 1993b pp.414, 420

Khumbu families continue to grow their own potatoes and vegetables. In the early 1990s, Stevens noted that "no [Khumbu] family has yet abandoned the cultivation of its lands to rely solely on earnings from tourism." He also pointed out that "every Sherpa family in Khumbu today farms. No matter how well-to-do many Khumbu Sherpa families have become from tourism they continue to produce as much of their household food supplies as they can."[49] The continued emphasis placed on agriculture in Khumbu is evidenced by the fact that, of over two thousand Khumbu residents surveyed in 1997, 71 percent considered themselves to be farmers.[50] Although Fisher noted that some of the higher altitude fields in Khumbu had been left abandoned in the latter 1980s, he also pointed out that a new strain of potato had been recently introduced with three times the yield of the older variety, which perhaps suggested that some marginally productive high-altitude fields had fallen out of use because they were no longer needed.[51] It has also been suggested that some remote Khumbu fields were not being cultivated any longer because they are more susceptible to the increased threat of crop depredation that has resulted from the growth of wildlife populations under the protection of the national park.[52]

While agriculture does not appear to have been affected much by the reorientation of the Khumbu economy toward tourism, several observers have reported significant changes in Khumbu herding practices in recent decades.[53] Because of the prestige associated with yak and yak-cattle crossbreed ownership in Khumbu Sherpa society, livestock owners have been reluctant to leave their valuable animals in the care of hired herders from lowland regions, who are considered to

49 Stevens 1993b p.419, 1993a pp.383, 387, 1991 pp.47-50
50 Sagarmatha Pollution Control Committee 1998 Annex 14. Note: This does not suggest that only 29 percent of Khumbu working residents are engaged in tourism, for clearly the percentage is much higher. Rather it implies that a high percentage of Khumbu residents remain engaged in farming as well as tourism.
51 Fisher 1990 p.122
52 Stevens 1993a pp.386, 501-502
53 Fürer-Haimendorf 1975 p.57; Brower 1990, 1991a, 1991b; Stevens 1993a pp.388-392

lack sufficient experience and knowledge to handle such an important responsibility. The reluctance to utilize outside labor for herding and the shortage of available labor in Khumbu due to local residents' involvement in tourism has constrained stockowners' ability to utilize remote high pastures and has reportedly resulted in overuse of grazing resources close to villages. This seems to have contributed to a decrease in the keeping of milk-producing female yak, although Stevens attributed the decrease more to the decline in trans-Himalayan trade than to the emergence of tourism. Despite the effects of tourism on pastoral practices in Khumbu, it should be pointed out that the keeping of livestock has not diminished in importance, and if anything has become even more economically rewarding due to the lucrative use of pack animals in tourism as discussed in Chapter Three.

While the traditional practices of farming and keeping livestock have continued thus far in Khumbu, the question remains whether the next generation of Khumbu Sherpas will have an interest in cultivating fields and herding animals. As Fisher pointed out,

> the younger generation [of Khumbu Sherpas] lacks interest in agriculture and animal husbandry because these occupations yield only meager returns. This generation prefers such novel economic activities as trekking and pays little attention to traditional occupations. A final disincentive to their pursuit of farming and animal grazing is that these activities have to be done in extreme highland conditions without the remuneration and amenities that tourists offer in such terrain.[54]

Stevens, however, refuted the loss of interest in agriculture among Khumbu residents, pointing out that women have remained very involved in farming, even if they have come to rely more on hired labor to help conduct the work than in the past. But although many Khumbu women have continued to remain involved with farming despite their contemporary involvement with running tourist lodges and shops, Stevens warned that if additional tourism-related demands

---

54 Fisher 1990 p.161

were placed on Khumbu women then their continued ability to engage in agricultural work might decline.[55]

Surprisingly, despite the absence of many Sherpa males due to tourism, it seems that some Khumbu families may actually be spending more time in Khumbu than in the past. Because they can make enough money from tourism to last the entire year, Khumbu families no longer need to migrate to lower altitude regions during the winter to seek wage labor opportunities or engage in trade. Instead, many families now spend the winter at home in Khumbu and use their income from tourism to make short winter trips to Kathmandu for shopping, religious pilgrimages, and socializing.[56]

Another perhaps unexpected effect of tourism has been the rising role of women in local government. In the 1970s, because of the increasingly frequent and prolonged absence of many Sherpa men from their communities, several Khumbu women were elected as *panchayat* village council members, and one woman was even elected chairperson of the powerful Namche-Thame village council. According to Fürer-Haimendorf, whose observations of Khumbu society spanned from the 1950s to the 1970s,

> the presence of women on the panchayat [village council] reflects their enhanced position resulting no doubt from the frequent absence of men on expedition and trekking business. In the 1950s women were vocal in the house and in purely social gatherings, but they never intervened openly in the discussions of the village assembly. Now [in 1971] they participate vigorously in panchayat [village council] meetings which are often held in public.[57]

Out-Migration

The profusion of local economic opportunities that have become available as a result of tourism has allowed more Sherpa families to continue living in Khumbu than otherwise would have been possible following the decline of trans-Himalayan trade in the 1960s. Most

---

55   Stevens 1993a pp.387-388
56   Stevens 1991 pp.48-49, 1993a pp.307-308
57   Fürer-Haimendorf 1975 p.96

communities in other parts of the Nepal Himalaya who had been reliant on trans-Himalayan trade prior to its decline did not have the opportunities in tourism enjoyed by the Sherpas of Khumbu. Many of these people were consequently forced to migrate to lowland regions to survive economically.[58] The Sherpas of Khumbu, on the other hand, were able to reorient their economy toward climbing and trekking tourism, enabling them to continue living in their native homeland.

Demonstrating the effect that involvement in tourism has had on enabling Sherpas to continue residing in Khumbu, Pawson pointed to the relatively high percentage of unoccupied dwellings in the Khumbu village of Thame, a situation he attributed to Thame residents' much lower involvement in tourism compared to other Khumbu villages. Because of Thame's location along the traditional trade route to Tibet but away from Khumbu's main tourist routes, the residents of Thame historically had been heavily involved in trans-Himalayan trade but generally have not had the opportunity to involve themselves as much in tourism. At the time of Pawson's research in 1982, 32 percent of houses in Thame were unoccupied, a much higher percentage than he found in the villages of Namche (11 percent), Khumjung (6 percent), or Kunde (12 percent), each of which offered much greater opportunities in tourism than Thame.[59]

Their ability to engage in tourism opportunities outside of the Everest region has also helped many Sherpa families to continue residing in Khumbu, although this often results in family members or even entire families being absent from Khumbu for part of the year. Over the past couple of decades, a significant number of Khumbu residents have moved to Kathmandu or abroad to establish or to work in trekking agencies, hotels, restaurants, shops, and other tourism-

---

58 Fürer-Haimendorf (1975) gives several examples of formerly thriving trading communities, including the people of Walungchung in northeastern Nepal and the people of Thak Khola in north-central Nepal, some of whose members were forced to migrate away from their home regions following the collapse of trans-Himalayan trade.

59 Pawson et al. 1984b p.244

related businesses. The growth of Kathmandu-based trekking agencies in particular has been an important factor drawing Sherpa men away from Khumbu. In some cases, entire families have moved to Kathmandu on a permanent basis, while others have split time between homes maintained in both Khumbu and Kathmandu. There are also many cases of Sherpa families spending considerable time apart because of the conflicting demands of tourism businesses in both Kathmandu and their home village. As an example, consider the case of a married Sherpa couple from Dingboche with whom I spoke in 1999. The husband lived year-round in Kathmandu running his own trekking agency while the wife remained in Khumbu operating their trekking lodge and raising their three small children. Outside of the tourist seasons, the wife and children joined the husband in Kathmandu for part of the year. The husband, who had decided to visit his family in Dingboche after the tourist season had ended, had not been to Khumbu in over a year. It is also worth mentioning that the wife told me that she was very unhappy with her husband spending so much time away from her and their children.

Of potentially even greater significance than the out-migration of family members pursuing economic opportunities, which, after all, is nothing new to the Sherpas when one considers their history of migration to Darjeeling and their engagement in long trade journeys, is the increasing out-migration of children whose families, because of affluence from tourism, can afford to send them to Kathmandu or abroad for a better education than is available in Khumbu. English language instruction in particular, which is seen by many Sherpas as the key to economic advancement in tourism, drives many parents to send their children away to better schools, even if it means that parents do not get to see their children very often. In some cases, entire families have chosen to move to Kathmandu because of the superior educational opportunities and their desire to keep their family together. But for some families this is not possible. For example, consider the case of a widow living in Pheriche with whom I spoke in 1999. She had sent all five of her children to attend school in Kathmandu for the past seven years while she remained in

Khumbu running a trekking lodge and cultivating potatoes. She told me that she only sees her children occasionally because she is forced to work year-round in Khumbu in order to pay for her children's education and boarding and because her children do not like visiting the remote, cold, and undeveloped village.

Fisher noted that many of the Sherpa children living and attending schools outside of Khumbu do not speak the Sherpa language and are unfamiliar with many Sherpa social, cultural, and religious traditions.[60] I question whether these children will ever return to Khumbu to live, especially since doing so would mean giving up many of the modern accoutrements to which they may have become accustomed. According to Stevens, local leaders in Khumbu have expressed concern that many of the children may not return.[61] Even if some of these children were to come back to live in Khumbu, it seems doubtful that they would continue many of the traditional practices historically identified with Sherpa society and culture. I am not making any value judgments here; I merely wish to point out the effect this could have on the continuity of Sherpa traditions.

Even some young people who return regularly to Khumbu end up spending very little time at home. For example, one Sherpa teenager from Thame with whom I spoke in November 1999 had just finished a two-month stint working for a climbing expedition and was on his way to Kathmandu for three months of school. He described his schedule over the previous twelve months, which he said was typical for him, as follows:

December, January, February – learning English and French in a private Kathmandu school
March, April, May – working for foreign climbing and trekking expeditions
June, July, August – in Switzerland improving his climbing and language skills
September – staying with his family in Khumbu

---

60   Fisher 1990 pp.175-177
61   Stevens 1991 p.54

October, November – working for a foreign climbing expedition

Thus, in the past year he had spent five months working for climbing and trekking expeditions, three months at school in Kathmandu, three months in Switzerland, and just one month with his family in Khumbu.

Skilled Professions & Local Crafts

The lure of lucrative tourism opportunities has resulted in a scarcity of Khumbu residents with an interest in filling skilled occupations in the community such as school teachers, carpenters, masons, and hydro-electric plant operators, to name a few. As a result, skilled jobs in Khumbu are typically the domain of immigrants from outside of Khumbu. For example, out of thirty-three teachers in the five Khumbu schools in the late 1980s, only two were Sherpas; the rest were Nepalis from outside the local area. Similarly, some traditional local crafts have reportedly been dying out because Khumbu Sherpas can make more money devoting their time to tourism work and because they can afford to import manufactured items instead of making things themselves. And while there is a thriving demand among tourists for Tibetan-style curios and paintings in the shops of Namche, most of the goods are actually made in Kathmandu, although some religious paintings (*thangka*) are the work of local artists.

Imported Foods & Clothing

Increased affluence from tourism has allowed Khumbu Sherpas to purchase more imported foods than in the past, diminishing to some degree the importance of the traditional foods produced in the region, although Stevens pointed out as late as 1991 that "potatoes and barley remain the preferred staples of even the wealthiest households. Families have broadened their food consumption, [...] but there has not been a fundamental break with former practices."[62]

---

62 Stevens 1991 pp.49-50

While, prior to the rise of tourism, barley flour (*tsampa*) was a local staple and wealthy households consumed rice primarily on special occasions, nowadays rice is the staple grain of practically every Khumbu household and barley flour is rarely eaten. Another aspect of local life that has changed with the times is the clothing worn by those involved with tourism. Nearly all Khumbu men have adopted Western-style clothing for everyday use, although some continue to wear traditional woolen robes on special occasions. While many Sherpa women have maintained their traditional style of clothing and ornamentation, jeans and other Western-style clothes have grown increasingly popular, especially among younger unmarried women and girls.[63] While younger Khumbu residents are today choosing to wear Western-style clothing because it is considered fashionable, their parents' earlier adoption of ready-made Western-style clothing was, as mentioned in Chapter Four, made necessary by the short supply of wool from Tibet following the decline of trans-Himalayan trade in the 1960s.

Westernization

Extensive association with foreigners has been a strong force in introducing Western tastes and culture to the Sherpas of Khumbu. There can be little doubt that their employment with foreign mountain climbing expeditions, a tradition among Khumbu Sherpas that dates back to the early 1900s, facilitated their early familiarity with Western attitudes and values.[64] Indeed, foreign climbers began to notice changes in Sherpa attitudes toward mountain aesthetics, adventure travel, and the recreational aspects of climbing even before the Khumbu region was opened to tourism. As Swiss climber and development expert Toni Hagen, who traveled extensively throughout Nepal while working for the United Nations, wrote in 1963: "that anyone should want to climb a high mountain solely for pleasure, is, at the present time, simply not understood by [Nepal's]

---

63   compare with Stevens 1991 pp.49-50
64   compare with Fisher 1990 p.106

mountain peasants. The exceptions are a few Sherpas who have developed a feeling for the beauty of the mountains and have discovered the pleasure of conquering peaks, owing to repeated participation in expeditions."[65]

Development worker cum anthropologist Jim Fisher, whose close firsthand experiences of Khumbu life span more than three decades, suggested that, over the years, Sherpas had come to admire Western ways because "Western contacts have opened new channels of mobility and access to power, wealth, and prestige. Sherpas honor the West because their experience of it has been so overwhelmingly positive financially."[66] One of the more explicit examples of adoption of Western practices by Khumbu Sherpas is the high use of Western medicine and care offered by the hospital in Kunde, which is staffed year-round by a pair of Western physicians. The widespread use of the hospital since it was began operations in 1967 is evidenced by the growth in the number of annual patient visits, the vast majority of which are by local residents, from about 2,000 in 1970[67] to nearly 9,000 in 1998.[68] Despite the Sherpas' high use of the hospital, however, Vincanne Adams and Susan Heydon both reported that many Sherpas continued to use traditional forms of medicine and shamanistic healing.[69] Heydon noted, however, that shamanistic practices were on the decline in Khumbu due to a decreasing number of new shamans and since "[Khumbu Sherpa] children no longer really believe in shamanism."

Another profound outside influence on Sherpa culture has not come from contact with Western visitors *per se*, but rather with Western technology and media. Along with electricity, which hydro-electric projects have brought to several Khumbu villages, has come satellite television. Although Nepal was one of the last countries in

---

65 Hagen *et al.* 1963, as quoted in Hornbein 1965 p. 64
66 Fisher 1990 p.133
67 Kunde Hospital annual reports, as cited in Heydon 1997 p.28
68 Litch & Bishop 1999, as cited by Dr. Jim Litch, Kunde Hospital physician, personal communication, 1999
69 Adams 1988 p.505, Heydon 1997 pp.29-30

the world to begin television broadcasts, which didn't begin there until 1985, now the Hong Kong based Satellite Television for the Asia Region (STAR TV) feeds Western movies and television programming to satellite dishes in Khumbu and elsewhere in Nepal. Regarding the effect of television in Khumbu, Ed Douglas wrote in a book about the effects of tourism in the Everest region that "tourism is often cited as having a major cultural impact but in many ways television has proved just as influential."[70]

Nepalization

The deeply felt influence of Nepali national interests, ideology, and culture in Khumbu, although not a direct result of tourism, has nonetheless been greatly facilitated and accelerated by the interest the Nepal government has focused on the Everest region because of tourism. The Everest region's economic and symbolic importance to the Nepal government since its development into a major international tourist destination has, over the past few decades, firmly attracted the government's attention to and increased presence in what had formerly been a remote, neglected, and relatively autonomous area. Indeed, the continually expanding influence of the Nepali presence in the Everest region prompted *National Geographic* writer Jim Carrier to warn that "assimilation into the Hindu majority threatens Sherpa culture even more than Western wealth."[71]

That the Nepali presence has risen dramatically in Khumbu during the past few decades is borne out by the following comparison. The early 1960s marked the beginning of the Nepal government's explicit presence in Khumbu with the establishment of the nationalized system of local panchayat government throughout Nepal and the establishment of a district government office in Namche in 1965. By 1970, there were 84 lowland Nepalis stationed in Khumbu. A decade later, the number had grown to 339, or 11 percent of the

---

70 Douglas 1997 pp.46, 96. Note: Luger (2000b) also discusses the role of television and movies on the Westernization of Sherpa youth.
71 Carrier 1992 p.85

region's total population, and of those, about 150 resided in Namche, comprising a whopping 20 percent of that village's population.[72] By 1999, the number of lowland Nepalis residing in Namche had again more than doubled to well over 300, including 37 national park staff and about 250 army personnel.

Although a significant number of Khumbu's non-native residents have been posted there by the government to serve as civil administrators, policemen, army personnel, national park staff, and school teachers, many others have migrated there in search of opportunities that have emerged as a result of the thriving tourism economy. With Khumbu Sherpas' own labor resources tapped by their involvement in tourism, outside laborers are counted upon to carry out domestic household chores, conduct farmwork, and perform skilled jobs such as carpentry. Such immigrant laborers are often ethnic Rai, Magar, Tamang, or Gurung peoples from lower lying areas to the south of Khumbu. In addition, Khumbu lodge owners have been increasingly hiring cooks from Kathmandu to run their lodge restaurants. Whether working in the fields or in a tourist lodge, such hired workers often reside in Khumbu for several months out of the year.

The presence of so many lowland Nepalis and the influence of the government authorities' Hindu-centric hegemony have had some very noticeable effects on local economic and social practices in Khumbu. For example, it is interesting to note that the weekly market bazaar (hayt) held each Saturday in Namche, which is the primary means by which Khumbu residents acquire imported goods from lowland Nepali merchants, was actually initiated in 1965 by Nepali government authorities stationed in Namche who were unsatisfied with the lack of consumer choices in Khumbu.[73] It is also no coincidence that the traditional Sherpa practice of polyandry, whereby two or more brothers share the same wife to avoid splitting their family inheritance, declined markedly in Khumbu after the

---

72 Fürer-Haimendorf 1984 p.32; Pawson et al. 1984a pp.74-75, 79. Note: 87 percent of the lowland Nepalis residing in Khumbu in 1982 were single males.
73 Fürer-Haimendorf 1975 p.75; Fisher 1990 pp.117, 188; Stevens 1993a p.449

arrival of Nepali government officials in the 1960s. That the practice of polyandry began declining before the rise of a significant tourism economy in Khumbu suggests that the decline was not solely due to economic factors. Polyandry was offensive and unlawful according to Hindu custom and as such was sharply discouraged by Nepali authorities stationed in Khumbu. The effect that the presence of Nepali government authorities had in this regard seems to be borne out by Fürer-Haimendorf's observation that the practice of polyandry continued longer in more isolated Khumbu villages such as Phortse that had fewer and less frequent contacts with Nepali authorities.[74]

In addition to the economic and social ramifications of their presence, Nepali civil servants associated with the national park and the district administration have also been the major conduits of the Nepal government's political and development agendas in the region. Although most local manifestations of Nepali civil society have been viewed by Khumbu Sherpas as either helpful or harmless, national park restrictions on the use of natural resources (particularly forests and pasturelands) have been viewed with disdain by local residents and have been the source of considerable friction in the past, as described in Chapter Five. A much less contentious means by which the Nepal government has endeavored to further its political agenda is in the staffing of local schools with Nepali teachers. Schools have been one of the main avenues through which the Nepal government has worked to promote a common sense of Nepali nationalism throughout the country. In Khumbu schools, many of which were built by and continue to receive support from foreign visitors, children are taught Nepali rather than their native Sherpa language, and the curriculum focuses on the Hindu dominated history and society of lowland Nepal rather than the country's Buddhist

---

74 Fürer-Haimendorf 1975 p.100. Note: Although Kunwar (1989 p.178) claimed that the practice of polyandrous marriages had completely disappeared from Khumbu by the 1980s, Fürer-Haimendorf (1984 p.44) reported that there were still a few polyandrous households remaining in Khumbu as late as 1983.

highlands.[75] To instill a sense of Nepali nationalism, classrooms have been adorned with national maps of Nepal and with portraits of Nepal's royal family, and a Kathmandu-centric perspective is promulgated. The preponderance of consumer electronics like radios, CD players, and televisions in Khumbu has also contributed to the ubiquitousness of lowland media bombarding local residents, for whom Nepali news broadcasts and Hindi films have become a regular part of daily life.[76]

But despite the growing popularity of Nepali and Hindi music, films, and radio and television programming, Stevens pointed out in 1991 that traditional Sherpa music and dancing remained an important facet of adult social life in Khumbu.[77] Indeed, although the unrelenting pressure of Nepali national interests and ideology and the seductive influence of Western material culture have certainly affected the Sherpas of Khumbu in many significant ways, the community has not melded into Nepal's dominant Hindu society or been swallowed up by the global monoculture of the West. As Stevens noted, "For all the socioeconomic and cultural change of recent decades, Khumbu Sherpas have not lost their sense of themselves as a people, and that to some degree may be due to their having maintained their language, religion, social structure, and homeland."[78] While incorporating change into their way of life, the Sherpas have retained their unique culture and identity, although it is a dynamic rather than static uniqueness. Some very basic and fundamental aspects of 'traditional' Sherpa culture and society persist to this day, and these continue to be distinguishing features of 'Sherpa-ness.' But perhaps the Sherpa characteristic that continues to be most relevant today is that of adaptability, and I think Stevens expressed this as well as anyone:

---

75 As Fisher (1990 pp.73-76) pointed out, any instruction that Khumbu children might receive in the Tibetan Buddhist tradition is left to the monasteries, or else to parents who may not have received any formal education themselves.

76 compare with Pawson *et al.* 1984a pp.79-80

77 Stevens 1991 p.49

78 Stevens 1993a p.38

The Sherpas of Khumbu are a people of remarkable adaptability, ingenuity, and persistence who thus far at least have been anything but another example of the tragedy of the demise of a traditional people and their culture following the impact of tourism and other new outside cultural, economic, and political pressures. There has been change during the past thirty years, more change, perhaps, than during any comparable period for a century or more. Khumbu Sherpas have reorganized some facets of their economy, their local political system, and their customs. They grow their crops, herd, and harvest forest products somewhat differently than they did during the 1950s, just as they dress somewhat differently, build slightly different houses, and have a somewhat different view of the world and its natural and supernatural beings, forces, and processes. But they remain Khumbu Sherpas, upholding a set of values, institutions, and practices that are rooted in the legacy of their cultural past and still order the tenor of social and cultural life in ways that give a distinctive cast to their way of life and set them apart as Khumbu Sherpas from other peoples of highland Asia. Khumbu Sherpas have changed but they have not been transformed. Instead they continue to adapt to new conditions, to experiment and innovate, and to reshape their land use and their culture with the same kind of inventive spirit, ingenuity, eye to opportunity, and reaffirmation of basic cultural values that has long characterized them.[79]

---

79   Stevens 1993a pp.424-425

CHAPTER 8

Key Factors Influencing Tourism

Tourism has developed quite differently in Khumbu than it has in other areas of Nepal and the Himalayan mountain regions of Pakistan, India, Bhutan, Tibet and China. And tourism has also had some very different effects in Khumbu than in other places in the world inhabited by indigenous peoples. Although a detailed comparison of tourism development and its effects on indigenous peoples in other areas of the world is beyond the scope of this book, this study has provided sufficient detail and breadth on the development of tourism and its effects in Khumbu for me to draw some general comparisons with other mountain regions with which I have had firsthand experience.[1]

In probably no other mountainous area within a developing country has international tourism developed in as concentrated a fashion as it has in Nepal's Everest region.[2] And I can think of no

---

1 Beyond the Nepal and Tibet sides of Mount Everest, other mountain regions with which I have firsthand experience include the Modi Khola, Lower Mustang, Manang, Nar-Phu, Nubri, Kutang, Tsum, Langtang, Rolwaling, Walung, and Kangchenjunga regions of Nepal; the Hunza, Nagar, Gilgit, Bagrot, Haramosh, Diamir, and Baltistan regions of Pakistan; the Ladakh, Zanskar, and Garhwal regions of India; the Nangzar, Shishipangma, Cho Oyu, Tingri, Chomo Gangar, and Nam Tsho regions of Tibet; the Pamir mountains of China; the Hoang Lien mountains of Vietnam; the Eastern and Western Cordillera of the Ecuadorian Andes; the Cordillera de Anahuac of Mexico; the Coastal and Rocky mountains of Canada; Alaska and much of the contiguous western United States.

2 Although Nepal's Annapurna region and India's Ladakh region draw larger overall numbers of international tourists than Khumbu, the concentration of tourists and of tourism development in Khumbu is much greater due to the region's relatively compact size.

other mountain locale within a developing country where the indigenous inhabitants have had as much involvement and control over tourism development, or where they have benefited as much economically, as has been the case in Khumbu. Neither can I think of a mountain environment that has had as much international attention consistently focused upon it over the past three decades.

Although some of the effects of tourism described in the previous chapters have parallels in other places in the world and particularly in other parts of the Nepal Himalaya, many of the effects that tourism has had in Khumbu are quite unique to the region and its people. Below, I have listed a number of concrete, identifiable factors that help explain why tourism has developed as it has in the Everest region. These 'key factors' have not only played important roles in influencing how tourism has developed in Khumbu, they also go a long way toward explaining the unique effects that tourism has had on the people who live there.

1) International draw of popular icons and scenery
2) Local hosts' characteristics suited to tourism
3) Local hosts' involvement in and control over tourism
4) Limited scale of tourism development
5) Limited economic leakage of tourism income
6) Types of visitors, their relations with local hosts, and their concerns
7) Protected area designation and management
8) Local hosts' participation in conservation and development activities
9) National government's encouragement of tourism development
10) Lack of local tourism planning and management

This chapter presents each of these key factors one-by-one and describes the manner in which each has influenced tourism development in Khumbu.

International Draw of Popular Icons and Scenery

The immense popularity of the Khumbu region among international tourist visitors can be largely attributed to a number of icons associated with the region. These icons have brought worldwide attention to the Khumbu region and the Sherpa people and, together with the area's well-deserved reputation for breathtakingly beautiful scenery, have attracted thousands of visitors each year from around the world.

Mount Everest

There is a deeply rooted and widespread fascination, particularly in more-developed countries, with Mount Everest as the highest point on Earth and therefore literally 'the top of the world.' In his book *Sacred Mountains of the World*, Ed Bernbaum wrote about Mount Everest and the importance it has assumed in Western society:

> As the highest point on earth, Mount Everest in particular has become for many a powerful symbol of ultimate goals. The importance the mountain has assumed in the West reflects a modern tendency to attribute ultimate value to the biggest, the best, the finest, the first. Whatever Western society regards as number one tends to take on an aura of ultimacy. [...] climbing the mountain has become a symbol of the value that Western civilization has put on the conquest of nature, a conquest that glorifies the spirit of man and establishes his dominion over the things of this world.[3]

Around Mount Everest and the attempts to reach its summit has emerged a richly symbolic history of humankind's struggle to overcome the challenges of Nature. George Mallory, a dashingly heroic and idolized figure who disappeared mysteriously on Mount Everest during an attempt to climb it in 1924, said about the mountain: "there is something in man which responds to the challenge of this mountain and goes out to meet it, [...] the struggle of life itself, upward and forever upward."[4] Over the past several

---

3   Bernbaum 1997 p.236
4   George Mallory, as quoted in Hornbein 1965 p.32

decades, hundreds of climbers have succeeded in reaching the summit but the mountain still frequently exacts a deadly toll, reminding humankind of Nature's power.[5] As William Siri wrote in introducing the account of the first American expedition to summit Mount Everest, the mountain has become "a universal symbol of human courage and endurance; an ultimate test of man's body and spirit."[6]

Because of the mountain's iconic status as the most difficult point to reach on Earth, surmounting Mount Everest has become inexorably fixed in the minds of people around the world as, in the words of some writers, "the pinnacle of achievement"[7] and "the ultimate trophy prize for adventurers."[8] As the head of the climbing department in Nepal's Ministry of Tourism put it, "Everest is still every mountaineer's ultimate dream, no matter how many times it has been climbed."[9] Indeed, even some of the world's leading mountain climbers have admitted an obsession with climbing Mount Everest, an obsession borne not from the mountain's beauty or technical challenge but rather from the prestige afforded the mountain due to its unsurpassed height and iconic status as the ultimate in climbing. For example, one of the world's more famous and accomplished mountain climbers, Chris Bonington, confided that "climbing Everest was a relief. I was happy to get it out of the way so that I could focus on [the other types of mountain climbing] I really loved."[10]

An important factor in Mount Everest's enduring notoriety is the overwhelming amount of media attention the mountain continues to attract on a regular basis. Indeed, the intense media coverage that Mount Everest climbers manage to draw year after year has probably contributed more than anything else to the Everest region's popularity as an international tourist destination. The Western media

---

5   As of June 2000, Mount Everest had been climbed 1,173 times by 874 different
     people and had claimed nearly 180 lives (source: HimalayaNet 2000).
6   Hornbein 1965 p.24
7   Bernbaum 1997 p.7
8   Carlson 1999 p.14
9   Shailendra Raj Sharma, as quoted in Associated Press 1999b
10   Chris Bonington 1999, as quoted in *Himalayan News* 1999 p.8

generally portrays the climbing of Mount Everest in a way that
romanticizes the climbers and dramatizes the danger in order to
continue to attract worldwide interest in the stories that emerge each
year from the mountain. Writing about the media's seeming
obsession with Mount Everest, climbing writer Ed Douglas pointed
out how "newspaper and television editors have come to expect an
Everest story during the peak climbing season of May, and with so
many [climbers and journalists] on the mountain each spring they are
rarely disappointed."[11] The climbing season of 1996 generated the
most attention the mountain had ever received, as the ultra-
publicized climbing disaster depicted in Jon Krakauer's best-selling
book, *Into Thin Air*, and David Breashears' IMAX film, *Everest*, as
one writer put it, "ushered mountaineering into the realm of pop
culture."[12]

The phenomenal popularity of the Krakauer book and IMAX
film launched a blitz of other books, articles, lecture tours, internet
websites, and television movies and news programs on Mount Everest
that publisher Michael Chessler referred to as "a major international
media and financial juggernaut that may have generated half a billion
dollars in spending."[13] The tremendous commercial appeal of Mount
Everest in Western society is illustrated by the enormous quantity of
books and videos related to the mountain carried by American
retailers. For example, Adventurous Traveler, an online mail order
bookstore focused on adventure travel, had 305 books, maps, and
video products on Mount Everest available for sale in April 2000.
Meanwhile, the on-line bookseller Amazon.com had 287 books and
videos on Mount Everest for sale, in addition to 923 other Mount

11 Douglas 1997 p.7
12 Bromet 1999 p.130
13 Chessler 1999 p.173. Note: Krakauer's book was on the best-seller list for over
    40 weeks and sold over 2.5 million copies in its first two years. Chessler (1999
    p.172) said the book "has had the greatest impact on the public's perception of
    climbing of any book in 50 years." Breashears' IMAX film set records for large
    format films by grossing US$60 million in its first year and was still playing in
    theaters four years after the disaster.

Everest products available from Amazon's retail partners.[14] A bibliography of Mount Everest published in 1993 listed 586 books on the mountain.[15] Of course, in the wake of the intense media attention generated by the 1996 disaster, the number has grown dramatically since then.

Another major 'Everest mega-story' hit the press in the spring of 1999 with the discovery high on the mountain of the body of famous British climber George Mallory, who disappeared while attempting to climb to the summit in 1924. The discovery revived the mystery surrounding whether Mallory and partner Andrew 'Sandy' Irvine were the first to reach the summit and again pushed Mount Everest into the international media spotlight. In the two weeks following the discovery of Mallory's body, the internet website MountainZone.com, which was providing daily coverage of the expedition that discovered the body, averaged a million 'hits' a day.[16] Photos taken of Mallory's frozen body were sold for thousands of dollars and featured on the covers of such widely read publications as *Newsweek* and *Time*, as well as many newspapers and magazines around the world.

Following the discovery of Mallory's body on Everest, *Climbing* magazine published a special issue dedicated solely to Mount Everest. In one of the magazine's articles, six-time Everest climber Pete Athans wrote: "Mount Everest has become a popular icon, generating more interest today than in the year of its documented first ascent [in 1953]. Everest is now a household word."[17] An announcement a few months later that the mountain's height had been recalculated to be two meters higher than previously believed was prominently featured on the front page of *USA Today*, one of the most widely read

---

14 Adventurous Traveler internet website http://www.adventuroustraveler.com, Amazon internet website http://www.amazon.com, April 2000
15 Salkeld & Boyle 1993
16 Anker & Roberts 1999 p.162. Note: The number of 'hits' is the number of times an internet website is visited by internet users.
17 Athans 1999 p.78

newspapers in America.[18] The following year, hoping to cash in on the incredible hype surrounding the mountain, a Canadian broadcasting company sponsored a climbing expedition to Everest in order to be the first to transmit live television coverage from the mountain's summit.[19] And the media's obsession with Mount Everest continues, as do the gimmicks to attract even more people's attention to the mountain. From opportunistic groups marketing themselves as environmental clean-up expeditions to media-savvy individuals of all ages and nationalities – and with all types of physical handicaps – attempting to be 'the first', 'the youngest', 'the oldest', 'the fastest', et cetera, everyone wants to take advantage of the world's fascination with Mount Everest in order to cash in on a corporate sponsorship deal.

Into Thin Air, Into Thin Hair, & Into Been There

A large number of the tourists I spoke with in Khumbu in 1999 attributed their interest in visiting the Everest region to the media blitz that followed the May 1996 disaster portrayed in Jon's Krakauer *Into Thin Air* book and the *Everest* IMAX movie. One trekker I talked with said that because of the attention given to Mount Everest by the Western media, "now everybody knows where Nepal is, and now everybody is going." Indeed, according to publisher Michael Chessler, the Krakauer book and IMAX film created "a stampede of climbers and trekkers to the Himalaya."[20]

The general increase in popularity of international adventure travel among the Western middle class during the 1990s has also

---

18 *USA Today*, 12 November 1999. Note: According to Wright (2000 pp.36-38), a global positioning system receiver placed on the snow surface of the mountain's summit on 5 May 1999 utilized radio signals from a network of satellites to determine the distance of the summit from the center of the Earth. A geoid model of the Earth's shape was then used to estimate the height of the summit above the inferred sea level at that location. The newly calculated height was 8850 meters (29,035 feet) above inferred sea level, with an error of plus or minus 2 meters.

19 Boone 2000

20 Chessler 1999 p.175

contributed to the surge in Khumbu visitor numbers, as has the aging of the 'baby boomer' generation. Hooman Aprin, a Western trekking agency owner and guide who visited the Everest region some forty times during the 1980s and 1990s, told me in 1999 that he had noticed a shift in Khumbu visitors in recent years. In the past, visitors to the Everest region were predominantly "younger people, hippie-types, and climbers," but lately there has been a marked increase in older and wealthier tourists, "a class of people who didn't come to Khumbu before."[21] He attributed this trend, at least among Americans, to the increased awareness and popularity of mountain recreation among the mainstream American public, a phenomenon that other observers have noted as well.[22] Aprin believes that effective marketing by adventure travel companies has played a big part in this, as has the attention drawn to Mount Everest and to climbing in general by the wildly popular *Into Thin Air* book and *Everest* IMAX film. According to Aprin, "Now the American public is looking at a trek in Nepal as something that yuppies do, one of the things you have to do in your lifetime. It's becoming more known to the [American] public. People hear that so and so went to Nepal, so they've got to go. It becomes a life mission."[23]

Shangri-La

Known around the world as the home of Mount Everest and the Himalaya, Nepal has been mystified by Westerners as a secret Shangri-La, a hidden kingdom, and an exotic sanctuary. Due to political and geographical isolation, Nepal's interior, and especially its remote high mountain regions, were virtually unknown to foreigners until the middle of the 20th century. As Barbara Brower wrote, "Nepal was an unknown land until 1950. In a century almost without its blank spots on the map, Nepal has been a place for exploration and discovery, where twentieth-century Hookers and von

21   Hooman Aprin, personal communication, 1999
22   Joseph 1999
23   Hooman Aprin, personal communication, 1999

Humboldts can pretend to be one of the first: virgin ground."[24] Because the country had been effectively sealed off from the rest of the world and the way of life there had changed little since medieval times, early Western visitors to Kathmandu must have felt as if they had stepped back in time. Even after the political barrier of isolationism was lifted, the rugged topography and lack of roads in the high mountains kept these areas insulated from outside influences. As stories of lush unexplored landscapes crowned by the world's loftiest peaks and inhabited by exotic peoples with archaic lifestyles, devout religious beliefs, and friendly demeanors made their way back to the West, Nepal gained a mythical stature in the Western imagination as a mysterious place of refuge untouched by the modern world, conjuring up images of the mountain paradise of Shangri-La in James Hilton's classic novel, *Lost Horizon*. The Khumbu region, by virtue of the outside world's obsession with Mount Everest, occupied center stage in the Western imagination of Nepal and came to symbolize humankind's adventurous quest to explore the exotic untrammeled reaches of the planet.

Tibetan Buddhism

Tibetan Buddhism and traditional Tibetan culture occupy a prominent place in the Western imagination. Since the 1960s, the Chinese suppression of Buddhist institutions and practices in Tibet has only added to the mystery and allure among Westerners of all things Tibetan. Westerners with an interest in Tibetan Buddhism and Tibetan Buddhist philosophy have found an outlet for their attention in the Buddhist monasteries of Nepal and especially those in Khumbu, which have thrived in recent decades and which have been much more easily accessible than their remaining counterparts in Tibet. As anthropologist Vincanne Adams noted, beginning in the

---

24   Brower 1991b p.67

1970s "Sherpas became for tourists (and others) some of the most accessible living representatives of the Tibetan Buddhist culture."[25]

Khumbu's significance among Buddhists is also bolstered by its being considered by some to be one of numerous traditionally sacred hidden valleys (*beyul*) that served as holy sanctuaries and places of refuge for Buddhists. As mentioned in Chapter Two, Padmasambhava, the Indian mystic who introduced Buddhism to Tibet in the 8th century, purportedly identified various places throughout the Himalaya for persecuted Buddhists to seek refuge. It is believed that these beyul are full of riches, both material and spiritual, and that from within a beyul it is easier to attain metaphysical enlightenment. The legendary Lama Sangwa Dorje, who established the first Buddhist monastery in Khumbu at Pangboche in the 17th century, is believed to have performed many miracles in the course of vanquishing the demons of the Bonpo religion that preceded Buddhism in Khumbu, and it is said that physical evidence of some of the miracles still exist to this day. The monastic leaders of Khumbu have taken advantage of Westerners' fascination with the legends and esoteric practices associated with Tibetan Buddhism by increasingly turning their monasteries into Western meditation retreats and tourist attractions and in turn collecting hefty fees and donations from foreign visitors.

The Abominable Snowman

Westerners have also been intrigued by the mystery of the *yeti*, or 'abominable snowman' as the enigmatic creature has become popularly known in the West.[26] As with the mysterious 'Bigfoot' in the American Northwest, the Western world's fascination with the yeti was fueled by reported sightings of a large, hairy, human-like creature and its large footprints in the mountains of the Himalaya. According to the world-famous climber Reinhold Messner, who

---

25 Adams 1996 p.129. Note: For a description of Western interest in Tibetan Buddhism and the attention that Westerners have focused on Khumbu Sherpa religious institutions and practices, see Adams (1996 pp.162-169).

26 see, for example, Choegyal 1998 pp.106-107

wrote a book about his decade-long search for the yeti, in the 1950s there were more expeditions in the Himalaya searching for the elusive creature than there were trying to climb mountains.[27] Stories of encounters with the yeti are a part of local lore among Khumbu Sherpas, and painted renditions of the creature are kept in local monasteries along with alleged relics such as a yeti scalp and hand. When some of these artifacts were taken on an international tour arranged by Edmund Hillary, the Khumbu region, which was already famous as the home of the world's highest mountain, became the focal point of the West's interest in the yeti as well.

The Sherpas

The Sherpa people whose homes lay in the shadow of Mount Everest have achieved iconic status as well among Westerners. The fame the Sherpas have enjoyed can primarily be attributed to their close geographical and historical association with Mount Everest, their reputation as proficient and courageous mountain climbers, and the West's depiction of them as a remarkably good-natured and devoutly religious people. As a result, the Sherpa people themselves have been a major draw for visitors from the very beginning of tourism in the Everest region. The renowned Himalaya climber and explorer Bill Tilman, who was among the very first Westerners permitted to visit the Khumbu region in 1950, expressed a "supreme interest" in visiting the home of the Sherpas, writing that "apart from viewing the south side of Everest there was the fun to be expected from seeing Sherpas, as it were, in their natural state."[28] Nowadays, travel companies use glossy brochures to market commercial tours of the Sherpa homeland, appealing to Westerners' fascination with the Sherpas' Tibetan Buddhist culture as well as their legendary reputation as friendly, welcoming hosts. Many brochures emphasize the opportunity for their clients to trek with Sherpas, pass through their villages, stay in their homes, attend local religious festivals, and

---

27 Messner 2000
28 Tilman 1951 p.210

'truly' experience the 'authentic' Sherpa ambiance. For example, one trekking agency brochure promoted an organized group trek to Khumbu as follows:

> It is much more than the nostalgia of those early tweed jacketed, hob-nailed booted explorers of the world's highest mountain that keeps drawing people to this area. Certainly the mountain itself attracts – the highest point on earth will always do that as long as it remains accessible. It also involves a combination of outstanding mountain scenery, stone-walled fields and houses, slate roofs, and above all – the Sherpas. These hardy traders, farmers and climbers who with patience, understanding and a barrel full of humor also manage our treks. A trek to the Khumbu provides a great opportunity to learn something of their culture.[29]

As one Western writer noted, the term 'Sherpa' has become "synonymous with the experience of trekking in Nepal."[30] As a result, members of other ethnic groups in Nepal have taken to referring to themselves as Sherpas in order to bolster their likelihood of obtaining tourism jobs or to raise their status in Nepali society.[31] The marketing power of the Sherpa label has not been lost on Nepalis engaged in tourism businesses outside of the Everest region either. For example, people trekking in the Annapurna region near Chhomrong village may be surprised to find that an ethnically Gurung family has baselessly named their lodge the 'Sherpa Guesthouse' in the hope of cashing in on the Sherpas' fame among foreign tourists. The acknowledged international recognition power of the Sherpa 'brand' has also been utilized well beyond the context of Himalayan tourism, with the Sherpa name having been used by Western corporations to promote a variety of products from cars to computer software to investment funds.[32]

---

29 Tiger Mountain Treks and Expeditions brochure by Mountain Travel Nepal, 1987, as quoted in Adams 1996 p.63
30 Parker 1989 p.11
31 compare with Parker 1989 pp.11-13, Stevens 1993a pp.37-38
32 Adams 1996 pp.44-47

Scenery

Even if Mount Everest and the Sherpa people had not become icons in the Western imagination, the breathtakingly spectacular Khumbu scenery would certainly still draw a large number of tourists to the area. The valleys of the Khumbu region offer remarkably easy access to and staggering close-up views of arguably the most impressive grouping of high mountain peaks anywhere on the planet. In a country famous for its natural beauty, the mountain scenery of Khumbu is generally considered the most stunningly sublime in all of Nepal. Photographs of the Khumbu landscape are regularly featured in postcards, magazines, and coffee table picture books, and many popular Khumbu images are instantly recognizable by mountain enthusiasts around the world. Indeed, many Khumbu tourists with whom I have spoken said that they came not only to see Mount Everest but to take in the Khumbu's famed scenery in general, and that their most valued souvenirs were the photographs they had taken of the region's magnificent natural environment.

Local Hosts' Characteristics Suited to Tourism

In his groundbreaking comparative study of a number of highland communities in the Nepal Himalaya historically involved in trans-Himalayan trade, Fürer-Haimendorf examined the circumstances and characteristics related to the various communities' different responses to the curtailment of trade in the 1960s.[33] While many groups were forced to abandon their home villages and adopt new ways of life in lowland areas, the Sherpas of Khumbu were able to completely reorient their economy around tourism. Fürer-Haimendorf noted that the Sherpas of Khumbu were unique among highland groups in their successful transition from trade to tourism and suggested that this was largely due to particular characteristics suited to an involvement in tourism:

> When travelling along the northern border of Nepal, I often wondered how one could explain the distinctive character of the

---

33 Fürer-Haimendorf 1975

Sherpas and their pattern of life, a pattern confined to one particular section of the vast Himalayan region. Neither among the Tibetan-speaking people on the upper course of the Arun and Tamur rivers in Eastern Nepal, nor among the Bhotias of such areas in Western Nepal as Thak Khola, Lo (Mustangbhot) or Dolpo does one encounter people comparable with the Sherpas in the combination of a high standard of living, spirit of enterprise, sense of civic responsibility, social polish and general devotion to the practice of Buddhism. It is not accidental that Sherpas have become the trusted guides and companions of innumerable foreign mountaineers and that no year passes without numerous Sherpas travelling with large and small expeditions over the length and breadth of Nepal. The physical prowess of these sturdy mountain people is matched by that of other Bhotias used to a hard life in inhospitable Himalayan valleys, but the Sherpas' moral fibre, reliability and charm of manner are qualities one does not meet to the same degree among any of the other Tibetan-speaking communities on Nepal's northern borders.[34]

This section describes several characteristics attributed to the Sherpas that have enabled them to excel in the business of tourism and, in turn, enabled tourism to become such an integral part of Sherpa life.

Familiarity with Travel

By virtue of their long involvement in trans-Himalayan trade, their history of migration to Darjeeling, and their previous experience working for Western climbing expeditions originating in British India, many Khumbu Sherpas were already accustomed to traveling for long periods of time and interacting with Westerners even before the first trekking tourists began coming to Nepal. In his multi-ethnography of Nepal's various ethnic groups, Nepali anthropologist Dor Bahadur Bista noted that the Sherpas, whom he had first began studying with Fürer-Haimendorf in the 1950s, "travel much more extensively than any other community [in Nepal], and it is quite common for the whole family of a Khumbu Sherpa to leave the house

---

34 Fürer-Haimendorf 1964 p.2

locked up for four or five months."[35] Fürer-Haimendorf himself was convinced that, although trekking tourism was a new enterprise for some Sherpas, they brought to it "all the skill and adventure they had developed as independent traders,"[36] and he noted that "being experienced in work with foreigners and themselves enterprising and used to long-distance travel, the Sherpas proved excellent guides and camp servants."[37] What's more, the seasonal nature of tourism work was similar to that of trans-Himalayan trade, adding to the ease with which Sherpas took up the new opportunities in tourism.

Cosmopolitan Perspective

Even before the first Westerners set foot in Khumbu in 1950, many Sherpas were already privy to the workings of the outside world and the peculiarities of Western ways. The larger traders had often traveled as far afield as Lhasa and Calcutta, while many poorer Sherpas had experience working on roads and tea plantations in the Darjeeling area of British India, with some having even worked directly for British climbing expeditions in Sikkim and Tibet. Anthropologist Robert Miller claimed that "Sherpas who stayed in Darjeeling [in the 1920s and 1930s] were impressed by the modern conveniences which they saw and used. Many arranged to bring their Khumbu relatives and parents to Darjeeling and to acquaint them with concepts of sanitation, of Western standards of dress and coiffure and other Western ideas."[38] Similarly, anthropologist Sherry Ortner suggested that "the centrality of long distance trade to Sherpa society enduringly produced individuals who had a sense of a larger world,"[39] while geographer Stan Stevens likewise pointed out that "Khumbu Sherpas were already a cosmopolitan people before the

---

35   Bista 1972 p.161
36   Fürer-Haimendorf 1975 p.104
37   Fürer-Haimendorf 1974 p.105, 1984 p.65
38   Miller 1965 (1997 reprint p.19). Note: Miller (p.22) went on to suggest that "the relatively long, easy and intermittent contact of Sherpas with Europeans may have been a critical factor in the development of change [in the Khumbu region] without extensive disruption [to Sherpa society and culture]."
39   Ortner 1998 pp.15-16

world began coming to them."[40] There can be little doubt that their historic exposure to the British in Darjeeling and to a steady stream of Western and Japanese climbers in Nepal during the 1950s helped Khumbu Sherpas become accustomed to the habits and preferences of foreigners before the Everest region was opened to trekking tourism in the mid 1960s. In fact, Nepali anthropologist Ramesh Kunwar contrasted the Sherpas of Khumbu with ethnic Sherpas from other regions of Nepal such as Solu and Helambu, who initially avoided pursuing opportunities in tourism because of what Kunwar termed an "unfamiliarity with Westerners."[41]

But although their previous experience with the British in India may have given Khumbu Sherpas an early advantage over members of other Nepali communities when it came to dealing with foreigners, what has really set the Sherpas of Khumbu apart has been their continued ability to adapt to and interact positively with a wide range of foreign visitors. Indeed, a Western trekking and climbing guide with whom I spoke in Khumbu in 1999 – an intelligent and articulate man who has traveled extensively throughout the Himalaya for the past twenty years – expressed his particular admiration for Khumbu Sherpas among Himalayan peoples and voiced an opinion that their success in tourism has been due to their energy and intelligence and how easily they have adapted to Western ways.[42]

Entrepreneurial Spirit

Because of their history of engaging in trade, a business in which many Khumbu Sherpas had excelled, the spirit of commercial enterprise was already well ingrained among Khumbu residents long before tourism began to develop there. In fact, many Khumbu Sherpas were already quite adept at cross-cultural communication and had an aptitude for taking advantage of new economic opportunities, and they aggressively seized upon tourism as such. As Fisher pointed out, "the Sherpas had a long tradition of dealing with and profiting

40 Stevens 1991 p.55
41 Kunwar 1989 pp.95-96
42 Hooman Aprin, personal communication, 1999

from foreigners; tourists and mountaineers are only the latest variety of outsider to do business with."[43] Similarly, Brower noted that "traditional Sherpa society and economy had a place for the enterprising individual; the spirit of free enterprise operating in trans-Himalayan trade is little different from that required to succeed in the contemporary tourism-dominated economy."[44] As perhaps further indication of the significant role that experience in trade played in the Sherpas' subsequent involvement in tourism enterprise, it is interesting to note that while the majority of Khumbu Sherpa households were historically involved in trade to some degree, the residents of Phortse were the least involved with trade of all the main Khumbu villages,[45] and today Phortse is also the village with the least involvement in tourism.

Fürer-Haimendorf pointed to certain underlying societal characteristics that he believed had contributed to the Khumbu Sherpas' success in trans-Himalayan trade. I would argue that these same characteristics have in turn helped them to succeed in the business of tourism. Fürer-Haimendorf pointed out that the Sherpas have "a social system which allows wide scope for individual choice both in economic activities and the ordering of social relations."[46] Relative to the Hindu castes occupying Nepal's lower elevations, he believed that the Sherpas had benefited in their business dealings from what he termed an "open society" characterized by minimal family obligations, freedom from kinship control over choices, and a lack of social restrictions based upon religious practices and caste distinctions.[47] In Fürer-Haimendorf's opinion, the relaxed, courteous, and tolerant nature of the Sherpas' Buddhist customs, in contrast to the guardedness of strict Hindu procedural rules focused on caste differences and ritual pollution, greatly facilitated the ability and the willingness of Sherpas to travel for extended periods in distant lands

---

43 Fisher 1990 p.163
44 Brower 1991b p.169
45 Fürer-Haimendorf 1964 p.15
46 Fürer-Haimendorf 1975 p.287
47 Fürer-Haimendorf 1964 pp.38-39, 94-97, 288; 1975 pp.287-290

inhabited by a variety of peoples with cultures different than their own.[48]

Fürer-Haimendorf also described Sherpa society as relatively egalitarian and homogenous and "preserving the ideal of the basic equality of all members despite a wide range in the wealth and political influence of individuals" and suggested that such a society allowed for economic and social mobility and therefore did not limit the opportunities of energetic and talented individuals.[49] Fürer-Haimendorf explained how the opportunities historically available in trade enabled poorer Khumbu residents who took effective advantage of them to advance economically and socially,[50] just as the opportunities more recently available in tourism have contributed to economic mobility among Khumbu residents.[51] Ortner echoed this sentiment in writing about the equality of opportunities available in the culturally egalitarian world of the Sherpas:

> Although there are significant differences of wealth and power in a Sherpa community, these differences are not given by birth but are achieved in a theoretically equal-opportunity system. Thus all unrelated Sherpa men are considered equal in principle if not in practice, and everyone in theory has the possibility of advancing himself or herself as much as he or she can.[52]

Fürer-Haimendorf also pointed out that Sherpa society "stresses the virtues of self-reliance and independence" among all members, from young people to the elderly, which he contrasted with the stress Hindu societies placed on obedience and conformity.[53] I suspect that these characteristics of self-reliance and independence have proven valuable in enabling so many Sherpas to start up and operate their own tourism businesses and hence maintain a great deal of control over tourism development in Khumbu, as will discussed below in the section on Local Hosts' Involvement In and Control Over Tourism.

---

48   Fürer-Haimendorf 1984 p.111
49   Fürer-Haimendorf 1975 p.289
50   Fürer-Haimendorf 1964 pp.30-31
51   Fürer-Haimendorf 1984 p.65
52   Ortner 1998 p.24
53   Fürer-Haimendorf 1964 pp.84-87

As Fürer-Haimendorf noted, "young boys and girls are encouraged to try their hand in small trade deals on their own account, and by the time a young Sherpa woman gets married she may already have considerable commercial experience."[54]

Fürer-Haimendorf considered the traditional independence and business acumen of Sherpa women in particular a great asset for the type of tourism that has developed in Khumbu where women are largely responsible for running lodges and shops, as well as maintaining households, farms, and livestock, while men are away for long periods with mountain climbing and trekking expeditions or operating trekking agencies in Kathmandu.[55] In the early 1960s, even before the Everest region had been opened to trekking tourism, Fürer-Haimendorf had commented on the characteristic independence and self-confidence of Khumbu Sherpa women:

> Much of the petty trade and of the disposal and allocation of agricultural and dairy produce lies in the hands of the wife. A man's long periods of absence from home necessitate the wife's effective control over the organization of the farm work, as well as over mercantile transactions and household finance. Many women are experienced in trade and money-lending, and will take on considerable commitments even when unable to consult their husbands. The independence of a Sherpa wife in the handling of economic matters is reflected in a sense of self-reliance and assurance.[56]

Fürer-Haimendorf also attributed the Khumbu Sherpas' well-developed entrepreneurial spirit and aptitude for enterprise to the geographical location and ecological conditions of their home region. He pointed out how their historical involvement in trans-Himalayan trade had been fundamentally dependent upon their location along a travel corridor linking Tibet and Nepal. And the widely traveled anthropologist also noted that all three of the more outstanding examples of successful trans-Himalayan trading communities in the

---

54 Fürer-Haimendorf 1964 p.97
55 Fürer-Haimendorf 1975 pp.287-288
56 Fürer-Haimendorf 1964 p.81

Nepal Himalaya – namely the Sherpas of Namche, the Thakalis of Tukche, and the ethnic Tibetans of Walungchung Gola – had inhabited areas of limited agricultural potential and as a result had been motivated to engage aggressively in the risky business of entrepreneurial trade in order to make a living.[57]

It also bears mentioning that, along with the important role that their geographic location played in their involvement in trade, the Sherpas' settlement along a major trans-Himalayan trade corridor put them in a position to provide food and lodging to other travelers and traders who passed through. This provided another form of economic opportunity for the Sherpas and resulted in their developing a tradition for providing hospitality to outsiders that far predates the advent of trekking tourism in Khumbu. The catering of services to trekking tourists over the past few decades has been a continuation of this tradition, albeit in a more intensive and commercialized manner.

Strong Identity, Self-Confidence, & Literacy

Frequent travel and interaction with a variety of other peoples also fostered a general awareness among Khumbu Sherpas of the distinctiveness of their own cultural identity. The success Khumbu Sherpas enjoyed in their dealings with outsiders while engaging in trade or climbing mountains also encouraged a sense of self-confidence and a desire to retain their distinctive identity. Nepali anthropologist Dor Bahadur Bista observed that "although Khumbu Sherpas travel widely in Nepal with expeditions, and visit many types of people on their way, once they arrive home in Khumbu they are amidst their own people and prefer to retain their particular customs. The outside contact does not change them much."[58] And Barbara Brower commented that the resilience of the Sherpas' cultural heritage "has helped the Sherpas meet the flood of visitors bringing novel ideas, values, expectations, products, and plans to their national park home with less loss of ethnic identity, less erosion of traditional

---

57   Fürer-Haimendorf 1975 pp.289-290
58   Bista 1972 p.164

values and practices, than that suffered by other Himalayan peoples in the face of the invasion of the Western world."[59]

Brower attributed a good part of the Sherpas' resilience to their lack of a colonial history. Since Nepal was able to avoid Western colonial rule, indigenous groups in the country were not subjected to the kind of colonization experiences that have ridden roughshod over the pride and self-determination of some indigenous groups in other parts of the world. As Brower put it,

> Sherpas themselves remain in control of their lives and environment to a greater extent than traditional peoples in many situations. The effects of a colonial heritage, so important in the recent history of many parts of the [South Asia] region, are muted here [in Khumbu]. The reach of the [British] Raj did not reach so high [in the Himalaya]; traditional Sherpa institutions were never preempted as were those of the Paharis of the Indian Himalaya, for instance. Until very recently, Sherpas did not experience the same sort of usurpation of land and resource control by the state [...] that afflicted the indigenous resource-control practices of groups easier to reach and in possession of more coveted resources.[60]

In addition, the remoteness of the Khumbu region from Nepal's capital of Kathmandu left the Khumbu region, for all practical purposes, politically autonomous until the 1960s, when the central government nationalized the country's forests and instituted the nationwide *panchayat* system of local governance.[61] As Fürer-Haimendorf pointed out,

> unlike many other [ethnic minority] communities in similar situations, [Khumbu Sherpas] were able to avoid entering into a

---

59 Brower 1991b pp.4-5
60 Brower 1991b p.10
61 According to Fürer-Haimendorf (1974 p.108), "as late as 1957 the villages of Khumbu were virtually autonomous except for the levy of a very modest land-tax by the government of Nepal. [...] Though in theory the laws of the state applied to Khumbu as much as to any other part of the kingdom, in practice no outside agency intervened in the affairs of the Khumbu people, as long as they arranged to pay the annual revenue to the appropriate government office, which was located at Okhaldunga, the district headquarters."

relationship of dependence with any numerically and politically superior population. They have not had to link their economy with that of any of the dominant castes of Nepal, but have developed their role in the tourist industry of Nepal in the spirit of potential entrepreneurs and not as labourers seeking work outside their own homeland. Sherpa climbers and tourist guides consider themselves as professionals and they have been able to establish a monopoly which is not seriously threatened by any other community of Nepal.[62]

Altogether, the Khumbu Sherpas' cosmopolitan character, well-defined sense of cultural identity, and historical self-determination left them relatively unsusceptible to intimidation, culture shock, or feelings of inferiority in their dealings with outsiders.

A further characteristic that aided the Sherpas' self-confidence in dealing with outsiders as tourism developed in Khumbu was their relatively high rate of literacy, at least among males. Due to the financial support local monasteries had received in the early and mid-1900s as a result of the Khumbu community's economic prosperity from trans-Himalayan trade, the introduction of the potato, and employment in Darjeeling, literacy in Khumbu in the 1950s was considerably higher than in other remote areas of the Nepal Himalaya.[63] As a result of their relatively high rate of literacy, Khumbu Sherpas had advantages in learning other languages and communicating with foreign visitors that proved very helpful in tourism. And, as pointed out in Chapter Six, the educational opportunities that have been made available to Khumbu Sherpas through the extensive school-building work of Edmund Hillary's Himalayan Trust and the generous support of foreign benefactors have played an important role in enabling Sherpas to take the lead in developing tourism businesses of their own rather than being forced to work for outsiders.

---

62 Fürer-Haimendorf 1974 pp.111-112, 1975 p.104
63 Fürer-Haimendorf 1960, as cited in Fisher 1990 pp.59-60

Physical Prowess & Drive

Yet another characteristic that was instrumental to Khumbu Sherpas' early and deep involvement in mountain tourism in the Himalaya is their widely acclaimed physical prowess at high altitude. From the early days of Himalayan climbing to the present, the Sherpas' physical strength and stamina have impressed foreign visitors. The admiration and respect earned by the Sherpas have assured them a place on virtually every climbing and trekking expedition undertaken in the mountains of Nepal, in addition to many in other Himalayan countries as well.[64] And the Sherpas continue to this day to earn praise for their physical abilities in the cold, harsh environment of the high Himalaya.[65]

When the British began pioneering Himalayan climbing in the early 20th century, however, the Sherpas had not yet built up their distinguished reputation among Westerners. The earliest British expeditions were organized from the colonial hill station of Darjeeling, and porters were initially hired with little regard to ethnicity. But British climbers soon learned that members of ethnic groups residing in lowland areas were not well suited to mountaineering work due to their unaccustomedness to high altitude and cold. As a result, the British made a point to instead hire peoples of Tibetan ancestry hailing from the highlands. Sherpas who had migrated to Darjeeling seeking wage labor opportunities were recognized as a highland group, and as such were hired to work as porters for British climbing expeditions.

According to Ortner, on the first British expedition to Mount Everest in 1921, the British climbers did not clearly distinguish between their Tibetan and Sherpa porters, finding both to be up to the physical challenge of carrying loads at high altitudes. It is unlikely that the Sherpas would have been able to differentiate themselves

---

64   compare with Ortner 1990, 1998 p.2

65   For example, as climber John Meyer wrote in an American Alpine Club newsletter in 1996, "Sherpas are some of the most hardy and resourceful people on earth. They thrive in an area that challenges even the strongest [Western] climbers."

from Tibetans and other Himalayan highlanders in the eyes of Western mountaineers if it had not been for the Sherpas' enterprising ethos and drive. For example, Ortner noted that, on the second British expedition to Mount Everest in 1922, the Sherpas "made it plain that they were competing with the Tibetans, volunteering for all the difficult high altitude jobs, and bringing themselves to the [British climbers'] attention as less superstitious, more willing, and more disciplined than the Tibetans."[66] After that 1922 expedition, the British expedition leader, Charles Bruce, described the Sherpas' competitive nature and drive by writing that "they backed themselves heavily to best the Tibetans. It was a pretty good race, but finally they came out well on top; in fact [...] all but one who reached 25,000 feet [altitude] and over were Sherpas."[67]

The Sherpas' continued involvement with Western mountain climbing expeditions enabled them to hone their climbing skills and gain confidence on steep and exposed mountain terrain even under difficult conditions, attributes that over time served to distinguish them from other Himalayan highlanders. By the 1930s, British mountaineers began to notice significant improvements in the climbing skills and confidence levels of their Sherpa porters relative to a decade earlier. On the 1924 British expedition to Everest, climber Edward Norton wrote that the Sherpas "are not really all-around mountaineers; they have little knowledge of snow and ice, and are as subject as other inexperienced amateurs to sudden loss of nerve if something goes wrong."[68] However, by the time of the 1938 British expedition to Mount Everest, expedition leader Eric Shipton wrote of the Sherpas, "[on previous expeditions] it has always been rather a question of driving these men to extreme altitudes; now the position was almost reversed."[69] By the 1950s, the Sherpas had so impressed their British employers that the British Himalayan Club recommended that Sherpa sirdars be given sole responsibility for

---

66   Ortner 1998 p.22
67   Bruce 1924 p.63, as quoted in Miller 1965 (1997 reprint p.17)
68   Norton 1925 p.59, as quoted in Miller 1965 (1997 reprint pp.19-20)
69   Eric Shipton , as quoted in Douglas 1999a p.123

arranging and hiring expedition porters.[70] Indeed, the eventual success of the British in reaching the summit of Everest in 1953 was largely attributed to the experience and skill of their Sherpa staff.

Good-Naturedness

Sherpas have regularly been characterized by foreign visitors as friendly, good-natured, affable, cheerful, and easily humored.[71] Other ethnic groups in Nepal have been similarly characterized by foreign visitors, but not nearly to the same extent as the Sherpas. For example, the renowned Himalayan anthropologist Fürer-Haimendorf, who during his long career studied a multitude of Himalayan peoples, singled out the Sherpas of Khumbu in writing that "the highlanders of Khumbu stand out as a people distinctive in their character," and described them as "sociable and uninhibited people, who greatly enjoy the pleasures of conviviality and abandon themselves whole-heartedly to the thrills of dancing and choral singing."[72] Even Nepali anthropologists have described the Sherpa people as jolly, sociable, and extremely hospitable, with an open policy (especially compared to orthodox Hindus) toward allowing guests into their kitchen and place of worship in the home.[73]

Based upon his ethnographic study of the Khumbu Sherpas in the 1950s, before many Westerners had ventured to Khumbu, Fürer-Haimendorf suggested that the Sherpas conducted themselves in a virtuous and agreeable manner because "the [Sherpas'] sentiments of tolerance and consideration for the interests and feelings of others, which are central to Sherpa morality, find their outward expression in courtesy and good manners."[74] Fürer-Haimendorf also placed a great deal of significance on the role of the Sherpas' Mahayana Buddhist tradition of compassion for all living-beings and their sense that "selfless activity in the wider interest of humanity complements the

---

70   Tobin 1954, as cited in Miller 1965 (1997 reprint p.20)
71   compare with Ortner 1990 pp.14-18, 1998 p.30
72   Fürer-Haimendorf 1964 pp.xix, 287
73   Shrestha, Singh, & Pradhan 1972 p.12 (1987 edition p. 29)
74   Fürer-Haimendorf 1964 p.285

striving for personal spiritual perfection."[75] Peter Matthiessen echoed Fürer-Haimendorf's religious-based explanation when he wrote of the Sherpas:

> as Buddhists, they know that the doing matters more than the attainment or reward, that to serve in this selfless way is to be free. Because of their belief in karma – the principle of cause and effect that permeates Buddhism – they are tolerant and unjudgmental. The generous and open outlook of the Sherpas, a kind of merry defenselessness, is by no means common, even among unsophisticated peoples.[76]

A different kind of explanation was put forth by anthropologists Michael Thompson and Sherry Ortner, who attributed the origin of the Sherpas' characteristic good-naturedness to their mercantile past. According to their argument, because a friendly and cheerful demeanor contributed to success in trade, such people were able to accumulate wealth and gain a high degree of respect and status in Sherpa society. As a result, maintaining a friendly and cheerful demeanor became the "culturally dominant style" of the Sherpas.[77] Fürer-Haimendorf also stressed the significance of wealth and the historical pervasiveness of mercantilism in Khumbu society:

> the acquisition of wealth and its proper utilization are basic to the average [Khumbu] Sherpa's idea of the good life. The instinct of traders is evident in most [Khumbu] Sherpas, even in those villages not greatly engaged in trade, and men and women, no less than half-grown boys and girls, seldom miss a chance when there is the opportunity to engage in some petty transactions or to sell their services for wages. This eagerness for gain has made it possible to recruit large numbers of porters for mountaineering expeditions, [just as it] accounts for the [Khumbu] Sherpas' unceasing and strenuous efforts to keep moving the flow of goods along one of the world's highest trade-routes.[78]

75　Fürer-Haimendorf 1963 (reprinted in Hornbein 1965 p.76), Fürer-Haimendorf 1964 p.288
76　Matthiessen 1978 pp.33-34
77　Thompson 1979 p.46; Ortner 1990 p.18, 1998 p.12
78　Fürer-Haimendorf 1964 pp.281-282. Note: By "proper utilization" of wealth, Fürer-Haimendorf was referring to the primary value placed by Sherpa society

Ortner has also made the claim that more impoverished Sherpas, having few other options available for economic advancement, consciously constructed a cheerful demeanor in order to gain favor with Western employers so that they could get jobs on mountaineering expeditions and reap the money, recognition, and respect this type of employment offered.[79] In this regard, Ortner compared the Sherpas with other highland peoples of the Himalaya, such as the Balti and Hunza people of northern Pakistan who were equally accustomed to living and working in cold, high-altitude mountainous terrain, and concluded that the Sherpas' more cheerful approach to mountaineering work was due to the frequently conscripted nature of Balti and Hunza portering labor versus the overwhelmingly voluntary nature of Sherpa labor.[80]

The stellar reputation that Sherpas earned from an early stage in their interactions with Westerners has not only withstood the test of time, it has grown to almost mythical proportions thanks to the accolades that have been heaped upon the Sherpas in Western literature. For example, consider what the famed Himalayan climber and explorer Bill Tilman wrote in *The Himalayan Journal* in 1935 about the Sherpas:

> For nearly five months we had lived and climbed together, and the more we saw of [the Sherpas], the more we liked and respected them. That they can climb and carry loads is now taken for granted; but even more valuable assets to our small self-contained party were their cheerful grins, their willing work in camp and on the march, their complete lack of selfishness, their devotion to our

on the prestige derived from the expenditure of wealth on hospitality to fellow villagers and generosity in the service of religion, as opposed to the mere possession of wealth or the use of wealth to provide only for one's own material comfort. According to Fürer-Haimendorf (1964 p.283), "second only to the prestige and admiration gained by generosity in the expenditure of wealth is the value placed on courtesy, gentleness and a spirit of compromise and peacefulness."

79 Ortner 1998 pp.13-23
80 Ortner 1998 pp.17-19

service. To be their companion was a delight; to lead them, an honour.[81]

Years later, Tilman was a member of the first Western group to visit Khumbu in 1950, and he described the Sherpas his group had hired as "sterling characters, dependable and solid as rocks, who worked for us with a will and cheered us by their company all the way."[82] Likewise, a Western doctor working with Edmund Hillary's Himalayan Trust in the 1960s wrote that the Sherpas were "resourceful people, with great charm and sense of humor. Their hospitality is rightly renowned; they strive to please and help, yet do so with quiet pride and dignity without a trace of servility so that it is easy to accept them as equals."[83] And Hillary himself commended the Sherpas for "their hardiness and cheerfulness, their vigor and loyalty, and their freedom from our [i.e. Westerners'] civilized curse of self pity."[84] Similarly, Malcolm Barnes wrote in his introduction to Tenzing Norgay Sherpa's autobiography that the Sherpas "are indeed a happy people, as anyone who has traveled with them will know, tolerant and good-humored to a high degree, finding enjoyment in almost anything they do, interested in everything and with a strong sense of fun."[85] And the renowned naturalist, George Schaller, who has spent considerable time traveling and conducting research in the Himalaya, wrote that "Sherpas have achieved world fame not just as mountaineers but also as self confident, amiable, and loyal people."[86]

Indeed, there seems to be no end to the amount of flattering praise that Western climbers, journalists, authors, and academics have piled onto the Sherpas over the years. In his academic tome on the Khumbu, geographer Stan Stevens claimed that the Sherpas "have won worldwide admiration for their strength, endurance, courage, indomitable good spirits and joy in life, deep faith in Buddhism, and

---

81 Tilman 1935 p.25, as quoted in Ortner 1998 p.5
82 Tilman 1951 p.219
83 Pearl 1965 pp.584-585, as quoted in Adams 1996 p.91
84 Hillary 1964 p.1, as quoted in Adams 1996 p.91
85 Sherpa 1977 p.20
86 Schaller 1980 p.178, as quoted in Kunwar 1989 p.101

their relatively egalitarian and open society."[87] In yet another example, but this time from the angle of the popular media, an internet website reporting on Everest climbing expeditions in the spring of 2000 featured among several articles on the Sherpas one that was entitled 'The Quiet Heroes of Everest', which described the Sherpas as:

> remarkable, courageous and generally unspoiled people of rare values, virtue and grace: generous in spirit, sacrificial in nature, brimming with modesty and humility, astonishing in strength and stamina. Selflessness is at the top of any Sherpa's job description. There's always a Sherpa there to save the day, like a guardian angel floating above the distress caused by the elements that can destroy a climber.[88]

Given the reams of both academic and popular literature extolling Sherpas' virtues, anthropologist Jim Fisher suggested that the positive stereotype Westerners have developed of Sherpas as "egalitarian, peaceful, hardy, honest, polite, industrious, hospitable, cheerful, independent, brave, heroic, compassionate people" had become something of a self-fulfilling prophesy based upon Westerners' expectations that have been fueled by a litany of "literary evidence, which has by now assumed epic proportions" and is then reinforced when things go well on a trek.[89] But irregardless of their origins, the reasons for their continuance, or the manner in which they are ascribed, the point is that Sherpa personal characteristics have not only been painted in a very positive light by foreigners, they have enabled Sherpas to build very amicable relations with visitors and significantly enhanced Khumbu Sherpas' ability to engage in and benefit from tourism.[90]

---

87 Stevens 1993a p.31
88 Quokka Sports and MountainZone internet website, http://everest2000.com
89 Fisher 1990 pp.123-125
90 compare with Ortner 1990 pp.14-18, Fisher 1990 pp.124-127

Local Hosts' Involvement In & Control Over Tourism

According to Pitamber Sharma, former coordinator of the Mountain Tourism for Local Development Program at the International Center for Integrated Mountain Development (ICIMOD) in Kathmandu, "the greater the voice that the local community can bring to bear in planning and managing tourism, the greater will the chances be of protecting and maintaining the cultural heritage."[91] In the case of Khumbu, local residents welcomed tourism as a means of filling the economic gap left by the curtailment of trans-Himalayan trade in the 1960s, and in many ways the Sherpas' involvement in tourism has enabled their culture to continue. As described in the previous section, Khumbu Sherpas possessed certain characteristics that made them particularly adept at developing tourism businesses of their own. What's more, involvement in tourism was generally open to the entire Khumbu population, although some people had advantages over others due to their location along the main tourist route and the availability of financial and labor resources to devote to tourism. But for all those engaging in tourism, it offered the potential for upward mobility, both economically and socially.

As early as 1970, tourism had overtaken farming as the leading primary occupation among Khumbu Sherpa men,[92] and the involvement of Khumbu men and women in tourism has grown considerably since then. Their high level of involvement and engagement in tourism has allowed Khumbu residents to dominate the tourism business in the Everest region, both in employment as wage earners (especially higher wage earners like sirdar and guide) and in providing services as owners of lodges, shops, and pack animals. Over the years, Khumbu Sherpas have expanded their involvement in

---

91 Sharma 1998b
92 Fürer-Haimendorf 1975 pp.93-94. Note: Fürer-Haimendorf performed a house-to-house census in 1970 in which 34 percent of the 775 working Khumbu Sherpa men reported their primary occupation as expedition work and tourism, compared to 32 percent as farming, 17 percent as monks, and 8 percent as trade. 771 working women also reported their primary occupations: 81 percent housewives and 19 percent farming.

tourism beyond guiding and hoteliering to own and operate many Kathmandu-based travel companies and even an airline. From a relatively early stage of tourism development in Khumbu, Fürer-Haimendorf noted how the Sherpas' involvement in and control over tourism had resulted in their "profiting from the tourist boom as entrepreneurs rather than as employees of an organization controlled from outside."[93]

Because local residents have largely controlled the development of tourism in the Everest region, visitors have had to fit into the local peoples' lifestyles and preferences instead of the other way around. Visitors trek on the same footpaths that have been used by Khumbu residents for centuries, buy supplies and souvenirs from locally owned shops, eat and sleep in locally owned lodges that have been built in the local architectural style, and employ local residents as their guides. Local business owners have reinvested their economic returns from tourism into moderately scaled and functional, revenue generating infrastructure. Nearly all lodge development in Khumbu has been by local residents who earned money from employment as a trekking or climbing guide, from operating a smaller lodge that they later expanded, and/or from funds loaned by a foreign sponsor. There are very few cases of lodge development by non-Khumbu residents.[94]

A major reason for the lack of outside involvement in and control over tourism in Khumbu is the region's remoteness from roads, as well as its rugged terrain, high altitude, and harsh climate. Together these characteristics have served to limit tourist numbers and, in turn, the expectations of financial returns by potential outside investors, as I will describe in the following section. But an equally important factor has been local residents' aggressive opportunism and

---

93   Fürer-Haimendorf 1975 p.92
94   As of 1999, the only non-Sherpa owned lodges in Khumbu of which I was aware included the Everest View Hotel and Panorama Hotel near Syangboche, the 8,000 Meter Inn near Lobuche, the Yak Lodge at Thukla, and the chain of Sherpa Guide Lodges owned by a group of California investors and Kathmandu businessmen as discussed by Stevens (1993a p.411).

entrepreneurial adeptness, which have left little room for outsiders to participate in or gain control over tourism development.

Because they have largely controlled tourism development themselves, Khumbu Sherpas have reaped significant economic benefits from tourism. And, due to the economic rewards, local residents have continued to enthusiastically welcome, embrace, and involve themselves in tourism. Following a 1982 survey of Khumbu residents, researcher Ivan Pawson stated that "there were few Sherpas who did not feel that tourism and the affluence it has brought to Khumbu was having a generally beneficial effect."[95] Likewise, Stan Stevens noted that "many Sherpas support continued tourism development and hope that tourist numbers will increase."[96] Indeed, of the numerous Khumbu residents with whom I have spoken, not a single one ever expressed a desire for a reduction of tourism in Khumbu.

Limited Scale of Tourism Development

Although it didn't take long for Western climbing expeditions to begin making their way to Khumbu after Nepal was opened to foreign visitors in 1949, for the first decade and a half Khumbu had only small numbers of visitors and almost no tourism infrastructure. But once the Nepal government opened the Everest region to trekking tourism in the mid 1960s, Khumbu residents began building tourist shops and lodges to cater to the growing number of visitors. Although tourist numbers and infrastructure in the Everest region have grown steadily since then, the overall scale of that growth has been kept in check by the difficulty of accessing the region and the rigors of Khumbu's high altitude environment.

These factors undoubtedly affected the decision made by the World Bank in the 1970s to forego financing a proposed multi-million dollar tourism development scheme in Khumbu after the bank had commissioned a study to investigate the potential for

95   Pawson *et al.* 1984a p.80
96   Stevens 1993b p.426

increasing tourism in the Everest region.[97] One can only wonder what Khumbu would be like today if the World Bank had decided to go forward with the scheme. Certainly it would be a much different place for Sherpas to live and a much different experience for visitors.[98] Perhaps more than anything else, the limited scale of tourism in Khumbu has allowed the Sherpas to remain as involved and as in control of it as they have been and to make their own choices about the direction their lives have taken.

Lack of Infrastructure in Nepal

An early factor limiting the scale of tourism development in the Everest region was the lack of transportation and accommodation infrastructure in the country of Nepal as a whole. As late as 1950, there was not a single airport in Nepal nor were there any motorable roads, and the number of hotels catering to foreign visitors remained severely limited throughout the 1950s and 1960s. With the support of foreign aid, in 1951 a rudimentary airport was constructed in Nepal's capital of Kathmandu, which later was expanded to accommodate commercial jets plying international routes. Although the number of hotels in the capital grew dramatically during the 1980s and 1990s, to this day there are few motorable roads in Nepal and none that provide direct access to the country's highland mountain regions.

The country's rugged topography and the national government's lack of funds have seriously constrained the building of modern transportation infrastructure such as roads, rails, cable cars, or airstrips in Nepal's highlands. As guidebook writer Stephen Bezruchka pointed out, Nepal has the fewest miles of roads in proportion to area or population of any country in the world.[99] As a

97   His Majesty's Government of Nepal 1977; Brower 1991b p.70
98   As Stevens (1991 p.52) and Rogers & Aitchison (1998 p.86) have pointed out, despite Namche's development as the hub of Khumbu tourism, up to now neither it nor any other village in the Everest region has been plagued by the problems of theft, prostitution, and begging that have been ushered in by heavy tourism development in many other places.
99   Bezruchka 1997 p.17

result, tourists are forced either to take a jarring bus ride through the hills and then walk into the mountains or else try their luck with pricey and often unreliable flights by helicopter or small plane. Bottlenecks related to the country's lack of transportation infrastructure continue to have a limiting influence on international tourism in Nepal in general, although, as will be discussed later in this chapter, Nepal's government (with help from foreign development agencies) has been working to expand the country's limited infrastructure and develop its tourism potential.

Limited Access to Khumbu

Without a doubt, the difficulty of accessing Khumbu has been the major limiting factor to the scale and growth of tourism in the Everest region over the past few decades. Although access to the region has improved markedly over the years, the limited availability of quick, inexpensive, and reliable transport between Kathmandu and Khumbu has remained the primary bottleneck, even as transportation and accommodation infrastructure has been expanded in Kathmandu to accommodate more foreign visitors to Nepal. Prior to the building of a small airstrip in 1964 at Lukla just to the south of Khumbu, reaching the Everest region from Kathmandu required an arduous walk of more than two weeks through the rugged hills of eastern Nepal. The completion of a road from Kathmandu to Jiri in the 1980s shortened the trip to a tortuous one-day drive followed by a still strenuous walk of one week. By flying to Lukla, one could theoretically reach Khumbu after a 40-minute flight and a one-day walk, but for many years flights were limited by a lack of suitable planes and frequently cancelled due to inclement weather. More recently, the availability of chartered helicopters has cut access time to about an hour, but helicopter flights are considerably more expensive and still apt to be cancelled by cloudy weather.[100]

---

100 The road to Jiri was constructed between 1971 and 1984 through a Swiss aid program. The Lukla airstrip was built by Edmund Hillary's Himalayan Trust to facilitate the building of the hospital at Kunde. According to guidebook writer Stan Armington (1997 p.173), Nepal's government lengthened the Lukla

In 1977, as part of a study of tourism in the Everest region commissioned by the World Bank, 259 visitors were sampled to determine their method of transport into and out of the region. The results clearly indicated the importance of air transport. Of those sampled, 68 percent flew in and flew out, 25 percent walked in and flew out, and only 7 percent walked both ways.[101] Due to the bottlenecks associated with air transport to Lukla, longtime Khumbu observer Jim Fisher predicted in 1988 that tourist numbers in Khumbu would not grow much beyond the then current level of about 7,000 tourists per year.[102] While Khumbu tourist numbers have more than tripled since then, the Lukla airstrip bottleneck has certainly kept the number of tourists from being higher. Lukla's short (450 meters) airstrip is not suitable for planes larger than the dual propeller, 15-passenger, Twin Otter style, short-take-off-and-landing (STOL) planes now used. Due to constraints imposed by typically windy and cloudy afternoon weather conditions in the mountains, a limited number of flights can be scheduled each morning; but even these are regularly cancelled because of poor visibility due to fog or clouds. Even so, during the tourist season Lukla is the third-busiest airport in Nepal, after Kathmandu and Pokhara.[103] Another airstrip sometimes used to access Khumbu is located at Phaplu, which is about a four-day walk from Namche, but it is subject to the same constraints of a short runway and unreliable weather conditions.

Beginning in the mid 1990s, a number of Nepal's domestic airline companies started using large, Russian-made, Mi-17 cargo helicopters to transport tourists between Kathmandu and Khumbu. Helicopter flights directly to and from the Khumbu village of

---

airstrip in 1977, and a control tower was added in 1983. The airstrip was subsequently paved in 2000. The availability of short-take-off-and-landing (STOL) planes in Nepal was alleviated somewhat when the government lifted its monopoly on domestic air travel in 1993. Large Russian-made helicopters came into charter use in Nepal in the mid 1990s, and today several private airlines in Nepal offer helicopter flights.

101 His Majesty's Government of Nepal 1977, as cited in Pawson *et al.* 1984b p.241
102 Fisher 1990 p.148
103 Armington 1997 p.173

Syangboche quickly became popular among tourists interested in shortening their travel time by avoiding the one or two-day walk between Lukla and Namche. However, Nepal's government halted the Syangboche helicopter flights in 1997 after lodge owners in Lukla protested their loss of business and national park authorities complained about the noise caused by the helicopters.[104] Helicopter flights between Kathmandu and Lukla, however, remained popular due to somewhat lower cancellation rates than planes in poor visibility conditions.

According to one trekking guidebook author, the increased frequency and reliability of helicopter service to Khumbu in the latter 1990s eased the tourist bottleneck and resulted in what he termed "serious overcrowding in the Everest region."[105] Citing safety concerns, Nepal's government subsequently prohibited the use of the popular Russian Mi-17 helicopters for regularly scheduled flights open to the public, although private charter flights were still permitted. Nepal's Ministry of Tourism and Civil Aviation mandated that the helicopters had to be retrofitted with front-facing seats to meet safety requirements, but the airline companies claimed the costly retrofit would be uneconomical for them because it would reduce the quantity of passengers and cargo the helicopters could carry.[106] The result was a significant reduction in air transport capacity and a return to the earlier reliance, except among private charter groups, on airplane flights to Lukla.

During the peak autumn tourist season in 1999, more than 30 scheduled flights landed daily at the Lukla airport, compared to about 6 per day in the off-season. In 2000, to further boost the capacity, reliability, and safety of flights to and from Lukla, Nepal's government extended and paved the Lukla airstrip and constructed a new terminal building. Funds for the project were secured through a loan from the Asian Development Bank, which Nepal's government

104 McGuinness 1998 p.161
105 Armington 1997 p.102
106 *Himalayan News* 1998 p.7

planned to pay back from the increased revenues that more tourist visas and higher airport taxes would bring in.

In addition to the improvements made to the Lukla airstrip, Nepal's government plans to build two separate motor vehicle roads to the village of Salleri, the administrative headquarters of the Solu-Khumbu district, as part of a larger government plan to connect all of the country's district headquarters with a road network. One of the planned roads is an eastward extension of the existing road between Kathmandu and Jiri, which currently serves as the primary trailhead for trekkers who choose to walk rather than fly to or from Khumbu. Since Namche can be reached on foot in 4 days of relatively easy walking from Salleri compared to 7 days of more difficult walking from Jiri, the extension of the road from Jiri to Salleri would likely result in an increased number of tourists willing to walk to and from Khumbu and would thereby loosen the air travel bottleneck. A second planned road would connect Salleri with the Mahendra Highway to the south, which serves as the main transportation artery along Nepal's east-west axis and which connects Nepal to its enormously populated southern neighbor, India. Indians already comprise roughly one-third of all visitors to Nepal, and improved road access between India and Solu-Khumbu could potentially bolster the number of Indian tourists visiting the Everest region.

Rigors of Altitude, Climate, Rustic Amenities, & Travel by Footpath

Even if all the issues limiting access to the Everest region were somehow completely resolved, the rigors associated with Khumbu's rugged high-altitude environment and the relatively rustic nature of travel there would continue to limit the number of visitors. Probably the biggest issue that stands in the way of the Everest region ever becoming a true mass tourism destination is the problem that many visitors experience with altitude. At elevations above roughly 3,600 meters (12,000 feet), the reduced oxygen level in the air due to the lower atmospheric pressure may cause people whose bodies are not sufficiently acclimated to the altitude to suffer headaches, nausea, and general malaise. The symptoms of altitude sickness are not only extremely uncomfortable, they can also lead to such life-threatening conditions as cerebral or pulmonary edema if an afflicted person does not descend to a lower elevation. Because of the Everest region's extreme altitude and the ease with which tourists can quickly ascend to elevations where they may be susceptible to altitude sickness, a considerable number of visitors experience altitude-related problems that force them to alter their plans and perhaps cut short their stay in the region. The need to ascend slowly while the body gets accustomed to higher and higher altitudes means that visitors who hope to trek to the popular destinations of Kala Patar or Gokyo for views of Everest generally have to have at least three weeks of holiday time, a requirement that quickly limits the number of tourists.

In addition to time constraints, reservations about the cold weather and relatively rustic nature of travel in the Everest region keep many potential visitors away, particularly those whose ideal vacation involves lying on a warm beach or taking in the sights from the comfort of an air-conditioned tour bus. In a place where nighttime temperatures are seldom above freezing and where mechanized transport is nonexistent, the rigors of traveling everywhere by foot on steep, rugged, dirt paths while bundled up in multiple layers of clothing make for a holiday that not every holidaymaker is cut out for. Indeed, the nature of travel in the Everest region has generally resulted in the self-selection of more hardy types of travelers and the exclusion of other less hardy types. Given the limited number of visitors willing to withstand the rigors of a trip to Khumbu, large international investors have generally shied away from tourism development there, preferring instead to invest in destinations favored by high paying luxury tourists. As a result, tourism development in the Everest region has been primarily left to local residents.

There have been a few exceptions to the general lack of outside investment in luxury tourism development in the Everest region, but overall these businesses have not met with resounding success. As described in Chapter Six, the best-known example of an outsider-owned tourism business in Khumbu, the Japanese-financed Everest View Hotel near Syangboche, closed down in the early 1980s after just a few years of operation. The primary reason cited for the hotel's failure was the frequency of altitude sickness among guests, who typically arrived by small plane at the private landing strip constructed specifically for the hotel, giving them no opportunity to gradually acclimate to the high altitude. Other hindrances to the hotel's business included the shortage of Cessna type planes in Nepal small enough to utilize the hotel's very short airstrip, frequent flight delays due to poor weather or visibility, and the high cost of providing luxury services in such a remote area. After being closed for several years, the hotel reopened in 1990 with the addition of two small pressure chambers (Gamow Bags) to help combat the altitude sickness problem, and with access enhanced by the increased availability of helicopters in Nepal. Despite these improvements, the twelve-room hotel still suffered from low occupancy, its guests primarily limited to wealthy Japanese patrons willing to pay twenty times the typical visitor's daily costs for food and lodging.[107]

Seasonality of Tourism

The relatively short duration of the spring and autumn tourist seasons in Khumbu, a product of the summer monsoon rains and the winter cold and snow, has also limited the attractiveness of tourism development by outside investors. For local residents, on the other hand, the seasonality of tourism has allowed for long periods of respite from the hectic schedule and disruption brought about by tourism. Some observers have suggested that this regular return to normalcy has contributed to the level of cohesion and continuity in the Khumbu Sherpa community and allowed local residents to blend tourism into their traditional way of life rather than having it take over.[108] The lower number of visitors during the summer months has

---

107 According to guidebook author Jamie McGuinness (1998 p.162), food and lodging at the Everest View Hotel runs about US$200 per day, compared to roughly US$10 per day for most Khumbu lodges.

108 Stevens 1991 p.55

also meant that the Sherpas' traditional agricultural practices have not been deeply affected by their engagement in tourism and has also lessened the strain on the natural environment relative to what a continual onslaught of tourist visitors might cause.

Limited Economic Leakage of Tourism Income

Unlike the residents of many other tourist locales in rural areas of developing countries, Khumbu Sherpas have been able to capture and retain a large portion of the money spent by tourist visitors. The limited 'leakage' of tourism revenues to outside interests is due to local residents' high degree of involvement in and control over tourism. Khumbu Sherpas have been able to derive economic benefits from tourism in a wide variety of ways, from their construction and operation of tourist shops and lodges, to their renting of pack animals, to their ownership of Kathmandu-based trekking agencies. Even local residents without sufficient capital to invest in a tourism-related business have been able to benefit from tourism through their employment as trekking and climbing staff and their sale of locally grown potatoes and vegetables for visitors' consumption. And many Sherpas have also benefited greatly from the relationships they have developed with Western sponsors they met through tourism. But despite the Sherpas' multi-faceted engagement in tourism and their efforts to capture as much of the economic benefit as possible, some leakage has still occurred, although it has remained at reasonable levels as described below.

Air Transport

A high percentage of Khumbu tourists come from North America, Europe, Australia, New Zealand, and Japan, with practically all visitors from these areas traveling to and from Nepal by air. The cost of an economy-class roundtrip plane ticket between the United States and Kathmandu generally costs somewhere around US$1,500. This constitutes a large but very necessary part of a typical Khumbu visitor's overall trip expenditure. Competition among international airlines, the services of discount airfare consolidators, and the availability of pricing information via the internet have helped keep down fares for international travel despite rising fuel costs, leaving travelers with more money to spend on other aspects of their trip.

A majority of international tourists visiting the Everest region also utilize air travel between Kathmandu and Lukla, with the fare paid by foreigners costing roughly US$100 for each leg of the roundtrip journey. Since the government of Nepal lifted its monopoly over the domestic air sector in 1993, a slew of private airlines have emerged, greatly increasing the coverage and capacity of domestic flights. Even after privatization, however, the government continued to regulate the price of fares, and despite ticket costs for foreigners running about three times that for Nepali passengers, fares for domestic flights are not cost prohibitive for most foreign tourists.[109] At least one Khumbu Sherpa businessman has countered the economic leakage arising from air transport by starting an airline of his own, which not only provides service between Kathmandu and Lukla but to several other destinations in Nepal as well.

Trekking Agencies

While prohibitively large investment requirements keep most Khumbu Sherpas from being able to counter the economic leakage that arises due to the provision of air transport by outsiders, an area where many Sherpas have been successful in competing with outside business interests is in running trekking agencies that organize visitors' trips to Khumbu. As mentioned in Chapter Three, a large number of the trekking agencies based in Kathmandu are owned and operated by Sherpas, and Sherpas also constitute a large portion of the staff of many Kathmandu-based trekking agencies. Even so, due to

---

109 Citing rising fuel costs, in 1999 Nepal's government decided to increase domestic airfares by 10 percent in January 2000 and a further 10 percent in September 2000. The government had originally planned a 20 percent price increase in January 2000, but the Trekking Agents Association of Nepal (TAAN) complained of the impact such a large sudden increase would have on their business and successfully lobbied the government to stagger the price increase.

the preponderance of non-Sherpa owned trekking agencies in Kathmandu, as well as the large role that foreign travel companies play in booking visitors on trips to the Everest region, some economic leakage still occurs.

In addition to the business lost to non-Sherpa owned trekking agencies, the proliferation of trekking agencies in Kathmandu has also created a highly competitive, price-sensitive business environment that limits the profitability of Sherpa-owned trekking agencies. Indeed, the highly competitive nature of Kathmandu's trekking agency sector has kept prices charged by trekking agencies nearly the same for well over a decade.[110] For foreign visitors with limited time and little or no experience trekking in Nepal, trekking agencies provide a welcome degree of convenience and peace of mind. For travelers with more flexibility and a greater desire and capacity for independence, however, the services offered by a trekking agency are largely superfluous, as the proliferation of Sherpa-run lodges and restaurants in the Everest region gives tourists the choice of foregoing the services of a trekking agency altogether. Indeed, Khumbu Sherpas' development of an extensive lodge infrastructure catering to tourist visitors has been the single most important factor in countering economic leakage to trekking agencies and keeping a significant portion of the economic benefits from tourism in local hands.

As described in Chapter Two, however, in 2006 the Trekking Agents Association of Nepal (TAAN) pushed for the adoption of a new tourism policy that promises to direct more business to urban-based trekking agencies and, in the process, increase the leakage of tourism revenues away from local areas like Khumbu. Under the proposed Trekking Registration Certificate (TRC) scheme, foreign tourists trekking in any area of Nepal would be required to obtain a TRC permit from a TAAN office and hire the services of a guide employed by a registered trekking agency. While the cost of the permit is only 250 rupees (about US$3.50), the added bureaucracy of

---

110 Murari Sharma, managing director of Kathmandu-based Everest Parivar Expeditions, personal communication, 1999 & 2006

the TRC scheme and its onerous and expensive requirement of hiring a registered guide in Kathmandu or Pokhara is unlikely to have any positive effects on the number of independent foreign travelers choosing to visit Nepal and will, if successfully implemented, undoubtedly hurt the ad hoc hiring of local guides in Lukla and potentially decrease the proportion of independent tea-house trekkers in the Khumbu region.

Employment, Provisions, & Lodges

Nepal tourism consultant Wendy Brewer Lama estimated in 1991 that tourism was generating about US$2.4 million annually for the local Khumbu economy, with tea-house trekkers spending an average of US$10 per day on locally purchased lodging and food and with self-contained trekkers spending an average of US$7-8 per day locally on supplemental food, camping charges, and incidentals.[111] In addition, both tea-house and self-contained trekkers spend considerable amounts on wages for their porters and guides, with many higher earning guides being Sherpas from the Solu-Khumbu region. Despite the large number of trekking staff and guides hailing from Solu-Khumbu, Nepali tourism researchers Kamal Banskota and Bikash Sharma estimated that porters comprised over 70 percent of trekking support staff,[112] and since nearly all porters are from outside Khumbu, their wages represent a form of economic leakage from the local area.

While a large portion of the money spent by self-contained trekking groups is spent on labor and provisions obtained outside of Khumbu, a significant amount of the money spent by tea-house trekkers goes to Khumbu residents who have established local tourism businesses. Indeed, probably the most significant way that Khumbu residents have succeeded in limiting leakage of tourism income has been through their opportunistic and aggressive development of lodges catering to tea-house trekkers. Even so, with tourism in the

---

111 Brewer 1991, as cited in Odell & Brewer 1998 p.196
112 Banskota & Sharma 1995 p.50

Everest region so heavily dependent upon outside labor and provisions, the necessary employment of non-Khumbu residents and sale of imported goods to tourists naturally result in regional economic benefits that, strictly speaking, represent leakage from the local Khumbu economy.

In the case of both tea-house and self-contained trekking, most of the food, drinks, and other supplies consumed by visitors are brought in from outside Khumbu. Although many Khumbu lodge owners cultivate 'kitchen gardens' that enable them to sell vegetables to their guests as well as to passing self-contained camping groups, Khumbu's high altitude environment limits both the amount and the variety of foods that can be grown locally to serve the tourism market. While agricultural limitations are what they are, economic leakage due to employment of outsiders is something that Khumbu residents can and have endeavored to control. In this regard, consider the power of the trekking sirdar – a large percentage of whom hail from Khumbu – relative to the porters under his or her employ. Due to the abundance of portering labor in Nepal, it is not uncommon for sirdars to extract for themselves a portion of their porters' budgeted wages as a 'commission' in return for hiring them for a trek. Furthermore, the frequent use by Khumbu sirdars of local yak and zopkio as pack stock has replaced the employment of considerable numbers of porters from outside the region, thereby helping to stem the leakage of revenues from Khumbu. Indeed, as described in Chapter Three, a sirdar typically enjoys a great deal of discretion over where a trekking group's money is spent. As such, the relations that local tourism entrepreneurs build with trekking agency staff are of critical importance to Khumbu residents' involvement in tourism because trekking agencies and their staff decide whether Sherpas (and which Sherpas) are hired to staff their trips as well as what lodges and shops their clients patronize while in Khumbu.

Fees Collected by the National Government
The fees collected by Nepal's government for tourist visas, trekking and climbing permits, and entrance to Sagarmatha National Park

represent an additional source of economic leakage of tourism dollars away from Khumbu. According to climbing writer Ed Douglas, "the Nepalese government sees trekking and mountaineering as a milch cow from which as much money has to be extracted as quickly as possible in Kathmandu."[113] Indeed, all of the visa, trekking and climbing permit, and national park entrance fees collected from visitors go directly to the government. The leakage represented by these government imposed fees has been limited, however, by the reasonably low cost of tourist visas, park entrance fees, and trekking permits, as well as by the government's allocation of a portion of Everest climbing permit fees back to conservation and development activities in the Khumbu region. In addition, as mentioned in Chapter Six, Nepal's government passed a law in 1993 that allows for up to fifty percent of national park entrance fees to be used for local community development projects in and around park areas, which, if this policy were followed for Sagarmatha National Park, would further reduce the degree of economic leakage arising from the government's collection of entrance fees from visitors.

Visas are required for foreign visitors to Nepal from all countries except India. Prior to 1999, a tourist visa cost US$15 for 15 days and could be extended for US$1 per day thereafter. In addition, a trekking permit was required to visit the Khumbu region at a cost of US$5 per week for the first 4 weeks and US$10 per week thereafter. Effective in 1999, the Nepal government changed the cost of a tourist visa to US$30 for 2 months and US$50 per month thereafter, and a trekking permit was no longer required to visit the popular Khumbu, Annapurna, and Langtang regions. Although the entrance fee for Sagarmatha National Park initially remained unchanged at 650 Nepali rupees (about US$10) per person, the government later raised the park entrance fee to 1,000 rupees.[114] The changes made in 1999

---

113 Douglas 1997 p.107
114 Likewise, the entrance fees for other popular trekking destinations in Nepal were also raised. In 2000, Nepal's King Mahendra Trust for Nature Conservation raised entrance fees for the Annapurna Conservation Area and the Manaslu Conservation Area from 1,000 to 2,000 Nepali rupees.

resulted in lower government fees for many Khumbu visitors. For example, under the new structure, government fees for a typical Khumbu trekker's 3-week stay in Nepal cost US$40 instead of US$46, and an 8-week stay cost US$40 instead of US$126. Despite the lower fees paid by longer staying tourists, Nepal's government expected its overall fee revenues to increase since short-term visitors, who comprise the majority of foreign visitors, paid higher visa fees under the new structure (e.g. a stay of less than two weeks required a US$30 visa rather than a US$15 visa).

It is also worth mentioning that when trekking permits were no longer required to visit Khumbu, Kathmandu-based trekking agencies lost a means of luring independent travelers to sign up for self-contained group treks. Prior to the elimination of trekking permit requirements for Khumbu, it was necessary for visitors to obtain trekking permits through a registered trekking agency, giving such agencies an opportunity to convince trekkers to join a self-contained tour organized by the agency. Since, relative to self-contained trekkers, a greater percentage of the money spent by tea-house trekkers generally stays in the Khumbu economy, the trekking permit policy change of 1999 may have indirectly served to limit some of the leakage from Khumbu tourism.

Permit fees for climbing Mount Everest have been a major exception to the Nepal government's maintenance of government-imposed fees at relatively low levels for Khumbu visitors. Between 1992 and 1996, Nepal's government raised the permit fee for climbing Mount Everest from a flat US$2,500 per group to a minimum of US$70,000 per group of up to seven climbers plus US$10,000 for each additional climber beyond seven. But while the high fees the government collects from Everest climbers represents a huge source of economic leakage from Khumbu, not all of these fees actually leak from the region. On paper at least, thirty percent of Mount Everest climbing permit fees are supposed to be used to fund the operation of Sagarmatha National Park,[115] and, as mentioned in

---

115 Gurung 1998

Chapter Five, between 1994 and 1998 a small portion of Everest climbing permit fees were allocated to the Sagarmatha Pollution Control Committee (SPCC), a local NGO staffed by Sherpas that has conducted a variety of community conservation and development projects in the Khumbu area.

Types of Visitors, Their Relations with Local Hosts, & Their Concerns

The kind of tourism that the Everest region is most famous for, namely climbing and trekking in the high mountains, has drawn a certain type of visitor to Khumbu, a self-selected lot not only willing to endure but attracted by the rustic facilities and physically rigorous nature of trekking and climbing in a rugged mountainous region. This self-selection process has served to filter out certain kinds of tourists and favored visitors who have generally been outdoor-oriented, environmentally conscious, and relatively non-materialistic and easy-going.

Although the demographics have changed somewhat in recent years due to the political turmoil in Nepal, the aftereffects of the September 2001 terrorist attacks in the U.S., and the increasing number of Asian tourists visiting Nepal, the bulk of Khumbu visitors have traditionally been middle class mountain enthusiasts from North America, Europe, Japan, Australia, and New Zealand. Unlike in the neighboring country of Bhutan where tourist visitors are charged a mandatory US$220 per day for a fixed itinerary or in the Nepal region of Upper Mustang where foreigners are charged US$70 per day merely for a trekking permit, Nepal's government has not charged exorbitant fees for visiting the Everest region. Meanwhile, competition among Khumbu lodge owners has kept prices for local food and lodging, even in the more remote locations, affordable by Western standards. As a result, middle class and even budget travelers have not been discouraged from visiting Khumbu. Sherry Ortner, an anthropologist whose research among the Sherpas of Solu-Khumbu spanned three decades, noted that the types of visitors who have primarily been drawn to the Everest region over the years include educated, liberal-progressive, conservation minded, socially aware, respectful, and friendly middle-class people from relatively egalitarian societies. Ortner went on to suggest that these visitor qualities, and especially their intersection with the good-natured qualities so often attributed to the Sherpas, have positively affected relations between foreign visitors and their Sherpa hosts.[116]

In addition to the process of self-selection that has influenced the type of tourists visiting Khumbu, the style of tourism that has developed in Khumbu has also played an important role in relations between visitors and hosts. Because of the length of time most foreign trekking and climbing visitors spend in Khumbu and the rustic nature of their travel there, visitors and Sherpas have a better chance to get to know each other than is typical of many tourist-host encounters elsewhere. Trekking and climbing visitors rarely stay for less than a couple weeks, and many stay for several weeks. This not only provides more time for getting acquainted, it also provides an incentive for getting along well. Since both visitors and Sherpas know they will spend a relatively long period of time together, a greater investment in the relationship seems warranted. Plus, the demanding nature of trekking, climbing, and rustic living at high altitude reduces barriers and establishes bonds of commonality and shared hardship. As anthropologist Jim Fisher noted about trekking in Khumbu, the "exigencies of living break down what might otherwise be a formal, distant relationship" between tourists and their Sherpa hosts and guides.[117] Nepal trekking guidebook author Stephen Bezruchka added his observation that "special bonds develop over the course of a trek between the trekker and his or her employees because the work involves social interaction as well as physical labor. These bonds are more like the implicit trust of kinsmen than of unrelated people and are not found in most other types of tourism exchanges."[118]

---

116 Ortner 1990 pp.8-13, 17-18
117 Fisher 1990 pp.132-133
118 Bezruchka 1997 pp.87-88

Given all the circumstances described above, it perhaps comes as no surprise that the majority of Khumbu visitors have treated the Sherpas and their culture with respect and sought out their company, friendship, and favor rather than treating them like lesser beings or exploiting them. For example, early British Himalayan climbing expeditions honored Sherpas who performed well under the hardships and dangers of mountain climbing by awarding them with so-called 'Tiger' medals as an expression of appreciation, respect, and admiration for the services they provided.[119] Although early British climbing expeditions of the 1920s and 1930s have been accused of exhibiting a colonial master-servant attitude toward their Sherpa and Tibetan employees, post-World War II European climbing expeditions were reportedly much more egalitarian in their treatment of the Sherpas, often including Sherpas as equal members of their summit teams. The effect this had on relations between foreign visitors and their Sherpa hosts can be seen in various accounts given by Sherpa climbers. For example, the famed Tenzing Norgay Sherpa, who began climbing with Western expeditions in 1935 and had been quite outspoken about his dislike for the way the colonial-era British had treated him and other Sherpa climbers,[120] wrote of a 1947 Swiss climbing expedition in northern India:

> I had enjoyed this expedition with the Swiss. For the first time on an expedition I felt on equal terms with my employers; indeed I felt towards them not as Sherpa to Sahib [i.e. master], but rather as friends.[121]

And, about a subsequent British expedition in 1950, Tenzing Norgay had the following to say:

---

119 Adams 1996 pp.13-15, Ortner 1998 p.30
120 Ortner (1998 p.28) noted that Tenzing Norgay (1955 p.204) had "a difficulty and a problem" with British climbers because they drew an essentially racist line between themselves and "Easterners." And Tenzing Norgay refused to attend a congratulatory reception at the British embassy in Kathmandu after his successful first ascent of Mount Everest because he had been snubbed previously by the British embassy.
121 Tenzing Norgay Sherpa 1955 p.135, as quoted in Ortner 1998 p.28

[...] this was one great thing about the expedition. There was no distinction at all between climbers and [Sherpa] porters. We did the same work, shared the same burdens, everyone helping everyone else when help was needed. We were not like employers and employees, but like brothers.[122]

Similarly, another Sherpa climber named Ang Tharkay recalled fondly in his autobiography the egalitarian style of the 1950 French expedition to Annapurna:

The [French climbers] like us put their shoulders to the wheel and made no distinctions between themselves and us concerning the work. It was a new and very agreeable experience; this mode of acting filled us with enthusiasm. Never, in any expedition we had been on, had we had such an impression of freedom and intimacy with the sahibs. We felt that a tight link of comradeship united us to them.[123]

Such egalitarian treatment of Sherpas by foreign visitors resulted in tremendous bonds formed between the visitors and their Sherpa hosts. Accordingly, over the past five decades relations between Sherpas and foreign visitors have generally been characterized by close friendships and mutual admiration, as exemplified by the following excerpts from accounts written by Western climbers. In one example, Gabriel Chevally, a member of the 1952 Swiss expedition to Mount Everest, recalled:

[...] we did well to treat [the Sherpas] as brothers. They didn't take long to understand that we were then friends. [...] between these people and ourselves a relationship has been clearly established that is something more than a material contract. [...] they bring us not only their muscles, but also their willingness, their pleasure and their participation [...] for deep within them is a taste and an aptitude for exceptional activities.[124]

Likewise, Will Siri, a member of the 1963 American expedition to Mount Everest, wrote:

---

122 Tenzing Norgay Sherpa 1955 p.142, as quoted in Ortner 1998 p.28
123 Ang Tharkay Sherpa 1954 p.148, as quoted in Ortner 1998 p.27
124 Dittert, Chevally, & Lambert 1954 pp.214-215, as quoted in Miller 1965 (1997 reprint p.21)

[...] once you start climbing with the Sherpas they become far more a part of the team, and friends, than they are on the approach march. There [is] less distinction between Sahib and Sherpa.[125]

While anthropologist Robert Miller observed in the mid-1960s:

[...] a Sherpa and one or another sahib could develop real comradeship. [...] those Europeans who accepted the Sherpas as individuals in a joint enterprise found that an almost mystic closeness could develop between them, even surmounting language barriers.[126]

And in the mid-1970s, after trekking tourism had been firmly established in Khumbu, anthropologist Christoph von Fürer-Haimendorf suggested that the good relations built between Sherpas and foreign climbers had positively affected the reputation and value of Sherpas among foreign trekkers as well:

[...] thanks to the admiration and affection felt by western mountaineers for their Sherpa companions, [Sherpas] have acquired a certain mystique, and western tourists have come to regard Sherpas as indispensable helpers not only in mountain-climbing but also on any trek in areas where experience in camping, resourcefulness and reliability are essential qualities in guides and tour-servants.[127]

To the present day, the egalitarian treatment of Sherpas by Western visitors has continued to positively influence relations between them, as climbing author David Roberts described in writing about Eric Simonson, a leading American expedition organizer, in 1999:

[Simonson's] care for the Sherpas is exemplary. He makes sure the Sherpas are treated as equals, puts the highest priority on their safety, and pays the best wages. As a result, his Sherpas are intensely loyal to him.[128]

---

125 Will Siri, as quoted in Hornbein 1965 p.66
126 Miller 1965 (1997 reprint p.21)
127 Fürer-Haimendorf 1974 p.112, 1975 p.104
128 Anker & Roberts 1999 p.58

While in Khumbu in 1999, I had the opportunity to talk with a Western trekking agency owner and guide who had visited Khumbu some forty times over the past 18 years. He stated that he had never during that time witnessed a "bad encounter" between a Sherpa and a tourist visitor (although he had heard of a few such instances attributed to visitors' drunkenness and aggressive behavior), and he contrasted this with the many negative interactions he had observed between hosts and visitors in tourist destinations in other parts of the world.[129]

Since the first scholarly research of the Sherpa people by Westerners began in the 1950s, Khumbu has been, according to a popularly quoted line by Edmund Hillary, "the most surveyed, examined, blood-taken, anthropologically dissected area in the world."[130] As mentioned in Chapter Seven, the nearly constant flow of academic researchers who have poured into the Everest region over the years has had the effect of encouraging continuity in Sherpa culture and reinforcing Sherpa self-confidence and pride by virtue of the researchers' interest in photographing, filming, interviewing, and writing about the Sherpas. There are few indigenous groups in the world that have been as studied or as celebrated as the Sherpas of Khumbu, and the wealth of photographs, films, books, and articles about the community has led to a keen appreciation of Sherpa culture among foreigners. As a result, visitors from around the world have shown the community a high level of respect and admiration, and some have even donated generous sums of money earmarked for supporting the continuation of Sherpa cultural traditions. In writing about interactions between tourists and Native Americans, Hollinshead suggested that successful cultural tourism depends, at least in part, on the development of an understanding of the indigenous culture by the visitor.[131] Regardless of how one might define 'successful' cultural tourism, there can be little doubt that

---

129 Hooman Aprin, personal communication, 1999
130 as quoted in Rowell 1980 p.61, Stevens 1993a p.1
131 Hollinshead 1992, as cited in Butler & Hinch 1996 p.7

visitors' respect and admiration for Sherpa culture have been a positive force in its vibrant continuity.

In addition to the respect they have shown for Sherpa culture, many visitors to the Everest region have also demonstrated their concern for the fragility of the natural environment by supporting local environmental conservation and restoration efforts.[132] Awareness and concern for tourism's impact on the environment were expressed by some visitors even before the Everest region was opened to trekking, as reflected in Thomas Hornbein's account of the first American climbing expedition to Mount Everest in 1963:

> [In Nepal's mountains,] wilderness, as western man defines it, did not exist. Here man lived in continuous harmony with the land [...]. He used the earth with gratitude, knowing that care was required for continued sustenance [...]. It was an enviable symbiosis. The expedition surely must have affected this balance: a thousand porters living off the produce of the land, a mixing of peoples, the economic stresses, the physical impact itself. Although we touched each place [along the approach to Mount Everest] for only a day and then moved on, I wondered how many such passings could be made before the imprint would become indelible.[133]

Since the early days of the environmental movement in the West, many visitors to the Everest region have been critical of the impacts tourism has had on the Khumbu environment.[134] Concern about the effects that trekking and climbing tourism were having on local environments in the Himalaya even prompted some Western visitors to publish environmentally conscious guidebooks with titles like *Trekking Gently in the Himalaya: Essential Tips for Trekkers* and *Gentle Expeditions: A Guide to Ethical Mountain Adventure*.[135] These books and others like them have educated and advised visitors about responsible ways to visit the Himalaya and encouraged the development of sustainable tourism practices among trekkers and

---

132 compare with Brower 1991b p.67
133 Hornbein 1965 p.58
134 compare with Fisher 1990 p.109
135 Brewer 1992 & McConnell 1996

climbers. In addition, a number of Khumbu visitors have gone beyond merely touring the area in a responsible fashion. As mentioned above, many foreigners have provided material support for local cultural and environmental conservation projects, and some have even founded or gone to work for NGOs carrying out conservation and/or development projects in Khumbu as well as other regions of the Himalaya.

Over the past couple of decades, the concept and to some degree the practice of a kinder, gentler, greener form of 'eco-tourism' has made inroads in Nepal and other Himalayan countries. Nowadays practically every trekking and climbing guidebook to Khumbu and other destinations in the Himalaya emphasizes the importance of responsible tourism. The result has been more educated, aware, and conscientious visitors and, in many cases, more responsible tour company policies and practices. Indeed, a number of Western travel companies, in addition to trying to improve working conditions and benefits for their Nepali employees and minimize negative impacts on local cultures and environments, are actively 'giving back' to the areas in which they operate trips by supporting local conservation and development projects.[136] These values are beginning to catch on, albeit slowly, among Nepali tour companies as well, and the Trekking Agents Association of Nepal (TAAN) has begun promoting responsible tourism practices among its members.[137]

---

136 Some examples of Western travel companies pledging to assist local areas in which they operate trips include Wilderness Travel funding fifty percent of the operating budget of the Namche Dental Clinic; Journeys International planting trees, supporting schools, and helping restore the Thame monastery; Peter Owens Treks and Tours subsidizing the installation of solar power systems and healthier, more efficient stoves with chimneys; KE Adventure Travel supporting schools; Geographic Expeditions (formerly Inner Asia) supporting orphanages; Erickson Travel funding the hiring of school teachers; and Summit Climb International supporting health care and education in Solu-Khumbu.
137 TAAN 1998 & 1999

Protected Area Designation & Management

As the popularity of trekking and climbing in the Everest region mushroomed in the early 1970s, concerns grew among Western observers regarding the effect that the rising numbers of tourists were having on the local environment. From 1970 to 1973 alone, the annual number of tourists visiting Khumbu rose from a few hundred to well over three thousand, while their accompaniment of porters and guides meant that the overall number of visitors was more than double that number. As described in Chapter Five, pressured by international donors to enact strict environmental conservation measures to preserve the world-renowned Everest region, the Nepal government gazetted the entire Khumbu watershed and declared the area a national park in 1976.

Given the pressure that the unprecedented number of visitors was putting on the environment, outside observers had feared that the Sherpas themselves were unable to provide effective stewardship over the area's fragile natural resources without outside help. Regardless of whether those fears warranted such draconian outside intervention, strict management of the Khumbu region as an environmentally protected area has served to check the decline of local natural resources such as forests and wildlife. Although the initial frictions that developed between local residents and park authorities could likely have been avoided or at least lessened if local residents had been given more opportunities to participate in early park planning and management, the park's protection, restoration, and education programs have undoubtedly benefited the Khumbu environment and in the process preserved the region's popularity among tourists.

The national park continues to be the watchdog for environmental problems in Khumbu and also plays a key role in regulating tourism development in the region. For example, park authorities expressed concern over the tremendous growth of visitor numbers during the latter 1990s and the effect this was having on the local environment. Park authorities I spoke with in 1999 referred to the rapid growth in visitor numbers over the previous two years as "unsustainable" and suggested that measures needed to be taken to curb the negative effects of continued growth. As mentioned in Chapter Five, park rangers pointed to the significant increase in the size of local zopkio herds due to their profitable use as pack stock for tourists and claimed that the zopkio were overgrazing rangeland resources relied upon by park wildlife such as Himalayan tahr and musk deer. In light of their primary objective to protect wildlife, park authorities had recommended to Nepal's government that it consider placing a limit on the annual number of visitors to Khumbu, despite the realization that imposing such a limit would be unpopular among local residents economically reliant upon tourism.[138] While the subsequent drop in Khumbu visitor numbers due to Nepal's Maoist insurgency rendered the park's concerns moot for awhile, the peace accord signed by Maoist and government leaders in November 2006 is likely to spur a resurgence of tourism in Nepal that could lead to record numbers of visitors in the Everest region. While the outcome of the park's recommendation to limit tourist numbers remains to be seen, one thing seems clear – the national park will continue to play an important role not only in regulating environmental impacts in Khumbu but also in influencing tourism there.

Local Hosts' Participation in Conservation & Development Activities

Khumbu Sherpas had developed their own unique forms of natural resource management long before tourists began visiting Khumbu. While the stress caused by thousands of annual visitors contributed to the demise of traditional resource management systems in many Khumbu villages, the nationalization of Nepal's forests and the creation of Sagarmatha National Park were even bigger factors. But a combination of initiative on the part of local residents and sensitivity on the part of park administrators to the rights of the local population has enabled the Sherpas to achieve a relatively high level of

---

138 Sagarmatha National Park rangers Uddhab Dhungana and Shyam Krishna Shrestha, personal communication, 1999

involvement in local conservation activities.[139] Sherpa conservation efforts have complimented those of the national park and in some areas, most notably pollution, have far surpassed what the park itself has been willing or able to do. Indeed, while park authorities place their priorities on wildlife and forest protection, local residents are motivated to focus on curbing pollution and cleaning up trash since these problems are highly visible to visitors and affect the popularity of tourism. As researcher Ivan Pawson noted in the 1980s, "most Sherpas are fully conscious of the direct relationship that exists between preservation of the natural environment and continued tourist expenditure in Khumbu."[140]

Since local residents established their own NGO, the Sagarmatha Pollution Control Committee (SPCC), in the early 1990s, Sherpas have been actively involved in local conservation activities. Through trash clean-up efforts, awareness campaigns, educational programs, and enforcement of local environmental policies on glass bottles and expedition trash, the SPCC has had a tremendously positive effect on the aesthetic environmental quality of Khumbu and, importantly for tourism, on visitors' perceptions of it. And the SPCC's efforts have extended beyond pollution control to include a number of community service activities, some of which have also benefited tourist visitors and positively influenced tourism in Khumbu. For example, the SPCC has helped with the construction of village water supply systems, the maintenance of trails and bridges, the building of toilets along trekking routes, and the enlargement of Namche's weekly market, which has itself turned into a tourist attraction. In addition, the SPCC has provided essential support to local monasteries, which also serve as major tourist draws, and has helped improve the service provided by tourist lodges by conducting training classes for lodge owners and workers. The SPCC has also played an important role in local reforestation efforts and in establishing local kerosene depots as an alternative to fuel-wood use. All in all, Sherpa

---

139 By 'relatively,' I mean in comparison to other indigenous groups whose homelands have become national parks and/or international tourist destinations.
140 Pawson *et al.* 1984b p.246

involvement in local conservation and development activities has played a significant role in enhancing the Khumbu environment as well as the amenities and services available to tourists.

National Government's Encouragement of Tourism Development

As illustrated by the chronological history of tourism, conservation, and development in Nepal and Khumbu presented in Chapter Two, Nepal's government has played an important role in encouraging and facilitating the development of tourism in Khumbu as well as other areas of the country. By opening the country's borders to foreign visitors in the 1950s, Nepal's government ushered the mountain kingdom into the 20th century and quickly attracted the attention of climbers, journalists, researchers, and development workers from around the world. And by allowing foreigners to climb the country's lofty mountains and to explore and publish information about areas previously unknown to the outside world, Nepal's government effectively whet the appetite of an entire generation of visitors enthralled by the mystery and grandeur of the country and drawn by the stories and photographs of its peoples and landscapes.

Following the visit of the first commercial tourists to Nepal in 1955, Nepal's king was reported to have quickly realized the great economic potential of tourism and the important role it could play in generating much needed foreign exchange earnings to finance the country's development. Soon thereafter, Nepal's government established its own national airline as well as a department of tourism to facilitate the development of this previously untapped asset. The door was opened to mass tourism in the Everest region when the government opened the area to trekking tourists in 1964, a move which coincided with the construction of an airstrip near Khumbu and the founding of Nepal's first trekking agency. It was also at this time that Nepal's government began including tourism in its official economic planning and began actively encouraging the development of tourism infrastructure by providing loans and tax breaks to hotel developers and seeking foreign aid for the expansion of the country's international airport. By the late 1960s, Nepal's king had created a high profile tourism development committee chaired by members of the royal family, and tourism development had risen in importance to become one of the top three priorities in the country's official development planning.

The 1970s were a time of tremendous growth for tourism in both Nepal and the Everest region. Annual tourist arrivals in Nepal grew by more than four-fold over the decade, while in Khumbu the annual number of visitors grew from just a few hundred to nearly five thousand. Nepal's growth in popularity as a tourist destination was helped by government efforts to promote tourism through more liberal visa policies, the creation of a system of national parks (including one in the Everest region), continued financing of hotel construction in Kathmandu, further expansion of the country's international airport and national airline fleet, and air service agreements with a growing number of international carriers. To facilitate these efforts, Nepal's king raised tourism planning and administration to the level of an official ministry within the government.

After a slowdown in the growth of visitor numbers in the 1980s, which was due at least in part to a political stand-off with India and Nepal's subsequent democratic revolution, tourism development was given renewed attention by the government in the 1990s. The government announced a goal of increasing the annual number of foreign visitors by four-fold, from about 250,000 in 1990 to one million by the year 2000. In trying to meet this goal, the government embarked on a series of tourism promotion campaigns aimed at easing restrictions due to transportation bottlenecks and administrative hassles. During this time, Kathmandu's airport was again further expanded to accommodate more international flights, and the government's monopoly on domestic air service was lifted to allow private carriers to expand the country's air service capacity. In the Everest region, the increased availability of flights to Lukla was a crucial factor in the tremendous growth of Khumbu tourist numbers during the 1990s. Bolstered by the government's promotional efforts, annual foreign tourist arrivals in Nepal nearly doubled over the course of the decade, and annual visitor numbers in Khumbu nearly tripled to well over 20,000.

At the turn of the new millennium, the growth in Khumbu tourist numbers showed no signs of slowing, with a record 25,000 visitors in 2001. The massive increase in tourists even led to concerns among national park staff about possible overcrowding and the effects this could have on the local environment. But this was by no means the first time such worries had arisen. In 1991, when annual Khumbu visitor numbers exceeded 10,000 for the first time, the respected Nepali scholar and civic leader Harka Gurung recommended that the yearly number of visitors to Khumbu should be limited to 15,000 with a monthly limit of 3,000.[141] And in 1993, researcher Stan Stevens claimed that, although the Khumbu environment and Sherpa culture had withstood the impacts of tourism thus far, many Sherpas themselves were concerned that continued tourism growth might overwhelm the adaptive capabilities of the local environment and culture.[142]

Whether Nepal's government will ever decide to impose limits on tourism in the Everest region will likely depend to a large extent on the length of the government's perspective. A shorter-term perspective would no doubt favor the government's continued milking of the Khumbu tourism cash cow with little heed for potential future problems. A longer-term perspective, however, would perhaps convince the government to acknowledge cultural preservation advocate David Robinson's warning about the growth of tourism in the Everest region:

> [...] tourism policy which places emphasis solely on increasing tourist volume and accumulating revenue is insufficient and potentially self-defeating. [...] the Nepalese government continues to operate either in ignorance of impacts, or in the belief that the

---

141 Gurung 1991, as cited in Rogers & Aitchison 1998 p.35
142 Stevens 1993b p.426

Sherpa culture is sufficiently resilient to withstand the presence of large, and increasing, numbers of tourists.[143]

Only time will tell what perspective the government will take in the future, but if the past is any indication, it will likely be a self-serving one, as the following example suggests.

In the early 1990s, citing growing environmental degradation on Mount Everest as a result of garbage left by climbing expeditions as well as what he termed overcrowding on the mountain, Sir Edmund Hillary lobbied Nepal's government to restrict the number of climbing expeditions allowed on the mountain each year and even proposed that all climbing on the mountain be halted for five years to let the environment recover.[144] In 1992, Nepal's government decided to limit the number of permits granted for climbing Mount Everest to one expedition per each climbing route on the mountain. The new restriction lowered the number of permits issued for Mount Everest from 20 in the 1992-1993 fiscal year (July to June) to 9 permits in 1993-1994. However, to more than make up for any lost revenues from a smaller number of expeditions paying permit fees for Mount Everest, the government simultaneously raised the permit fee four-fold, from a flat fee of US$2,500 per group to a minimum fee of US$10,000 per group plus US$1,200 for each additional climber beyond nine.[145] The very next year, upon realizing that foreign climbing expeditions were perfectly willing to pay higher fees for the now limited number of permits available to climb the world's highest mountain, Nepal's government raised the permit fee again, this time to a minimum of US$50,000 per group plus US$10,000 for each additional member above five. By the next year, Nepal's government could not resist the temptation of cashing in on the pent up demand for Mount Everest permits. It abolished the number limit on permits and once again raised the permit fee, this time to a minimum of US$70,000 per group plus US$10,000 for each additional climber beyond seven. As a result, the number of permits issued for Mount

143 Robinson 1992 p.128
144 Ali 1994, as cited in Bishop & Naumann 1996 p.323
145 National Geographic Society 1992 p.142, Banskota & Sharma 1995 pp.34-35

Everest rose from 4 in 1994-1995 to 18 the following year, and the revenues collected by the government for climbing permits in the Everest region more than quadrupled to well over US$1 million.[146] As an aside, it is interesting to note that the May 1996 disaster on Mount Everest, which resulted in the deaths of eight climbers, was blamed on overcrowding on the mountain as well as the guiding of wealthy but inexperienced clients willing to pay the higher permit costs.

Lack of Local Tourism Planning & Management

In his foreword to a book presenting several case studies of tourism in the Himalaya, Egbert Pelinck, the former director of the International Center for Integrated Mountain Development (ICIMOD) in Kathmandu, wrote: "with few exceptions, the promotion of tourism [in the Himalaya] until recently has lacked a specific focus on local community development and environmental stability."[147] I would argue that tourism in Khumbu is no exception to this. Although Nepal's government has broadly encouraged tourism development by expanding transportation infrastructure in the country and national park authorities have mitigated environmental impacts by regulating local natural resource use, there has been no tangible planning or management of tourism *per se* in Khumbu. Neither the national government, the national park, local government authorities, nor local residents have formulated any definitive, comprehensive plans for managing tourism in the Everest region at a local or regional level.

As a result, tourism in Khumbu has largely developed in an ad hoc fashion as determined by demand-driven market forces and according to the initiative of whoever has possessed sufficient will, connections, and capital to start a tourism business. In many ways, the lack of planning and management of tourism development has favored entrepreneurial Sherpas and allowed them to involve

---

146 information from Reuters' Kathmandu climbing correspondent Elizabeth Hawley, as cited in Rogers & Aitchison 1998 pp.43-44
147 Pelinck 2000 p.vii

themselves in it according to their own ambitions, abilities, and preferences. This may seem to have been a blessing for the Sherpas, and indeed some Sherpas have grown extremely wealthy through the unstructured and individualistic development of tourism in the Everest region. However, the lack of tourism planning and management has not been a blessing for all Khumbu residents. For some it has actually made life more difficult than might have been the case if tourism had been more carefully planned and managed with the egalitarian ideals of widely spread benefits and community betterment in mind. As the many examples provided in this book should have made clear by now, tourism in the Everest region has been accompanied by a plethora of negative implications for the Sherpa people and the Khumbu environment. But it didn't necessarily have to be that way, nor does it need to be that way in the future. What I am suggesting is that many of the negative effects of tourism could be avoided or at least tempered through enlightened and effective planning and management that is focused on widespread community benefit rather than individual gain.

Former ICIMOD tourism expert Pitamber Sharma recognized the important role the private sector can play in tourism development when he wrote that "the private sector, guided as it is by the motive of profit, has the advantage in providing competitive services, running facilities and, given a conducive policy environment, taking advantage of the entrepreneurial opportunities opened up by tourism."[148] But Sharma also pointed out "the importance of proactive intervention and supply-side planning to make tourism relevant to the concerns of local economic, environmental and socio-cultural development"[149] and suggested that planning and intervention were necessary to guide and regulate market-driven tourism development since "the social cost of damaging the fragile ecological and cultural system of the mountains is rarely internalized by the private sector."[150] As Kurt

---

148 Sharma 2000b p.174
149 Sharma 1998 p.34
150 Sharma 2000b p.174

Luger, a Himalayan tourism researcher and chairman of the Austrian NGO, Eco-Himal, noted:

> [...] the laissez-faire development of tourism is capable of excesses that can lead to severe environmental damage. [...] tourism as a development agent requires careful planning in order to avoid possible negative effects. It has to focus on the ecological aspect of all activities, should be considered not as the central business but rather as a side income to the existing subsistence economy, and should establish a partnership with the local communities and make them responsible actors, all with the objective of long-term benefit for those who live in tourist areas.[151]

And, as researchers Paul Rogers and John Aitchison concluded in their study of Khumbu tourism, "under free-market conditions, the various actors involved are unable to guide the tourism economy towards the social and environmental ideals of ecotourism. In this regard there is a need for stronger planning and coordination."[152]

As this book has shown, unplanned and unmanaged market-driven tourism development in the Everest region has led to a number of problems for local residents and for the environment. Many of the economic and social problems in particular have stemmed from an unequal distribution of tourism's economic benefits, a situation that Nepali tourism researchers Kamal Banskota and Bikash Sharma have generally associated with poor or inadequate planning of tourism development.[153] For example, not all Khumbu residents have had the same opportunities to participate in tourism, and the resulting disparities in income have increased economic differentiation in the region. And since tourism has led to significant inflation of local prices for food and other goods and services, life has become more difficult for those with little or no involvement in tourism. Meanwhile, those local residents who are involved in tourism have become heavily reliant upon it and are therefore vulnerable to the potential for a downturn in tourism business or an increase in

---

151 Luger 2000a pp.ix-x
152 Rogers & Aitchison 1998 p.74
153 Banskota & Sharma 1995 pp.2, 123

economic leakage. It is possible that differences in the tourism opportunities available between and within villages could have been (and still could be) smoothed out through a sensitive and egalitarian approach to regional planning and management of tourism development. And it is also possible that local economic disparities could be lessened through an equitable investment of fees collected from tourists into community development projects aimed at benefiting all residents of the region.

In addition to lessening economic differentiation, enlightened planning and management of tourism development could also prove useful in diminishing other problems that have arisen in Khumbu. For example, purely market-driven tourism development has had a number of negative sociocultural implications for Sherpas, as suggested by the elevated levels of stress, competitiveness, and friction that have arisen from the individualistic pursuit of tourist dollars. Longtime Khumbu observer Christoph von Fürer-Haimendorf contrasted Khumbu Sherpa society before and after the opening of the region to trekking tourism and claimed that, because of the private and uneven nature of economic opportunities available through tourism, Sherpa individuals had begun focusing on their own personal economic success at the expense of the social solidarity that had previously reigned supreme:

> Sherpa villages [in the 1950s] used to be characterized by their unity of purpose and the absence of factionalism. The interests of the villagers were seldom in conflict [...] and economic advancement and the build-up of prestige were considered in the terms of a man's position within the village-community. Now [in the 1970s], however, the focus of many Sherpas' interests has shifted to the [personal] economic possibilities provided by tourism and success in this sphere.[154]

Fürer-Haimendorf offered as an example the building of the luxury Everest View Hotel near Syangboche in the 1970s by Japanese developers. According to Fürer-Haimendorf, the project created

---

154 Fürer-Haimendorf 1975 p.98

considerable conflict among local residents as individuals took positions supporting or opposing the project according to the personal benefits they expected to receive from it. Likewise, Khumbu researcher Barbara Brower claimed that "the economic opportunities of the tourist era [...] are opportunities available to the individual entrepreneur [and as a result] individuals have flourished at the expense of community interests." Brower went on to suggest that a system was needed "to address this incompatibility of private and public interest."[155]

In the absence of careful, community-oriented planning or management of tourism, local residents have suffered from the intrusive and insensitive behavior of some visitors, which in certain cases has resulted in conflict and discord, and Sherpa culture has come under considerable pressure to adapt to Western and Nepali influences brought about through or as a result of tourism. In addition, the individualistic pursuit of tourism has done little to counteract, and instead probably has exacerbated, the dangerous and often exploitative working conditions associated with climbing and trekking tourism. Furthermore, the Khumbu's local natural resources and environment initially suffered from unsustainable use and pollution in the absence of comprehensive planning and management, and local residents were given little say in the resulting knee-jerk restrictions that protection-oriented national park authorities placed upon local resource use.

---

155 Brower 1991b p.169

CHAPTER 9

Conclusion: Lessons from the Everest Region

This study of tourism in the Everest region has covered a lot of ground, and perhaps it would be helpful to look back at where it has taken us. Chapter One started with a general introduction to the value of mountain regions and the threats faced by such areas and their indigenous inhabitants, as well as the concept of tourism as an alternative means of economic development and environmental conservation. The second chapter presented a geographical and historical background of the Khumbu and its indigenous Sherpa residents, as well as an overview of contemporary tourism in the Everest region. Upon this foundation, the next six chapters delivered a proverbial mountain of information on the effects that tourism has had in Khumbu and the key factors that have influenced tourism development there. So much information, in fact, that I think it would be helpful to summarize the more notable findings before drawing some overall lessons from the study.

Summary of Tourism Effects in the Everest Region

As illustrated by the wealth of material presented in Chapters Three through Seven, tourism has had myriad effects on the environment of the Everest region and on the economy, personal well-being, self-determination, and sociocultural continuity of its inhabitants. Perhaps most important of all, tourism has provided local residents with welcome economic opportunities that helped make up for the decline of trans-Himalayan trade beginning in the 1960s. Many Khumbu Sherpas have achieved significant economic benefit from their involvement in tourism, as they have consistently been able to secure the highest paying tourism jobs and have nearly monopolized local tourist lodge and shop development. Some Khumbu Sherpas have further expanded their involvement in tourism by investing in pack animals and by starting trekking agencies based in Kathmandu. And a large number of Khumbu Sherpas have also been successful in establishing relationships with foreign benefactors who have assisted them with a variety of business, education, healthcare, and other expenses.

In many ways, their heavy involvement in tourism has enabled the Sherpas of Khumbu to maintain a relatively high degree of self-determination. If economic opportunities in tourism had not become widely available to the Sherpas following the curtailment of trans-Himalayan trade, they would certainly not have the same level of economic independence they enjoy today. Tourism allowed the Sherpas to continue inhabiting the high valleys of Khumbu as landowners and entrepreneurial business people rather than being forced to migrate to the lowlands as landless laborers dependent upon employment by others. And the Sherpas' enthusiastic welcoming of and enterprising involvement in tourism allowed them to largely control its development rather than having it control them, as it likely would have had tourism development been left to outsiders.

Due to their heavy involvement in tourism, many local residents have become extremely reliant on tourism economically and therefore vulnerable to any downturn in the tourism market. Despite their reliance on tourism, Sherpas living in Khumbu have not given up traditional agricultural practices and local food production has not diminished. But although they have continued to grow and consume potatoes, cash earned from tourism also enables them to import large amounts of food grains and other goods from outside the region.

Through their participation in tourism, many formerly poor Khumbu residents have been able to improve their economic and social status. Despite this, the more rewarding opportunities in tourism have been largely limited to entrepreneurs with ample capital and social connections, and thus tourism has actually widened the degree of economic differentiation in the region. Tourism has also caused considerable inflation in the prices of goods and services purchased by both tourists and local residents. Although locally produced goods have also increased in price due to high demand caused by tourism, inflation has especially affected imported goods. Because of the inherent limitations of agropastoral production in Khumbu, local residents have long been unable to meet all of their own needs and must rely on imported foods and other items. Thus, economic differentiation and inflation caused by tourism have made life more difficult for those Khumbu residents who have not had the opportunity to become heavily involved in tourism.

For those Khumbu Sherpas who have been involved in tourism, increased affluence has improved their ability to satisfy basic needs and has raised the quality of their diets, clothing, and housing. In addition, because of the attention their home region has received as a result of tourism, Khumbu residents have been the beneficiaries of an inordinate amount of externally sponsored development projects. Some of the more noteworthy among these include electrification projects providing household electricity to most villages, a well equipped hospital and health clinic both staffed by Western doctors, a modern dental clinic, schools in every village, a plethora of modern bridges and village water supply systems, and a busy airport just a day's walk away.

Despite these and other improvements to local facilities and services, involvement in tourism seems to have raised levels of stress, competitiveness, and unhappiness among at least some Khumbu Sherpas. In addition, dangerous work with mountain climbing expeditions has resulted in a great many deaths among Sherpas, while the rigors and unfair labor relations of trekking tourism have also subjected many Nepalis from outside of Khumbu to frequent exploitation and occasional injury or death.

Although the amount of deforestation in Khumbu attributable to tourism pales in comparison to the historical clearing of local forests to create pasturelands for livestock, if it were not for strict natural resource conservation measures imposed by outside authorities, it is likely that tourism-related tree-felling would eventually have had a serious impact on forest cover in Khumbu. As the number of tourist visitors grew, demand increased for firewood as well as for lumber used in constructing tourist lodges and the new larger homes of Sherpas who have grown wealthy from tourism. But while tourism may have posed an environmental threat, it should also be pointed out that tourism and the conservation concerns of foreign visitors were actually the driving forces behind the designation and management of the Khumbu region as a national park. But while national park regulations have been largely successful in reducing the problems of deforestation and wildlife poaching in Khumbu, this has transferred pressure to forests outside the park in the adjacent Pharak region, which now serves as the source of firewood and lumber for Khumbu tourism businesses. In addition, the growth of tourism has put added pressure on shrub cover in alpine regions of Khumbu where juniper has been collected for use as fuel.

Although successful from a conservation perspective, the restrictions on local resource use imposed by the national park have formed the single greatest impediment to Sherpa self-determination, which has led to considerable conflict and distrust between local residents and park staff. Though the national park was forced upon the indigenous residents of Khumbu with neither their consent nor their significant participation in its early planning or management, park planners made unprecedented efforts to accommodate the Sherpas' continued inhabitance and use of their homeland, and Sherpas who received training abroad were later given lead roles in the park's administration. And, in recent years, efforts by park authorities to increase local participation have allowed the Sherpas greater community-level involvement in regulating local forest use. From the start, tourism played a key role in the progressive nature of the park's policies, which can be attributed not only to the widespread attention given to the area because of tourism but also to the involvement of foreign visitors in the park's development.

The growth of tourism has increased the popularity among Khumbu Sherpas of keeping yak-cattle crossbreeds for use as pack stock and led to a significant change in the composition of Khumbu livestock herds as well as in local pastoral practices. These changes have put added pressure on lower altitude pastures in the proximity of villages. The effect of this increased pressure on grazing resources within the national park has caused concern among park officials charged with protecting wildlife that are also reliant upon those resources.

The development of tourism has resulted in greatly expanded local infrastructure (primarily tourist lodges), as well as increased pollution and sanitation problems in Khumbu. The pollution problems have in recent years been lessened by the clean-up efforts of a Sherpa-run NGO, as well as national government policies regulating the handling of trash by mountain climbing expeditions. Although tourism has been a primary cause of pollution in the region, tourism has also been an important factor in raising awareness of and ensuring attention to pollution problems.

While the influx of nearly 400,000 foreign visitors and a markedly increased Nepali presence over the past fifty years have had undeniable and lasting effects in the Everest region, Khumbu Sherpas have not abandoned their traditional culture or fundamentally reoriented their society. Rather, the Sherpas seem to have gradually adapted to modern Western and Nepali influences by choosing to adopt certain features of those societies while steadfastly maintaining many aspects of their own unique cultural identity. Although tourism has been intrusive and has hastened the spread of Western and Nepali influences in Khumbu, it has in many ways also served to encourage, preserve, and strengthen local cultural traditions. Foreigners' interest in, praise for, and financial support of Sherpa culture and religion have reinforced their value among Sherpas and been important factors in their vibrant continuity. In addition, increased wealth from tourism has allowed many Khumbu Sherpas themselves to afford greater financial support of local cultural and religious institutions, which have flourished in Khumbu during the past couple of decades.

Involvement in tourism has taken many Sherpas away from home for long periods, either to climb or trek in other regions of the

Himalaya or to attend to trekking businesses based in Kathmandu. Despite the regular, prolonged absence of many Sherpas, success in tourism has served as an important means for Sherpas to gain recognition and respect in their communities, and many successful tourism entrepreneurs have also managed to serve as local civic leaders. Since trekking and climbing employment among Khumbu Sherpas has generally been dominated by males, females have taken on a greater portion of household labor and families have increased their reliance on hired agricultural labor, with cash wages paid out of tourism earnings. Because of the absence of many Khumbu men working in tourism and the increased importance of women in the household and in running tourist lodges, Khumbu women have achieved higher public status in Sherpa society, and it has become more common for Sherpa women to hold important positions in local government.

Money earned through involvement in tourism has allowed many Khumbu families to send their children to Kathmandu or abroad for a better education than is available in Khumbu. The widespread raising of children outside of Khumbu may prove to bring the most change of all to Khumbu society, as there is concern among older Khumbu Sherpas that these children are not learning the Sherpa language and will not wish to return to live in Khumbu. In addition to the out-migration of children, entire families have left Khumbu, primarily to pursue business opportunities in Kathmandu or abroad. However, it is hard to blame tourism for the increasing out-migration of affluent Sherpas when one considers that without tourism there would likely have been instead an out-migration of impoverished Sherpas.

As this study has shown, tourism has had an incredibly broad variety of effects in Khumbu, some which could be considered detrimental to the local people or environment and others which could be considered beneficial. It is also important to keep in mind that tourism has affected different local residents in different ways. Indeed, some people have benefited tremendously from tourism, while others have hardly benefited at all. Likewise, some facets of the environment have been harmed, while others have actually been helped as a result of tourism. If anything, what this study has illustrated is that the effects of tourism in Khumbu present a mixed picture. As such, it would be far too simplistic a generalization to conclude that tourism has been 'good' or 'bad' or that it has 'succeeded' or 'failed.' Even if one were to somehow conclude that tourism had been 'good' for Khumbu thus far, threats of additional and more significant detrimental effects certainly persist. Acknowledging both the beneficial and the detrimental impacts of tourism, Khumbu researcher Stan Stevens suggested in the early 1990s that it was "too early to proclaim that the region is a model for achieving local development through tourism."[1] A few years later, in recognition of the growing problem of deforestation in Pharak, researchers Paul Rogers and John Aitchison concluded that "in spite of many encouraging features, tourism as it has developed in Solu-Khumbu could not be described as a model form of eco-tourism."[2]

But even if Khumbu does not provide the ideal model for other areas to emulate, it does at least provide a clear example of the myriad ways that tourism development can affect the local population and environment of a formerly remote mountain region. And it also provides an excellent opportunity to learn from the mistakes and successes that have marked tourism development there over the past fifty years.

Summary of Key Factors Influencing Tourism in the Everest Region

In Chapter Eight, I presented a set of ten key factors that have influenced the development of tourism in the Everest region and that help explain the manner in which tourism has evolved there as well as the ways it has affected local residents and the environment. Similar to the way the above section summarized the more noteworthy effects

---

1   Stevens 1993b p.426
2   Rogers & Aitchison 1998 p.95

of tourism, this section summarizes the key factors that have influenced the way tourism has developed in Khumbu.

The Everest region has become recognizable around the world based upon a number of popular icons associated with the area, including the world's highest mountain, the legendary Sherpa people, the esoteric practice of Tibetan Buddhism, the mythical sanctuary of Shangri-La, and the mysteriously elusive abominable snowman. These icons, together with a well-deserved reputation for breathtakingly scenic beauty, have drawn legions of tourists to Khumbu. Looking for adventure and/or epiphany, streams of foreign visitors have brought along their pocketbooks and their good intentions and left behind their trash and the example of a way of life that has seemed as exotic and appealing to the Sherpas as the Sherpas' way of life has seemed to visitors.

Realizing the potential of tourism as a means of generating revenue and foreign exchange earnings, the government of Nepal has given high priority to encouraging tourism development in the country. When Nepal's doors were first opened to foreign visitors in the 1950s, the country's transportation infrastructure and accommodation facilities were woefully inadequate to support significant numbers of tourists. In the decades that followed, Nepal's government, with the support of foreign aid, focused on expanding the country's tourist facilities and also promoted tourism by liberalizing visa policies, creating a system of national parks, and opening additional areas of the country to foreign visitors. The government's efforts to expand infrastructure and encourage tourism have been a critical factor in the growth of Khumbu tourist numbers over the past few decades.

The Sherpas of Khumbu were motivated out of necessity to engage whole-heartedly in tourism in order to replace their previous economic reliance on trans-Himalayan trade, a business that declined markedly just as tourism was getting its start in Khumbu. The Sherpas' success in this regard was aided by a bundle of characteristics that made the group particularly well suited to tourism. Their initiative and spirit of enterprise, familiarity with Westerners, and cultural self-confidence, together with a charming manner, paved the way for the Sherpas' unrivaled degree of involvement in Himalayan mountain climbing and trekking tourism. The group's virtual domination of tourism employment and service provision in Khumbu enabled them to largely control the development of tourism there.

The Sherpas' effective control over tourism development in the Everest region was also helped to a great degree by several factors that limited the scale and growth of tourism there and that, in turn, dissuaded most outside business interests from investing in the region. Among the factors that limited the scale and growth of tourism development in Khumbu were the general lack of infrastructure in Nepal, the physically demanding nature of travel in the Everest region, the limited duration of the tourist season due to seasonal weather extremes, and the limited and difficult access to Khumbu (which has become less of an issue in recent years due to improved air service).

The Sherpas' great involvement in and control over tourism in Khumbu has also enabled them to retain a significant amount of the money spent by tourist visitors. While airline tickets and permit fees collected by Nepal's government represent significant tourist expenditures that are not captured locally, economic leakage from Khumbu's tourism economy has been considerably less than in many other tourism destinations. This has been largely due to the Khumbu Sherpas' domination of higher paying tourism jobs, their widespread use of local pack animals to transport loads for tourists, their development of an extensive tourist lodge and shop infrastructure, and their ownership of many Kathmandu-based trekking agencies.

Although the Sherpas have played a prominent role in shaping tourism development in Khumbu, they have not been alone in this process. The tourists who have visited Khumbu have had much to do with the way tourism has developed and the manner in which it has affected local residents and the environment. The rugged nature and reasonably affordable cost of travel in the Everest region have attracted certain types of visitors over others. The typically middle-class, outdoor-oriented, environmentally-conscious, and non-materialistic visitors have, over the course of relatively long stays in the area, generally formed friendly, respectful relations with their hosts and been sensitive to and concerned about the effects of tourism on the local culture and environment. Indeed, many Khumbu visitors have donated money for and some have even become personally involved with projects focused on local conservation and development issues. As a result of concerted efforts by visitors of this type, the concepts of environmentally and culturally responsible tourism have begun to make a mark among visitors, hosts, and travel companies not only in the Everest region but throughout the Himalaya.

Concerns raised by Westerners about the effect that tourism was having on the local environment were a primary factor in the designation of Khumbu as a national park. Another factor was the Nepal government's desire to attract foreign aid and promote tourism. Whatever the original motivations may have been, the national park's protection of local forests and wildlife have significantly benefited the Khumbu environment and, in the process, contributed to the region's continued popularity among tourists. But while the national park's environmental conservation efforts have been laudable, the park has done little to counteract the growing problem of pollution. Realizing that increasing amounts of trash were threatening the popularity of tourism, local residents took the initiative in forming a grassroots NGO, the Sagarmatha Pollution Control Committee (SPCC), to address the problem of waste disposal by conducting periodic clean-ups and raising awareness of waste disposal issues among both local residents and visitors.

Although Nepal's government has sought to encourage tourism development and, at the same time, protect the Khumbu environment from the effects of tourism, the actual planning and management of tourism in the Everest region has been virtually nonexistent. The resulting ad hoc tourism development that has occurred has been driven almost entirely by market forces and the initiative of enterprising local residents. The lack of planning and management of tourism has had important consequences for the style of tourism that has developed, as well as the effects that tourism has had on local residents and the environment. On the one hand, the lack of planning and management has allowed entrepreneurial Sherpas the freedom to pursue tourism enterprise according to their own abilities and ambitions. Driven by the potential rewards available from individualistic involvement in tourism, Khumbu residents have enjoyed a great deal of self-determination in their pursuit of wealth, status, and improved personal well-being. On the other hand, the lack of planning and management has also allowed a plethora of negative effects to develop unchecked, not the least of which includes disparate access to tourism opportunities exacerbating economic differentiation among the local population. If careful planning and management of tourism had occurred and been driven by sensitive and egalitarian community priorities, many of the negative effects associated with tourism might have been averted, tempered, or at least dealt with more effectively.

Lessons from the Everest Region

A cynic is not merely one who reads bitter lessons from the past;
he is one who is prematurely disappointed in the future.
(Sydney Harris, prominent American journalist, 1917-1986)

Lessons are gained from an understanding of the problems and successes of the past, and this study has described a number of problems and successes associated with tourism in the Everest region. I would like to end by pointing out several lessons that can be gleaned from this study and, from those lessons, making some recommendations regarding the future direction of tourism in Khumbu that I believe could prove helpful in avoiding similar problems and spreading the benefits of success among the entire local community.

Limited Scale & Gradual Growth of Tourism along with Environmental Protection

The limited scale and relatively gradual growth of tourism in the Everest region during its first four decades and the environmental protection conferred through national park designation have limited the negative effects often associated with tourism in fragile mountain environments occupied by indigenous peoples. Because tourism developed gradually in Khumbu, local residents were able to consciously adapt their culture and society to the changes that gradually came with it instead of being overwhelmed. The great degree of local involvement and control over tourism development, and hence the limited amount of economic leakage, would not have been possible if tourism had grown quickly and attracted a throng of outside business interests. The gradual expansion of tourism allowed local residents to refine the skills and build the capital necessary to succeed in establishing tourism businesses of their own without having to compete at an early stage with (and perhaps lose out to) more politically powerful and heavily capitalized outsiders. And the gradual growth and small scale of Khumbu tourism during its first couple of decades had a rather small effect on the environment. As tourism went through a growth phase in the early 1970s, however, signs of mounting environmental pressures were noticed. But these were countered by the establishment of a national park and the policies put forth to protect the area's natural resources.

Although the growth of tourism in Khumbu was relatively gradual during its infancy, visitor numbers began growing much more rapidly in the latter 1990s, especially just before the downturn in Nepal tourism that began in 2001 as a result of the country's Maoist insurgency. While tourist numbers had grown at an annualized rate of just 6 percent per year between 1974 and 1992, growth increased to 11 percent per year between 1992 and 1998, before exploding by 18 percent in 1999. With the marked improvement in Nepal's political situation following the rapprochement between government and Maoist leaders in 2006, a return to rapid, unmanaged growth in tourist numbers could bring renewed challenges for Khumbu residents and for the environment in both Khumbu and the neighboring region of Pharak.

In the latter 1990s, national park officials in Khumbu became alarmed by the rapid growth of visitor numbers and concerned that continued tourism expansion could exceed the region's carrying capacity and result in severe environmental degradation. Based on these concerns, national park officials recommended to Nepal's government that the entrance fee paid by tourist visitors to the park be raised and a limit on tourist numbers be imposed. Such actions would undoubtedly be unpopular with local residents economically reliant on tourism and could cause discord between Sherpas and the national park. In addition, a limit on visitor numbers would necessitate the development of a potentially unwieldy and difficult to manage entry permit quota system that could be subject to favoritism and corruption. Such a system would likely play to the power and government connections of influential Kathmandu-based trekking agents who might require Khumbu visitors to join their self-contained group treks in order to obtain entry permits, thereby reducing the proportion of tea-house trekkers and further hurting the local tourism economy.

Rather than charging exorbitant entrance fees to visitors and placing a limit on visitor numbers, I believe the tourism carrying capacity of the Everest region could be increased through better planning and management of the effects of tourism.[3] As one example of how this could happen, the harmful effect of tourism on the forests of Pharak could be lessened if all lodges were required to use electricity, kerosene, or other alternative sources of energy instead of burning wood.

In recommending a higher park entrance fee and a limit on visitor numbers, it seems that national park officials are suggesting that it is the visitors themselves who cause the bulk of the impact on the local environment. Based upon my understanding and experience of tourism in Khumbu and other areas of the Himalaya, I would argue that the numerous support staff, porters, and pack animals employed by visitors cause a greater environmental impact than the visitors themselves. Thus, the numbers of support staff, porters, and

---

3   Banskota & Sharma (1995 p.78) pointed out in their overview of mountain tourism in Nepal that tourism carrying capacity can generally be increased through proper planning and management of tourism.

pack animals employed need to be considered as well as the number of tourists when assessing the effects of tourism and proposing an appropriate carrying capacity for the Everest region. In the case of Khumbu, it might be wise to charge entrance fees according to the numbers of support staff, porters, and pack animals accompanying tourist visitors into the park. In this way, entrance fees might more accurately reflect the true environmental costs of tourist visits, and the additional entrance fee revenues could be used by the park and by local communities to counter the detrimental effects caused by the support staff, porters, and pack animals employed by tourists. Such an entrance fee scheme would also encourage tourist visitors and trekking agencies to minimize the number of support staff, porters, and pack animals employed on treks and therefore lessen the overall impact on the region. And entrance fees based upon numbers of support staff, porters, and pack animals might sway some potential self-contained trekkers to opt for tea-house style trekking instead, which would result in less leakage from the Khumbu economy, deliver more economic benefit to local residents, and reduce the exploitation of porters by trekking agencies and their staff.

Visitor Awareness & Responsibility

Because of the rustic and physically demanding nature of tourism in the Everest region, it has attracted tourists who don't mind enduring a little hardship and discomfort and who revel in close contact with nature and with a culture different from their own. The type of visitor generally drawn to Khumbu has contributed to the positive effects of tourism there, and many visitors have also conscientiously tried to minimize the negative effects of their visits. Relations between visitors and Sherpas have generally been marked by friendliness and mutual respect, and a number of visitors have even become Sherpa benefactors, providing financial assistance for things like education, health care, and starting a business. Most visitors have displayed a reverence for traditional Sherpa culture, and the respect and admiration that foreigners have shown for Sherpas have bolstered many Sherpas' self-confidence and self-esteem and aided their high degree of self-determination. What's more, a number of visitors have advocated and even championed local development projects that have significantly improved the well-being of Khumbu residents. In addition, many visitors to the Everest region have expressed concern for the environment, doing their utmost to minimize the negative effects of their visit by disposing of trash responsibly and discouraging the use of firewood.

As the popularity of climbing and trekking in the Everest region has grown, however, so have the demographics and diversity of the visitors. Around the world, mountain tourism has been thrust into the mainstream of popular culture by the international media's seeming obsession with Mount Everest, and as a result the types of visitors drawn to Khumbu have become more varied. What's more, as the number of comfortable lodges in Khumbu and the availability of flights to Lukla have grown, visiting the Everest region has become more desirable for and within the reach of more and more people. Fortunately, this demographic widening of the Khumbu tourist profile has coincided with a green revolution in the adventure travel business. Guidebook sermons, changing societal norms, and the peer pressure of fellow travelers have turned regular tourists into eco-tourists by promoting culturally and environmentally responsible behavior. Even so, an increase in the number of visitors to the Everest region poses the threat of greater pressure on the local environment and culture and greater potential for misunderstanding and discord between visitors and hosts.

Because of the central role visitors play in the effects tourism has on the local economy, environment, and culture, building and maintaining awareness and responsibility among visitors should be an important goal in the management of Khumbu tourism. I would suggest the production of a brief video (like the educational videos that visitors to Denali National Park in Alaska are required to watch) aimed at informing park entrants about the uniqueness and fragility of the local environment and culture, educating about the potential negative effects of irresponsible tourism, and encouraging tourists to take responsibility for their hired staff. The video could be made available in several languages, and every tourist as well as their support staff and porters could be required to watch the brief video upon entering the national park. Nepali trekking staff and porters do not have the same opportunities as foreign visitors to learn about responsible trekking practices, and they do not have the same societal norms or peer pressures influencing their behavior. As such, education is a critical element of minimizing the impact of hired staff. Another critical element is the expectations of tourists. If tourists directed their business toward lodges, trekking agencies, and hired staff that acted responsibly, then irresponsible ones would be forced to improve their standards or lose business. Visitors should see it as their responsibility to ensure that their money goes to lodges, trekking agencies, and hired staff that act conscientiously because, perhaps more than anything else, visitors' spending decisions can make a difference. Rhetoric alone is not enough. The responsible trekking guidelines advocated in Kathmandu by the Trekking Agents Association of Nepal have not translated into responsible behavior in the mountains, nor will they until responsible behavior and economic reward are linked together.

Empowerment of Local Residents

> Much of the current instability in the Himalaya is due to the fact that the forces of change that affect local communities have their genesis in distant societies and therefore lie outside the experiences of mountain people.
>
> (David Zurick & P. P. Karan, 1999,
> *Himalaya: Life on the Edge of the World*)

> Without including the people in the process of decision-making, success will remain elusive irrespective of how well-meaning the strategies are.
>
> (Syed Sadeque, 2000, *Issues in Mountain Development*)

The importance of involving local residents in directing the changes that affect their communities cannot be overstated. Many conservation and development schemes in the mountains of Nepal have failed because they did not consult with or gain the support and participation of local residents. And even those externally driven projects that have been considered successful have been so only in a qualified sense because the success has generally not been self-sustaining. Without establishing stewardship among local residents through involvement in and ownership of the project, a situation of dependency emerges in which local residents assume no responsibility for the project or its continuance. Even better than involving local residents in schemes developed by external agents is the empowerment of local residents to develop their own ideas and mold their own programs within the framework of local social and cultural institutions, beliefs, and norms. Empowered local residents are much more likely than external agents to realize, understand, and overcome problems facing their local economy, society, and environment and are much more likely to gain and maintain the support and cooperation of the entire community.

Since the 1950s, when Nepal began opening its doors to the world in order to enlist foreign aid to support the country's economic growth, conservation and development in Nepal has generally been an externally driven project. Only in recent years have conservation and development schemes begun to be initiated and run by Nepalis, although still largely with the support of foreign funding and expertise. The situation has been no different in the Everest region.

With the nationalization of Khumbu forests in the 1960s and the establishment of Sagarmatha National Park in the 1970s, the Sherpas' ability to manage their own resources was essentially stripped away. National authorities bowed to the environmental conservation imperatives of international funding agencies with little regard for local residents' natural resource needs or their knowledge of the environment. In Khumbu, traditional systems that had been used to manage local resources for centuries were undermined along with the Sherpas' sense of stewardship for the land. As a result, access to local natural resources became dependent upon the policies of the national park. But the national park had to rely on army patrols to enforce regulations that did not have the support of the local population, and relations between local residents and the park were marked by strife and distrust. Although Edmund Hillary's Himalayan Schoolhouse Expeditions of the 1960s endeavored to enlist the participation of the local population in their development projects, waves of similarly well-intentioned projects over the ensuing decades failed to empower or even to gain the participation of local residents in their schemes. Over time, many Sherpas grew dependent on the benevolence and initiative of outside assistance in charting the course of development in Khumbu. As a result, not only were the Sherpas disempowered to determine their own path of development, many lost any sense of responsibility for it and came to expect outsiders to provide things freely for them.

But the conservation and development dependencies that developed in Khumbu were not due to the Sherpas' inability to handle their own affairs. Indeed, the initiative, adeptness, self-determination, and control they have exhibited in tourism enterprise certainly suggest otherwise. Without undue interference from outsiders, local residents were independently empowered in tourism and took pride in its fruitful development. And when given the opportunity, the Sherpas have shown the same aptitude with conservation and development. Since a grassroots Sherpa-run NGO, the Sagarmatha Pollution Control Committee (SPCC), was established (albeit with outside support) in the early 1990s, local residents have accomplished a number of extremely laudable clean-up and community service projects that have helped to re-establish the Sherpas' sense of stewardship over their homeland.

I would argue that local residents of the entire Solu-Khumbu area (as well as elsewhere in Nepal and the Himalaya) should be intimately involved with and empowered to direct the planning and management of local tourism, conservation, and development activities. To accomplish this, Nepal's government should follow through and actually allocate a full fifty percent of national park entrance fees to local communities in the Solu-Khumbu area for community-oriented development projects, as was stipulated under Nepal's 1993 Buffer Zone Amendment. And to keep tourism development in the hands of local residents rather than outside business interests, perhaps policies should be considered that would protect the economic opportunities and self-determination of local residents by prohibiting outside developers from owning local tourism businesses.

Planning & Management of Tourism for the Benefit of the Community

This study has revealed a number of problems that have been associated with tourism in Nepal's Everest region, many of which I believe can be attributed to the lack of planning and management of tourism with the goal of widespread community benefit in mind. Despite the widely acknowledged problems it has brought to local communities and natural environments around the world, international tourism remains a significant and growing force affecting many developing countries, and it will almost certainly continue to be a major force in Nepal. Rather than discrediting tourism as a means of bringing about community development and environmental conservation, proponents of responsible tourism development have focused their efforts on reconceptualizing and reprioritizing the underlying goals of tourism. For example, Himalayan tourism expert Pitamber Sharma proposed that tourism development in mountain regions should facilitate what he referred to as the three cardinal concerns of community development: alleviation of poverty, regeneration of the environment, and empowerment of the local community.[4] In particular, Sharma stated that tourism could have positive implications for mountain regions

> if it contributed towards enhancing income as well as capabilities of the poor and the disadvantaged, if it encouraged the regeneration of the environment and an enhanced awareness for safeguarding the environment, and if it facilitated in empowering local communities by enabling them, as stakeholders, to have a say in the planning, prioritisation, implementation, monitoring and risk/benefit sharing of all common resource management and development activities, including tourism.[5]

---

4   Sharma 1998a p.24, Sharma 2000a pp.8-9
5   Sharma 2000a p.9

Sharma went on to point out that a number of studies in the Himalayan regions of Nepal, India, and Pakistan[6] have indicated that "the positive linkages between mountain tourism and the central development concerns in the mountains [...] are not spontaneous processes, but need to be deliberately planned and managed through an effective partnership with all concerned stakeholders and actors."[7]

Because of the unique character of the Everest region and the inordinate amount of outside attention it receives, any planning and management of tourism there will most likely involve a large number of stakeholders with a diversity of interests and opinions. But when it comes to involving people in decision making and setting goals, the indigenous local residents (including the people of Pharak as well as Khumbu) must remain the primary stakeholders for whose benefit any planning and management is done and whose voices are heard above all others. They are the ones with the most at stake, for they are the ones who will have to endure the costs of poor or short-sighted planning and management. The mistakes of the past should not be repeated. In all too many cases in Nepal, indigenous peoples have not been included in the planning and management of tourism, conservation, or development programs in their homelands. Instead, such planning and management, if they have occurred at all, have generally been carried out by self-interested government authorities together with whatever foreign agency has come up with the requisite funding. As an example, one need only look at the lack of involvement given to Khumbu residents in the initial planning of Sagarmatha National Park.

Tourism in the Everest region seems to be coming to an important juncture. As the Maoist insurgency that has hampered tourism in Nepal over the past several years appears to have drawn to an end, it seems likely that Khumbu tourist numbers will return to and exceed the record growth experienced prior to the escalation of violence in 2001. Prior to the downturn in tourism, the rapid growth

---

6   As examples, Sharma cited Banskota & Sharma 1995, Nazeer & Al Zalaly 1995, Sharma 1995 & 2000b, Sreedhar 1995.

7   Sharma 2000a p.9

of visitor numbers in the Everest region had begun to trigger a series of responses with the potential to radically change the future path of tourism in Khumbu. Perhaps the most portentous of these was the national park's recommendation to Nepal's government to set a limit on tourist numbers in order to protect local natural resources and wildlife. In addition, researchers and land managers had begun to acknowledge the amount of deforestation Khumbu tourism growth was creating in the neighboring region of Pharak and were considering ways to address the problem. Now, with a return to peace in Nepal, outside business interests will surely be taking another, closer look at the potential returns to be gained from their involvement in tourism in the Everest region. With tourism, the environment, and further business development at such crossroads, the need for planning and management of tourism is perhaps greater than ever. And indeed, the wheels have already been set in motion.

With the support and influence of funding from the United Kingdom, the future of Khumbu tourism and Pharak forest management is being mapped out by Western tourism, conservation, and development experts and Nepal government authorities. The importance of the funding for this process should not be ignored. Khumbu has been a national park for some thirty years, but a comprehensive tourism management plan had never before been created because of a lack of sufficient funding. And the implications the source of the funding has for this process should not be ignored either. The location of the initial meetings – London – did not augur particularly well for the likelihood of significant participation by Khumbu residents in the planning. I think the important question that needs to be asked is who and what exactly are the plans intended to benefit. If the planning is intended to benefit the local community, as I hold that it absolutely should, then it should be conducted locally with the full input and participation of local residents and with full appreciation of the many effects that tourism has had in the Everest region and the key factors that have influenced tourism there. And *that*, I put forth, is the bottom line on tourism on top of the world.

Bibliography

Adams, Vincanne. 1988. "Modes of Production and Medicine: An Examination of the Theory in Light of Sherpa Medicinal Traditionalism." *Soc. Sci. Med.* 27(5): 505-513.

Adams, Vincanne. 1996. *Tigers of the Snow and Other Virtual Sherpas: An Ethnography of Personal Encounters*. Princeton University Press: Princeton, New Jersey.

Ahluwalia, Major H.P.S. 1982. *Eternal Himalaya*.

Ali, Aamir. 1994. "Introduction." *Environmental Protection of the Himalaya*. Edited by Aamir Ali. 9-28. Indus Publishing: New Delhi.

Anker, Conrad and David Roberts. 1999. *The Lost Explorer: Finding Mallory on Mount Everest*. Simon & Schuster: New York.

Aris, Michael. 1975. "Report on the University of California Expedition to Kutang and Nubri in Northern Nepal in Autumn 1973." *Contributions to Nepalese Studies*. 2(2): 45-87. Kathmandu.

Aris, Michael. 1979. *Bhutan: The Early History of a Himalayan Kingdom*. Aris & Phillips: Warminster, England.

Aris, Michael. 1990. "Man and Nature in the Buddhist Himalayas." *Himalayan Environment and Culture*. N.K. Rustomji & Charles Ramble (eds). Indian Institute of Advanced Study in association with Indus Publishing Company: New Delhi.

Armington, Stan. 1997. *Trekking in the Nepal Himalaya*. Lonely Planet Publications: Hawthorne, Australia.

Arnold, David. 1998. "A Sherpa Breaks Barriers." *The Boston Globe* (newspaper). 13 November 1998.

Associated Press. 1998. "King Birendra Decides Against Early Elections." 17 December 1998. The Associated Press: Kathmandu.

Associated Press. 1999a. "Sherpa Sits Atop Everest 21 Hours." 10 May 1999. The Associated Press: Kathmandu.

Associated Press. 1999b. "Even After 800 Climbs, Everest Still Attracts Adventurers." 8 June 1999. The Associated Press: Kathmandu.

Associated Press. 2000a. "Sherpa Women Set Out for Mount Everest." 8 April 2000. The Associated Press: Kathmandu.

Associated Press. 2000b. "Tibetans Protest in Nepalese Capital." 10 March 2000. The Associated Press: Kathmandu.

Athans, Peter. 1999. "The Big E: 800 People Have Climbed It and So Can You." *Climbing: The Everest Issue* (magazine). September 1999. 188: 78. Primedia Publications: Carbondale, Colorado.

Bajracharya, D. 1983. "Deforestation in the Food/Fuel Context: Historical and Political Perspectives from Nepal." *Mountain Research and Development.* 3(3): 227-240.

Baker, Ian. 2004. *The Heart of the World: A Journey to the Last Secret Place.* Penguin Press: New York.

Banskota, Kamal & Bikash Sharma. 1995. *Mountain Tourism in Nepal: An Overview.* Mountain Enterprises and Infrastructure Series 95/7. Center for Resource and Environmental Studies. ICIMOD: Kathmandu.

Banskota, K. & M. Upadhyay. 1991. "Impact of Rural Tourism on the Environment, Income, and Employment in the Makalu-Barun Area." *The Makalu-Barun Conservation Project.* Report 17. Nepal Department of National Parks and Wildlife Conservation and Woodlands Mountain Institute: Kathmandu.

Basnet, Khadga. 1992. "Sagarmatha (Mt. Everest) National Park: Conservation for Sustainable Development." *Contributions to Nepalese Studies.* 19(1): 121-127. Tribhuvan University Centre for Nepal and Asian Studies: Kirtipur, Nepal.

Basnet, Khadga. 1993. "Solid Waste Pollution Versus Sustainable Development in High Mountain Environment: A Case Study of Sagarmatha National Park of Khumbu Region, Nepal." *Contributions to Nepalese Studies.* 20(1): 131-139. Tribhuvan University Centre for Nepal and Asian Studies: Kirtipur, Nepal.

Bass, Dick, Frank Wells, & Rick Ridgeway. 1986. *Seven Summits.* Warner Books: New York.

Baumgartner, F. *et al.* 1978. "Tourism and Development in Nepal: Impacts of Trekking-Tourism in Hill Areas." Report of a field survey in Autumn 1977. Zurich, Switzerland.

BBC News. 1998a. "Everest Bottle Ban." 15 August 1998. BBC World News Service: South Asia.

BBC News. 1998b. "Nepal: Instability Breeds Poverty." 31 December 1998. BBC World News Service: South Asia.

BBC News. 1998c. "Nepal's Power Struggle Set to Continue." 06 November 1998. BBC World News Service: South Asia.

BBC News. 1999a. "Nepal Heads for Early Poll." 15 January 1999. BBC World News Service: South Asia.

BBC News. 1999b. "Nepal To Ban Cigarette and Alcohol Ads." 05 January 1999. BBC World News Service: South Asia.

Bernbaum, Edwin. 1980. *The Way to Shambhala: A Search for the Mythical Kingdom beyond the Himalayas.* Anchor Press/Doubleday: New York.

Bernbaum, Edwin. 1997. *Sacred Mountains of the World.* University of California Press: Berkeley, California. Originally published in 1990 by Sierra Club Books: San Francisco, California.

Bezruchka, Stephen. 1997. *Trekking in Nepal: A Traveler's Guide.* The Mountaineers Press: Seattle, Washington.

Bishop, Barry C. 1963. "How We Climbed Everest." *National Geographic* (magazine). 124(4): 477-508. National Geographic Society: Washington, D.C.

Bishop, Brent. 1999. "How Green Are We?" *Climbing: The Everest Issue* (magazine). September 1999. 188: 56. Primedia Publications: Carbondale, Colorado.

Bishop, Brent & Chris Naumann. 1996. "Mount Everest: Reclamation of the World's Highest Junk Yard." *Mountain Research and Development.* 16(3): 323-327.

Bishop, Brent & Chris Naumann. 1998. "The Mountain Environment." *The American Alpine Journal.* 40(72): 177-182. The American Alpine Club: Golden, Colorado.

Bishop, Brent & Chris Naumann. 1999. "The Mountain Environment." *The American Alpine Journal.* 41(73): 182-188. The American Alpine Club: Golden, Colorado.

Bishop, Naomi. 1998. *Himalayan Herders.* Harcourt Brace College Publishers: Fort Worth, Texas.

Bista, Dor Bahadur. 1972. *People of Nepal.* Second edition. Ratna Pustak Bhandar Publishers: Kathmandu.

Bjønness, Inger-Marie. 1979. *Impact on a High Mountain System.* Sagarmatha National Park: Kathmandu.

Bjønness, Inger-Marie. 1980a. "Animal Husbandry and Grazing, A Conservation and Management Problem in Sagarmatha (Mt. Everest) National Park, Nepal." *Norsk Geografisk Tiddskrift* 34: 59-76.

Bjønness, Inger-Marie. 1980b. "Ecological Conflicts and Economic Dependency on Tourist Trekking in Sagarmatha (Mt. Everest) National Park, Nepal: An Alternative Approach to Park Planning." *Norsk Geografisk Tiddskrift* 34: 119-138.

Bjønness, Inger-Marie. 1983. "External Economic Dependency and Changing Human Adjustment to Marginal Environment in the High Himalaya, Nepal." *Mountain Research and Development.* 3(3): 263-272.

Blaikie, Piers, John Cameron, & David Seddon. 1980. *Nepal in Crisis: Growth and Stagnation at the Periphery.* Clarendon Press: Oxford, United Kingdom.

Blower, John H. 1971. "Proposed National Park in Khumbu District." Unpublished report to the Secretary of Forests, His Majesty's Government of Nepal.

Blum, Arlene. 1980. *Annapurna: A Woman's Place.* Sierra Club Books: San Francisco, California.

Boone, Mike. 2000. "Peak Performance: Canadian Byron Smith Will Report Live from Top of Everest." *Montreal Gazette* newspaper, 18 March 2000. Montreal.

Bourdillon, F.W. 1908. "Another Way of Mountain Love." *The Alpine Journal.* 24(180): 160. London.

Brauen-Dolma, Martin. 1985. "Millenarianism in Tibetan Religion." *Soundings in Tibetan Civilization: Proceedings of the 1982 Seminar of the International Association for Tibetan Studies held at Columbia University.* Barbara Nimri Aziz & Matthew Kapstein (eds). Manohar Publications: Delhi.

Brewer, Wendy. 1991. "Tourism Report: Environmental Management and Sustainable Development in the Arun Basin." King Mahendra Trust for Nature Conservation: Kathmandu.

Brewer, Wendy. 1992. *Trekking Gently in the Himalaya: Essential Tips for Trekkers.* Sagarmatha Pollution Control Project & Sagarmatha National Park, Nepal.

Bromet, Jane. 1999. "The Days After: Going Home After Everest 1996." *Climbing: The Everest Issue* (magazine). September 1999. 188: 128-133, 192-195. Primedia Publications: Carbondale, Colorado.

Brower, Barbara. 1990. "Range Conservation and Sherpa Livestock Management in Khumbu, Nepal." *Mountain Research and Development.* 10(1): 34-42.

Brower, Barbara. 1991a. "Crisis and Conservation in Sagarmatha National Park, Nepal." *Society and Natural Resources.* 4(2): 151-163. Taylor and Francis: United Kingdom.

Brower, Barbara. 1991b. *Sherpa of Khumbu: People, Livestock, and Landscape.* Oxford University Press: New Delhi.

Brower, Barbara. 1996. "Geography and History in the SoluKhumbu Landscape, Nepal." *Mountain Research and Development.* 16(3): 249-255.

Bruce, C.G. 1924. *The Assault on Mt. Everest, 1922.* Second printing. London.

Burger, Viet. 1978. "The Economic Impact of Tourism in Nepal: An Input-Output Analysis." Ph.D. dissertation. Cornell University.

Butler, Richard & Thomas Hinch. 1996. "Indigenous Tourism: A Common Ground for Discussion." *Tourism and Indigenous Peoples*. Edited by Richard Butler & Thomas Hinch. 3-19. International Thomson Business Press: London & Boston.

Butt, Nathalie & Martin Price. 2000. *Mountain People, Forests, and Trees: Strategies for Balancing Local Management and Outside Interests*. Synthesis of an Electronic Conference of the Mountain Forum, April 12-May 14, 1999. The Mountain Institute: Harrisonburg, Virginia.

Byers, Alton. 1986. "A Geomorphic Study of Man-Induced Soil Erosion in the Sagarmatha (Mount Everest) National Park, Khumbu, Nepal: Report on the Activities of the UNU/MAB (Nepal) Mountain Hazards Mapping Project, Phase II." *Mountain Research and Development*. 6(1): 83-87.

Byers, Alton. 1987a. "An Assessment of Landscape Change in the Khumbu Region of Nepal Using Repeat Photography." *Mountain Research and Development*. 7(1): 77-81.

Byers, Alton. 1987b. "Landscape Change and Man-Accelerated Soil Loss: The Case of The Sagarmatha (Mt. Everest) National Park, Khumbu, Nepal." *Mountain Research and Development*. 7(3): 209-216.

Byers, Alton. 1996. "Historical and Contemporary Human Disturbance in the Upper Barun Valley, Makalu-Barun National Park and Conservation Area, East Nepal." *Mountain Research and Development*. 16(3): 235-247.

Byers, Alton. 1997. "Landscape Change in Sagarmatha (Mt. Everest) National Park, Khumbu, Nepal." *Himalayan Research Bulletin*. 17(2): 31-41.

Byers, Alton. 2003. "Landscape Change in Sagarmatha National Park." *Triumph on Everest: A Tribute from the Sherpas of Nepal*. Edited by Ang Rita Sherpa & Susan Höivik. 91-99. Mandala Bookpoint: Kathmandu.

Byers, Alton & Lhakpa Sherpa. 1991. "Review of Sherpas: Reflections on Change in Himalayan Nepal by James F. Fisher." *Mountain Research and Development*. 11(2): 170-171.

Byers, Elizabeth & Meeta Sainju. 1994. "Mountain Ecosystems and Women: Opportunities for Sustainable Development and Conservation." *Mountain Research and Development*. 14(3): 213-228.

Cameron, Ian C. 1984. *Mountains of the Gods: The Himalaya and the Mountains of Central Asia*. Century Publishing: London.

Carlson, Timothy. 1999. "Into Thick Air: Interview with Mt. Everest Climber Rick Wilcox." *RailRiders* (magazine). Summer 1999. 14-15. RailRiders: Cambridge, Massachusetts.

Carrier, Jim. 1992. "Gatekeepers of the Himalaya." *National Geographic* (magazine). December 1992. 182(6): 70-89. National Geographic Society: Washington, D.C.

Centre for Economic Development and Administration (CEDA). 1991. "Workforce Survey of the Accommodation and Catering Industry in Nepal." A project of the Hotel Management Tourism Training Centre with the technical cooperation of the International Labour Organization (ILO) and funding from the United Nations Development Programme (UNDP).

Chalmers, John. 1999a. "Maoist Violence Mounts Ahead of Nepali Polls." 02 May 1999. Reuters International News. Kathmandu.

Chalmers, John. 1999b. "Nepal Votes Amid Tight Security and Maoist Clashes." 03 May 1999. Reuters International News. Kathmandu.

Chessler, Michael. 1999. "After Thin Air: The Legacy of the 1996 Mount Everest Tragedy." *American Alpine Club Journal*. Edited by Christian Beckwith. 41(73): 171-177. The American Alpine Club: Golden, Colorado.

Childs, Geoffrey. 1999. "Refuge and Revitalization: Hidden Himalayan Sanctuaries (Sbas-yul) and the Preservation of Tibet's Imperial Lineage." *Acta Orientalia*. 60:126-158.

Choegyal, Lisa. 1998. *Nepal*. Insight Guides. APA Publications: Singapore.

Coburn, Broughton. 1997. *Everest: Mountain Without Mercy*. National Geographic Society: Washington, D.C.

Cravitz, Karen. 1999. "Off the Beaten Track: Monsoon Trekking in Nepal." *Himalayan News* (newsletter). 11: 3-7. The Himalayan Explorers Club: Boulder, Colorado and Kathmandu.

D'Amore, Lou. 1988. "Tourism: The World's Peace Industry." *Tourism: a Vital Force for Peace, Proceedings of the First Global Conference*. Edited by L. D'Amore & J. Jafari. 7-14. Lou D'Amore Associates: Montreal.

Denniston, Derek. 1995. *High Priorities: Conserving Mountain Ecosystems and Cultures*. Worldwatch Institute: Washington, D.C.

Diemberger, Hildegard. 1991. "Lhakama and Khandroma: The Sacred Ladies of Beyul Khenbalung." *Tibetan History and Language: Studies Dedicated to Uray Geza on His Seventieth Birthday*. Ernst Steinkellner (ed). Arbeitskreis fur Tibetische and Buddhistische Studien, Universitat Wien: Vienna.

Diemberger, Hildegard. 1993. "Gangla Tshechu, Beyul Khembalung: Pilgrimage to Hidden Valleys, Sacred Mountains and Springs of Life

Water in Southern Tibet and Eastern Nepal." *Anthropology of Tibet and the Himalaya.* C. Ramble & M. Brauen (eds). Ethnological Museum of the University of Zurich: Zurich.

Diemberger, Hildegard. 1997. "Beyul Khenbalung, the Hidden Valley of the Artemisia: On Himalayan Communities and their Sacred Landscape." *Mandala and Landscape.* A.W. Macdonald (ed).

Dittert, Rene, Gabriel Chevally, & Raymond Lambert. 1954. *Forerunners to Everest: The Story of the Two Swiss Expeditions of 1952.* Harper and Brothers: New York.

Douglas, Ed. 1997. *Chomolungma Sings the Blues: Travels round Everest.* Constable: London.

Douglas, Ed. 1999a. "Bittersweet Success: Tenzing Norgay Struggled from Humble Beginnings to the Top of the World and Thought Good Fortune Would Follow." *Climbing: The Everest Issue* (magazine). September 1999. 188: 122-123. Primedia Publications: Carbondale, Colorado.

Douglas, Ed. 1999b. "The Sherpas: Changing Times for Climbing's Unsung Heroes." *Rock and Ice* (magazine). June 1999. 93: 76-83. North South Publications: Boulder, Colorado.

Eckholm, Erik. 1975. "The Deterioration of Mountain Environments." *Science.* 189: 764-770.

Eckholm, Erik. 1976. *Losing Ground: Environmental Stress and World Food Prospects.* Worldwatch Institute. W.W. Norton & Company: New York.

Eco-Himal. 1995. *The Thame Hydro Power Plant: A Development Cooperation between Austria and Nepal.* Jagadamba Printing: Patan, Nepal.

Eco-Himal. 1999. *Eco-Himal in Khumbu.* Austrian Development Cooperation (Austrian Ministry of Foreign Affairs): Salzburg, Austria.

Ehrhard, Franz-Karl. 1994. "The Role of 'Treasure Discoverers' and Their Writings in the Search for Himalayan Sacred Lands." *The Tibet Journal.* 19(3).

Ehrhard, Franz-Karl. 1997. "A 'Hidden Land' in the Tibetan-Nepalese Borderlands." *Mandala and Landscape.* A.W. Macdonald (ed).

Fickeler, Paul. 1947. *Fundamental Questions in the Geography of Religions.* Translated from *Erdkunde: Archiv fur Wissenschaftliche Geographie.* 1: 121-144.

Fisher, James F. 1987. "Comments on Professor Dor Bahadur Bista's paper on 'Nepal's Society and Culture: Ethnic and Regional Diversity'." *Nepal: Perspectives on Development Issues.* Edited by Leo Rose, 17-22.

Occasional Paper No. 12, Center for South and Southeast Asia Studies. University of California: Berkeley, California.

Fisher, James F. 1990. *Sherpas: Reflections on Change in Himalayan Nepal.* University of California Press: Berkeley, California.

Fürer-Haimendorf, Christoph von. 1960. "The Role of the Monastery in Sherpa Society." *Ethnologica.* 2: 12-28. Cologne.

Fürer-Haimendorf, Christoph von. 1963. "Formation, Population and Exploration of the Everest Region." *Mount Everest.* Edited by Toni Hagen, Gunter-Oskar Dyhrenfurth, Christoph von Fürer-Haimendorf, & Erwin Schneider. Oxford University Press: London. Chapter reprinted as "The Sherpas of the Khumbu Region" in *Everest: The West Ridge,* by Thomas Hornbein. 1965. Sierra Club: San Francisco, California.

Fürer-Haimendorf, Christoph von. 1964. *The Sherpas of Nepal: Buddhist Highlanders.* University of California Press: Berkeley, California.

Fürer-Haimendorf, Christoph von. 1974. "The Changing Fortunes of Nepal's High Altitude Dwellers." *The Anthropology of Nepal.* Edited by Christoph von Fürer-Haimendorf. 98-113. Aris and Phillips: Warminster, England.

Fürer-Haimendorf, Christoph von. 1975. *Himalayan Traders: Life in Highland Nepal.* John Murray: London. 1988 paperback edition published by Time Books International: New Delhi.

Fürer-Haimendorf, Christoph von. 1984. *The Sherpas Transformed: Social Change in a Buddhist Society of Nepal.* Sterling Publishers: New Delhi.

Garratt, K.J. 1981. *Sagarmatha National Park Management Plan.* The New Zealand Department of Lands and Survey for the Nepal Department of National Parks and Wildlife Conservation: Kathmandu.

Ghimire, K. 1992. *Forest or Farm? The Politics of Poverty and Land Hunger in Nepal.* Oxford University Press: Oxford, United Kingdom.

Graburn, Nelson H.H. 1989. "Tourism: The Sacred Journey." *Hosts and Guests: The Anthropology of Tourism.* Edited by Valene Smith. First edition in 1977, revised edition in 1989. 21-36. University of Pennsylvania Press: Philadelphia, Pennsylvania.

Gray, Denis D. 1980. "Crossroads in Kathmandu." *International Wildlife* (magazine). July-August. 10(4).

Gray, Denis D. 1999. "Everest Conqueror Has Ongoing Quest in Himalayas." Associated Press. 29 April 1999. Kathmandu.

Guido, Michelle. 2000. "Everest Team Conquers Peak, Trash." *San Jose Mercury News* (newspaper). 25 May 2000. Mercury Center and Knight Ridder News Service.

Gurubacharya, Binaj. 1999. "Nepal Bans Glass Bottles to Protect Everest." Associated Press. 01 February 1999. Kathmandu.

Gurung, Ghana, David Simmons, & Patrick Devlin. 1996. "The Evolving Role of Tourist Guides: The Nepali Experience." *Tourism and Indigenous Peoples.* Edited by Richard Butler & Thomas Hinch. 107-128. International Thomson Business Press: London & Boston.

Gurung, Harka. 1991. *Tourism Carrying Capacities in the Mountain Regions of Nepal.* United Nations Development Program: Kathmandu.

Gurung, Harka. 1998. *Mountaineering in Nepal: Some Reflections.* Himalayan Association of Japan: Tokyo.

Gurung, Harka. 2003. "What's in a Name: The 'Everest' Story." *Triumph on Everest: A Tribute from the Sherpas of Nepal.* Edited by Ang Rita Sherpa & Susan Höivik. Mandala Bookpoint: Kathmandu.

Guthman, Julie. 1997. "Representing Crisis: The Theory of Himalayan Environmental Degradation and the Project of Development in Post-Rana Nepal." *Development and Change.* 28: 45-69.

Hagen, Toni, Gunter-Oskar Dyhrenfurth, Christoph von Fürer-Haimendorf, & Erwin Schneider. 1963. *Mount Everest.* Oxford University Press: London.

Hamilton, Lawrence. 1993. "Status and Current Developments in Mountain Protected Areas." *Mountain Research and Development.* 13(3): 311-314.

Hardie, Norman, *et al.* 1987. "Nepal-New Zealand Project of Forest Management in Khumbu-Pharak." Unpublished report to the Himalayan Trust and Volunteer Service Abroad.

Herzog, Maurice. 1953. *Annapurna.* E.P. Dutton: New York.

Heydon, Susan. 1997. "Change and Continuity: A History of Kunde Hospital, Solukhumbu, Nepal … A Work in Progress." *Himalayan Research Bulletin.* 17(2): 27-30.

Hillary, Edmund. 1964. *Schoolhouse in the Clouds.* Doubleday: New York.

Hilton, James. 1933. *Lost Horizon.* William Morrow & Company: New York.

Himalayan News. 1998. "Himalayan Notes and Travel Tips." *Himalayan News* (newsletter). 3(3)9: 7. The Himalayan Explorers Club: Boulder, Colorado and Kathmandu.

Himalayan News. 1999. "Factoids from Nepal." *Himalayan News* (newsletter). 11: 8. Fall 1999. The Himalayan Explorers Club: Boulder, Colorado and Kathmandu.

HimalayaNet. 1999. "New Mount Everest Measurement Announced." *HimalayaNet* (newsletter). No. 64. November 1999. The Himalayan Explorers Club: Boulder, Colorado and Kathmandu.

HimalayaNet. 2000. "Everest Round-Up." *HimalayaNet* (newsletter). No. 71. June 2000. The Himalayan Explorers Club: Boulder, Colorado and Kathmandu.

Hinrichsen, D., P.H.C. Lucas, B. Coburn, & B.N. Upreti. 1983. "Saving Sagarmatha." *Ambio.* 11(5): 274-281.

His Majesty's Government of Nepal. 1973. *National Parks and Wildlife Conservation Act 2029.* His Majesty's Government of Nepal: Kathmandu.

His Majesty's Government of Nepal. 1977. *Khumbu Region Tourism Study.* His Majesty's Government of Nepal: Kathmandu.

Hollinshead, K. 1992. "White Gaze, Red People – Shadow Visions: The Disidentification of Indians in Cultural Tourism." *Leisure Studies.* 11(1): 43-64.

Honey, Martha. 1998. *Ecotourism and Sustainable Development: Who Owns Paradise?* Island Press: Covelo, California & Washington, D.C.

Hooker, Joseph Dalton. 1855. *Himalayan Journals.* John Murray: London. 1905 edition by Ward, Lock & Co.: London.

Hornbein, Thomas F. 1965. *Everest: The West Ridge.* Sierra Club Books: San Francisco, California.

Houston, Charles S. 1987. "Deforestation in Solu Khumbu." *Mountain Research and Development.* 7(1): 76.

Hunt, John. 1954. "Triumph on Everest: Siege and Assault." *National Geographic* (magazine). 106(1): 1-44. National Geographic Society: Washington, D.C.

Inside China Today. 1999. "Police Shoot Tibetan Boy on Escape to Nepal." *Inside China Today* (newspaper). 02 February 1999. Agence France Presse: Beijing.

Ives, Jack & Bruno Messerli. 1989. *The Himalayan Dilemma: Reconciling Development and Conservation.* Routledge: New York & London.

Joseph, Patrick. 1999. "New Heights of Interest in Everest." *The Bergen Record.* 11 April 1999. The Bergen Record Corporation.

Joshi, D.P. 1982. "The Climate of Namche Bazar: A Bioclimatic Analysis." *Mountain Research and Development.* 2(4): 399-403.

Kansakar, Vidya Bir Singh & Rajani Shrestha. 1998. "Development of Air Transportation and its Impact on Tourism in Nepal." *The Himalayan Review.* 29: 10-19. Nepal Geographical Society: Kathmandu.

Karan, Pradyumna P. & Cotton Mather, 1985. "Tourism and Environment in the Mount Everest Region." *The Geographical Review.* 75(1): 93-95.

Kathmandu Post. 1999. "NTC Plans to Go Rural." *The Kathmandu Post* (newspaper). 11 December 1999. Kathmandu.

Kauder, Carol. 1996. "Are You Experienced? Have You Ever Really Been Experienced?" *Himalayan News* (newsletter). The Himalayan Explorers Club: Boulder, Colorado and Kathmandu.

Kauder, Carol. 1999. "Green Teams: Controversy over Removing Garbage from Everest." *Himalayan News* (newsletter). 10: 2, 8. Spring 1999. The Himalayan Explorers Club: Boulder, Colorado and Kathmandu.

Khadka, R.B. 1990. "Environmental Impact Assessment of Mountain Tourism." *Everest Voice.* 1(2): 11.

Kharel, Fanindra. 1997. "Agricultural Crop and Livestock Depredation by Wildlife in Langtang National Park, Nepal." *Mountain Research and Development.* 17(2): 127-134.

Kholi, M.S. & B.G. Vergese. 1962. "The Sherpas." *Himalayan Endeavor.* Edited by M.S. Kholi. Times of India Publications: Bombay.

Krakauer, Jon. 1997. *Into Thin Air: A Personal Account of the Mount Everest Disaster.* Villard Books: New York.

Kunwar, Ramesh Raj. 1989. *Fire of Himal: An Anthropological Study of the Sherpas of Nepal Himalaya Region.* Second edition 1999. Nirala Publications: New Delhi, India.

Lachapelle, Paul. 1998. "Managing Sanitation in Protected Areas: Problems and Challenges in Sagarmatha (Mt. Everest) National Park, Nepal." *Himalayan Research Bulletin.* 17(1): 53-57.

Lang, S.D.R. & Ann Lang. 1971. "The Kunde Hospital and a Demographic Survey of the Upper Khumbu, Nepal." *New Zealand Medical Journal.* 74(470): 1-8.

Levine, Norma & Tia Rinpoche. 1993. *Blessing Power of the Buddhas: Sacred Objects, Secret Lands.* Harper Collins: United Kingdom.

Litch, J.A. & R.A. Bishop. 1999. *Kunde Hospital and Community Health Program Annual Report.* Himalayan Trust: Kathmandu.

Lohani, Vikash. 1999. "Tourist Arrivals Increase by 7 Percent." *The Kathmandu Post* (newspaper). 27 November 1999. Kathmandu.

Lucas, P.H.C., N.D. Hardie, & R.A.C. Hodder. 1974. "Report of the New Zealand Mission on Sagarmatha (Mount Everest) National Park." Nepal Department of National Parks and Wildlife Conservation: Kathmandu.

Luger, Kurt. 2000a. "Foreword." *Tourism as Development: Case Studies from the Himalaya.* Edited by Pitamber Sharma. ix-xi. Himal Books: Lalitpur, Nepal and Studien Verlag: Innsbruck, Austria.

Luger, Kurt. 2000b. *Kids of Khumbu: Sherpa Youth on the Modernity Trail.* Eco-Himal and Mandala Bookpoint: Kathmandu.

Lustgarten, Abrahm. 1996. "The Unbearable Burden: What Can You Do About Porter Abuse?" *Climbing* (magazine). August 1996. 162: 183-184. Primedia Publications: Carbondale, Colorado.

MacCannell, Dean. 1976. *The Tourist: A New Theory of the Leisure Class.* Revised edition 1989. Schoken Books: New York.

Macdonald, Alexander. 1973. "The Lama and the General." *Kailash: A Journal of Himalayan Studies.* 1(3): 225-233. Kathmandu.

Mason, Kenneth. 1955. *Abode of Snow: A History of Himalayan Exploration and Mountaineering.* Rupert Hart-Davis: London.

Matthiessen, Peter. 1978. *The Snow Leopard.* 1996 edition. Penguin Books: New York.

McConnell, Robert. 1991. "Solving Environmental Problems Caused by Adventure Travel in Developing Countries: The Everest Environmental Expedition." *Mountain Research and Development.* 11(4): 359-366.

McConnell, Robert. 1996. *Gentle Expeditions: A Guide to Ethical Mountain Adventure.* The American Alpine Club Press: Golden, Colorado.

McConnell, Robert. 1999. "Legacy of the Everest Environmental Project." *American Alpine News* (newsletter). January 1999. 32-33. American Alpine Club: Golden, Colorado.

McGuinness, Jamie. 1998. *Trekking in the Everest Region.* Nepal Trekking Guide Series. Trailblazer Publications: Surrey, United Kingdom.

McKinnon, John. 2003. "Health in Khumbu – And Sir Edmund's Contribution." *Triumph on Everest: A Tribute from the Sherpas of Nepal.* Edited by Ang Rita Sherpa & Susan Höivik. 119-121. Mandala Bookpoint: Kathmandu.

McLaren, Deborah. 1998. *Rethinking Tourism and Ecotravel: The Paving of Paradise and What You Can Do to Stop It.* Kumarian Press: West Hartford, Connecticut.

Menocal, Armando. 1999. "Cashing in on Trash: Everest Expeditions Clean Up by Milking the Green Public." *Climbing: The Everest Issue* (magazine). September 1999. 188: 54. Primedia Publications: Carbondale, Colorado.

Messner, Reinhold. 2000. *My Quest for the Yeti.* St. Martins Press.

Meyer, John. 1996. "A Flight to Remember." *Continental Alpine Club Newsletter.* November 1996. Reprinted in *American Alpine News* (newsletter). April 1999. 27-28. American Alpine Club: Golden, Colorado.

Miller, Robert. 1965. "High Altitude Mountaineering, Cash Economy, and the Sherpa." *Human Organization.* 24(3): 244-249. Reprinted in *Himalayan Research Bulletin,* 1997, 17(2): 17-22.

Mishra, H. 1973. *Conservation in Khumbu: the Proposed Mt. Everest National Park*. His Majesty's Government of Nepal: Kathmandu.

Moran, Kelly. 1996. *Nepal Handbook*. Moon Publications: Chico, California.

Mountain Forum. 1995. "Summary Report and Recommendations to the United Nations Commission on Sustainable Development." International Non-Governmental Organization Consultation on the Mountain Agenda. Lima, Peru. In response to Agenda 21, Chapter 13, entitled "Managing Fragile Ecosystems: Sustainable Mountain Development," at the 1992 United Nations Conference on Environment and Development ('The Earth Summit') in Rio de Janeiro, Brazil.

Mountain Agenda. 1999. *Mountains of the World: Tourism and Sustainable Mountain Development*. SDC/CDE: Bern, Switzerland.

Mowforth, Martin & Ian Munt. 1998. *Tourism and Sustainability: New Tourism in the Third World*. Routledge: London & New York.

Nash, Dennison. 1989. "Tourism as a Form of Imperialism." *Hosts and Guests: The Anthropology of Tourism*. Edited by Valene Smith. First edition in 1977, revised edition in 1989. 37-52. University of Pennsylvania Press: Philadelphia, Pennsylvania.

National Geographic Society. 1989. "Rebuilding a Monastery on the World's Roof." *National Geographic* (magazine). September 1989. 176(3). National Geographic Society: Washington, D.C.

National Geographic Society. 1992. "Steep Price Hike Aids Mount Everest Cleanup." *National Geographic* (magazine). April 1992. 181(4): 142. National Geographic Society: Washington, D.C.

Nazeer, M. & Al Jalaly. 1995. *Mountain Tourism in NWFP and Northern Areas of Pakistan: An Overview*. Mountain Enterprises and Infrastructure Series 95/8. Center for Resource and Environmental Studies. ICIMOD: Kathmandu.

Nepal, Sanjaya K. 1997. *Tourism Induced Environmental Changes in the Everest Region: Some Recent Evidence*. Centre for Development and Environment, Institute of Geography, University of Bern: Bern, Switzerland.

Nepal Ministry of Finance. 1997. *Economic Survey 1995-1996*. His Majesty's Government of Nepal: Kathmandu.

Nepal Ministry of Finance. 1999. "Budget Speech of the Fiscal Year 1997-1998." Delivered by Finance Minister Mahesh Acharya to the 16th Session of the Nepal Parliament. 11 July 1999. Translated and published by *Nepal News* (newspaper). Mercantile Communications Pvt. Ltd.: Kathmandu.

Nepal Ministry of Tourism. 1989. *Nepal Tourism Statistics*. His Majesty's Government of Nepal: Kathmandu.

Nepal Ministry of Tourism. 1992. *Nepal Tourism Statistics*. His Majesty's Government of Nepal: Kathmandu.

Nepal Ministry of Tourism. 1996. *Nepal Tourism Statistics*. His Majesty's Government of Nepal: Kathmandu.

Nepal Ministry of Tourism. 1998. *Nepal Tourism Statistics*. His Majesty's Government of Nepal: Kathmandu.

Nepal Mountaineering Association. 1997. *Parbat* (Journal of the Nepal Mountaineering Association). ICM 1997 Special Issue. May-June 1997. Nepal Mountaineering Association: Kathmandu.

Nepal News. 2000. "Nepal Calls for Help to Fight Terrorism." *Nepal News* (newspaper). 09 June 2000. Kathmandu.

Norton, E.F. 1925. *The Fight for Everest, 1924*. London.

O'Connor, Bill. 1989. *The Trekking Peaks of Nepal*. Crowood Press: Wiltshire, United Kingdom. Cloudcap Press: Seattle, Washington.

Odell, Malcolm J. & Wendy Brewer Lama. 1998. "Tea House Trekking in Nepal: The Case for Environmentally Friendly Indigenous Tourism." *Sustainability in Mountain Tourism: Perspectives for the Himalayan Countries*. Edited by Patricia East, Kurt Luger, and Karin Inmann. 191-206. Oeko Himal Publication. Studienverlag: Innsbruck-Vienna, Austria (Reprinted by Book Faith India: Delhi).

Oppitz, Michael. 1974. "Myths and Facts: Reconsidering Some Data Concerning the Clan History of the Sherpa." *The Anthropology of Nepal*. Edited by Christoph von Fürer-Haimendorf. 232-243. Aris and Phillips: Warminster, England.

Ortner, Sherry. 1989. *High Religion: A Cultural and Political History of Sherpa Buddhism*. Princeton University Press: Princeton, New Jersey.

Ortner, Sherry. 1990. "Who Shapes the Text?: Sherpas and Sahibs on Mount Everest." Comparative Study of Social Transformations Working Paper No. 56. University of Michigan: Ann Arbor, Michigan.

Ortner, Sherry. 1998. "The Making and Self-Making of 'The Sherpas' in Early Himalayan Mountaineering." *Studies in Nepali History and Society*. 3(1): 1-34. Mandala Book Point: Kathmandu.

Pant, G.P. 1991. *Foreign Aid, Economic Growth and Social Cost-Benefit Analysis*. Avebury: Aldershot.

Parker, Anne. 1989. "The Meanings of 'Sherpa': an Evolving Social Category." *Himalayan Research Bulletin*. 9(3): 11-14.

Pawson, Ivan, Dennyse Stanford, & Vincanne Adams. 1984a. "Effects of Modernization on the Khumbu Region of Nepal: Changes in

Population Structure, 1970-1982." *Mountain Research and Development.* 4(1): 73-81.

Pawson, Ivan, Dennyse Stanford, Vincanne Adams, & Mingma Norbu Sherpa. 1984b. "Growth of Tourism in Nepal's Everest Region: Impact on the Physical Environment and Structure of Human Settlements." *Mountain Research and Development.* 4(3): 237-246.

Pearce, Fred. 1999. "Flooded Out." *New Scientist.* 5 June 1999.

Pearl, Max. 1965. "Kiwi in the Khumbu." *New Zealand Journal of Medicine.* 64: 584-588.

Peirce, R. 1996. *News from Nepal.* December-January (citing A. Samacharpatra in Spotlight).

Pelinck, Egbert. 2000. "Preface." *Tourism as Development: Case Studies from the Himalaya.* Edited by Pitamber Sharma. vii-viii. Himal Books: Lalitpur, Nepal and Studien Verlag: Innsbruck, Austria.

Pye-Smith, Charlie. 1988. *Travels in Nepal: The Sequestered Kingdom.* 1990 edition. Penguin Books: London.

Poore, D. 1992. *Guidelines for Mountain Protected Areas.* IUCN Publications: Gland, Switzerland.

Rawls, John. 1971. *Theory of Justice.* Harvard University Press: Cambridge, Massachusetts.

Reinhard, Johan. 1978. "Khembalung: The Hidden Valley." *Kailash: A Journal of Himalayan Studies.* 6(1): 5-35. Kathmandu.

Reuters. 2000. "Nepal Doubles Tourist-Site Fees." Reuters News Service. 25 May 2000. Kathmandu.

Robinson, David. 1992. "Sociocultural Impacts of Mountain Tourism on Nepal's Sagarmatha (Everest) World Heritage Site: Implications for Sustainable Tourism." *World Heritage Twenty Years Later.* Edited by J. Thorsale. 123-134. IUCN: Gland, Switzerland.

Rogers, Paul & John Aitchison. 1998. *Towards Sustainable Tourism in the Everest Region of Nepal.* IUCN Nepal: Kathmandu.

Rowell, Galen. 1980. *Many People Come, Looking, Looking.* The Mountaineers: Seattle, Washington.

Rowell, Galen. 1983. *Mountains of the Middle Kingdom: Exploring the High Peaks of China and Tibet.* Sierra Club Books: San Francisco, California.

Sacherer, Janice. 1981. "The Recent Social and Economic Impact of Tourism on a Remote Sherpa Community." *Asian Highland Societies in Anthropological Perspective.* Christoph von Fürer-Haimendorf (ed). Humanities Press: New Delhi.

Sadeque, Syed Z. 2000. "Poverty and Social Exclusion in the South Asia Highlands: State of the Social Sector and Opportunities for Poverty

Reduction and Social Inclusion." *Issues in Mountain Development.* Edited by Shahid Akhtar & Archana Karki. ICIMOD: Kathmandu.

Sagarmatha Pollution Control Committee. 1998. *Annual Progress Report for the Fiscal Year 1997-1998.* Sagarmatha Pollution Control Committee: Namche, Nepal.

Sagarmatha Pollution Control Committee. 1999. *Annual Progress Report for the Fiscal Year 1998-1999.* Sagarmatha Pollution Control Committee: Namche, Nepal.

Salkeld, Audrey & John Boyle. 1993. *Climbing Mount Everest: The Bibliography.*

Sardar-Afkhami, Hamid. 1996. "An Account of Padma-Bkod: A Hidden Land in Southeastern Tibet." *Kailash: A Journal of Himalayan Studies.* 18(3-4): 1-21. Kathmandu.

Sardar-Afkhami, Abdol-Hamid. 2001. "The Buddha's Secret Gardens: End Times and Hidden Lands in Tibetan Imagination." Harvard University.

Schaller, George B. 1980. *Stones of Silence: Journeys in the Himalaya.* Vikash Publishing House: New Delhi.

Sharma, Pitamber (editor). 1995. *Tourism for Local Community Development in Mountain Areas: Perspectives, Issues and Guidelines.* ICIMOD: Kathmandu.

Sharma, Pitamber. 1998a. "Approaches to Promoting Mountain Tourism for Local Development: Experiences from Nepal." *The Himalayan Review.* 29: 20-36. Nepal Geographical Society: Kathmandu.

Sharma, Pitamber. 1998b. "Environment, Culture, Economy, and Tourism: Dilemmas in the Hindu Kush-Himalayas." *Issues in Mountain Development.* ICIMOD: Kathmandu.

Sharma, Pitamber. 2000a. "Mountains, Tourism and Development." *Tourism as Development: Case Studies from the Himalaya.* Edited by Pitamber Sharma. 1-19. Himal Books: Lalitpur, Nepal & Studien Verlag: Innsbruck, Austria.

Sharma, Pitamber. 2000b. "Common Issues in Mountain Tourism for Local Development." *Tourism as Development: Case Studies from the Himalaya.* Edited by Pitamber Sharma. 169-179. Himal Books: Lalitpur, Nepal & Studien Verlag: Innsbruck, Austria.

Sherpa, Ang Rita & Susan Höivik (editors). 2003. *Triumph on Everest: A Tribute from the Sherpas of Nepal.* Mandala Bookpoint: Kathmandu.

Sherpa, Ang Tharkay. 1954. *Memoires d'un Sherpa, recuiles par Basil P. Norton.* Translated into French by Henri Delgrove. Amiot Dumont: Paris.

Sherpa, Lhakpa Norbu. 1985. "Management Issues in Nepal's National Parks." Paper presented to the International Workshop on the Management of National Parks and Protected Areas of the Hindu Kush-Himalaya. Kathmandu.

Sherpa, Lhakpa Norbu. 1992. "The High Profile Dump." *Himal* (magazine). 5(6): 28-29.

Sherpa, Lhakpa Norbu. 1993. *Sagarmatha National Park Working Paper: Implementation Status and Priorities.* Nepal Department of National Parks and Wildlife Conservation: Kathmandu.

Sherpa, Nawang Doka. 2003. "Healthy Smiles at the Top of the World: The Highest Dental Clinic." *Triumph on Everest: A Tribute from the Sherpas of Nepal.* Edited by Ang Rita Sherpa & Susan Höivik. 123-125. Mandala Bookpoint: Kathmandu.

Sherpa, Tenzing Norgay. 1977. *After Everest: An Autobiography.* As told to Malcolm Barnes. George Allen & Unwin: London.

Sherpa, Tenzing Norgay & James Ramsay Ullman. 1955. *Tiger of the Snows.* G.P. Putnam's Sons: New York.

Shrestha, D.B, C.B. Singh, & B.M. Pradhan. 1972. *Ethnic Groups of Nepal and Their Ways of Living.* Third edition printed in 1987. Madhab Lal Maharjan Himalayan Booksellers: Kathmandu.

Singh, Kedar Man. 1981. "Not Yet Cleared for Take-Off." *Far Eastern Economic Review.* 113: 130.

Smith, Valene. 1981. "Controlled vs. Uncontrolled Tourism: Bhutan and Nepal." *Royal Anthropological Institute News.* 46: 4-6.

Smith, Valene. 1989. "Introduction." *Hosts and Guests: The Anthropology of Tourism.* Edited by Valene Smith. Second edition. 1-17. University of Pennsylvania Press: Philadelphia, Pennsylvania.

Smith, Valene, & William Eadington (editors). 1992. *Tourism Alternatives: Potentials and Problems in the Development of Tourism.* University of Pennsylvania Press: Philadelphia, Pennsylvania.

Snellgrove, David. 1957. *Buddhist Himalaya: Travels and Studies in Quest of the Origins and Nature of Tibetan Religion.* Cassirer: Oxford, United Kingdom.

Stephens, Tony. 1998. "Vision Is Clearer For Mountain Kingdom." *Sydney Morning Herald* newspaper. 27 November 1998. Sydney, Australia.

Stevens, Stan. 1988. "Tourism and Development in Nepal." *Anthropological Research on Contemporary Tourism: Student Papers from Berkeley.* Edited by Nelson H.H. Graburn. 67-80. Kroeber Anthropological Society Papers 67-68. University of California: Berkeley, California.

Stevens, Stan. 1991. "Sherpas, Tourism, and Cultural Change in Nepal's Mount Everest Region." *Journal of Cultural Geography.* 12(1): 39-58. Bowling Green University Popular Press: Bowling Green, Ohio.

Stevens, Stan. 1993a. *Claiming the High Ground: Sherpas, Subsistence, and Environmental Change in the Highest Himalaya.* University of California Press: Berkeley, California.

Stevens, Stan. 1993b. "Tourism, Change, and Continuity in the Mount Everest Region, Nepal." *The Geographical Review.* 83(4): 410-427. American Geographical Society of New York: New York.

Stevens, Stan. 1997. "Consultation, Co-Management, and Conflict in Sagarmatha (Mount Everest) National Park, Nepal." *Conservation Through Cultural Survival: Indigenous Peoples and Protected Areas.* Edited by Stan Stevens. 63-97. Island Press: Covelo, California & Washington, D.C.

Stevens, Stan & Mingma Norbu Sherpa. 1992. "Tourism and Local Development in Sagarmatha (Mount Everest) National Park, Nepal." Paper presented at IUCN 4th World Congress on National Parks and Protected Areas. Caracas, Venezuela.

Stiller, Ludwig F. 1973. *The Rise of the House of Gorkha: A Study in the Unification of Nepal 1768-1816.* The Patna Jesuit Society: Patna, India.

TAAN. 1998. "Second TAAN National Eco-Trekking Workshop." *TAAN Newsletter.* 5(1): 5. Trekking Agents Association of Nepal: Kathmandu.

TAAN. 1999. *TAAN's Third National Eco-Trekking Workshop.* Program brochure published by Trekking Agents Association of Nepal: Kathmandu.

The Hindu. 2000a. "Nepal Seeks Resumption of Indian Airlines Flights." *The Hindu* (newspaper). 26 February 2000. The Hindu & Tribeca Internet Initiatives: New Delhi.

The Hindu. 2000b. "Indian Airlines to Resume Flights to Nepal from June 1." *The Hindu* (newspaper). 15 May 2000. The Hindu & Tribeca Internet Initiatives: New Delhi.

Thomas, Bryn. 1996. *Trekking in the Annapurna Region.* Nepal Trekking Guide Series. Trailblazer Publications: Surrey, United Kingdom.

Thompson, Michael. 1979. "Sahibs and Sherpas." *Mountain* (magazine). 68: 45-49.

Thompson, M. and M. Warburton. 1988. "Uncertainty on a Himalayan Scale." *Deforestation: Social Dynamics in Watersheds and Mountain Ecosystems.* Edited by J. Ives & D.C. Pitt. 1-53. Routledge: New

York. (The article also appeared under the same title in 1985 in the journal *Mountain Research and Development*. 5(2): 115-135.)

Tilman, H.W. 1935. "Nanda Devi and the Sources of the Ganges." *The Himalayan Journal*. 8: 1-26. The Himalayan Club: Bombay.

Tilman, H.W. 1951. *Nepal Himalaya*. Reprinted in 1998. Book Faith India: Delhi.

Tobin, H.W. (editor) 1954. *The Himalayan Journal*. Volume 18. The Himalayan Club: Calcutta.

Travers, Don and Stacy Kelly. 1999. *Everest Epic Trivia*.

Tuladhar, Tirtha. 1970. "Recent Trends in Tourism Development." *Nepal: A Profile*. Edited by Nepal Council of Applied Economic Research. 229-232. His Majesty's Government of Nepal: Kathmandu.

Unsworth, Walt. 1981. *Everest: A Mountaineering History*. Houghton Mifflin: Boston, Massachusetts & Penguin Books: Middlesex, England.

Upadhyay, M.P. 1984. *Environmental Impact on Mountain Ecosystem by Trekkers and Mountaineers: Mt. Everest Trek Route Survey Report*. Nepal Institute of Development Studies: Kathmandu.

Upadhyaya, Ramesh. 1999. "Maoists Spreading Terror in Nepal." *The Hindu* (newspaper). 13 March 1999. Kathmandu.

Upreti, Hari K. 1998. "Eco-Tourism with People's Participation for Sustainable Development." *The Himalayan Review*. 29: 53-63. Nepal Geographical Society: Kathmandu.

Van Slambrouck, Paul. 2000. "American Heads to Nepal: It's Trash Day on Mt. Everest." *The Christian Science Monitor* (newspaper). 13 March 2000. The Christian Science Publishing Society.

Vuichard, Daniel and Marcus Zimmermann. 1986. "The Langmoche Flash-Flood, Khumbu Himal, Nepal." *Mountain Research and Development*. 6(1): 90-94.

Vuichard, Daniel and Marcus Zimmermann. 1987. "The 1985 Catastrophic Drainage of a Moraine-Dammed Lake, Khumbu Himal, Nepal: Cause and Consequences." *Mountain Research and Development*. 7(2): 91-110.

Watanabe, Teiji, Jack Ives, & June Hammond. 1994. "Rapid Growth of a Glacial Lake in Khumbu Himal, Himalaya: Prospects for a Catastrophic Flood." *Mountain Research and Development*. 14(4): 329-340.

Watanabe, Teiji, Satoshi Kameyama, & Tatsuaki Sato. 1995. "Imja Glacier Dead-Ice Melt Rates and Changes in a Supra-Glacial Lake, 1989-1994, Khumbu Himal, Nepal: Danger of Lake Drainage." *Mountain Research and Development*. 15(4): 293-300.

Weir, Tom. 1955. *East of Katmandu*. Oliver & Boyd: London.

Whelan, Tensie. 1991. *Nature Tourism: Managing for the Environment*. Island Press: Covelo, California & Washington, D.C.

World Tourism Organization. 1999. *Tourism Highlights 1999*. WTO: Madrid, Spain.

Wright, Karen. 2000. "Measuring Mount Everest." *Discover* (magazine). May 2000. 36-38.

Yamada, T. & K.C. Sharma. 1993. "Glacier Lakes and Outburst Floods in the Nepal Himalaya." *IAHS Publication*. 218: 319-330.

Zhu, B., W.S.F. Kidd, D.B. Rowley, B.S. Currie & N. Shafique. 2005. "Age of Initiation of the India-Asia Collision in the East-Central Himalaya." *Journal of Geology*. 113: 265-285.

Zurick, David & P.P. Karan. 1999. *Himalaya: Life on the Edge of the World*. Johns Hopkins University Press: Baltimore, Maryland.

About the Author

The author, who holds a Ph.D. and an M.A. in Cultural Geography and an M.B.A. in Business, all from the University of California at Berkeley, has traveled and conducted research in the mountains of Nepal, India, Pakistan, Tibet and China for the past ten consecutive years. He spent more than four years living in Nepal while carrying out doctoral and post-doctoral research in Manang and Samdo and traveling in the Himalayan highland regions of Mustang, Nyishang, Nar-Phu, Nubri, Tsum, Langtang, Rolwaling, Khumbu, Walung, and Kangchenjunga. Dr. Rogers' previous book, *Secrets of Manang*, told the fascinating story behind the emergence of a remarkably successful entrepreneurial culture among a Tibetan Buddhist community residing in northern Nepal's remote and starkly beautiful trans-Himalaya region.